Conversations on Early Childhood Teacher Education

Voices from the Working Forum for Teacher Educators

Andrew Gibbons and Colin Gibbs, *Editors*

WORKING FORUM
FOR TEACHER EDUCATORS

Conversations on Early Childhood Teacher Education
is a project of the World Forum Foundation
in partnership with New Zealand Tertiary College.

Where possible grammar and spelling preferences that are unique to each author's culture, and style of writing, have been preserved by the editors.

The views expressed by the contributors to this publication are not necessarily those of New Zealand Tertiary College.

Cover Photograph by Karen Knighton

Printed in the United States
through support from Teaching Strategies, Inc.

TABLE OF CONTENTS

FOREWORD

Teaching Strategies is delighted to be able to sponsor the printing of *Conversations on Early Childhood Teacher Education* to help make the ideas and concepts discussed available to a wider audience. It's hard to imagine a topic of greater importance to the care and education of young children than the issues that were explored at the first Working Forum for Teacher Educators. Teachers are the critical factor in achieving the kind of quality programs that create rich childhoods for children and nurture their development and learning. It is the quality of teacher-child interactions that matter the most—how teachers build positive and responsive relationships with children, promote thinking and reasoning, teach important skills and concepts, and generate excitement about learning.

Teaching is an art as well as a science, and those of us who work with pre-service teachers before they enter a classroom and provide support and guidance to teachers on-the-job have an enormous responsibility. What should be taught in teacher education courses? How should it be taught? How do we address the learning styles and needs of a very diverse group of students and teachers? We have much to gain from an opportunity to share our collective stories, learn from each other's successes, and struggle with the dilemmas that confront us in our work. That is what took place at the inaugural Working Forum for Teacher Educators and what is captured in this book.

The *Conversations on Early Childhood Teacher Education* documents the presentations, conversations, and real-life experiences of teacher educators from all over the world who came together in New Zealand to learn from each other and enhance their work. It is a gift for those of us who are immersed in teacher education, but were not able to participate. If you have been to other World Forums, you know how valuable it is to be immersed in the conversations that go on throughout, and between the panels; they are all interesting and open a window into the experiences and programs in parts of the world we may never visit. Now we don't have to choose! It is all here for us, organized into topics, with leading questions to guide and challenge us to think more deeply about our work. The participants who wrote up their presentations—along with Selena, Chip, Colin, and Andrew, who undertook the challenging job of capturing the rich diversity of the presentations and putting them into a cohesive format—have given all of us a chance to participate and learn.

There is something in the book for everyone. You can focus on the dilemmas and important questions that are raised on each of the major topics and use them to promote dialogs with colleagues in your own settings. You can gain insights into the ways that culture affects how and what teachers learn by reading firsthand accounts from culturally diverse parts of the world. If you are looking for new and creative ways to help teachers use responsive language in their interactions with children, or seeking ways to cultivate an understanding of math concepts in order to teach it effectively, you can go right to those chapters and gain practical strategies you can immediately put to use. Coaches and mentor teachers will find thoughtful ideas for enhancing their work. And when you want to put up your feet and read some personal journeys of teacher educators, there are wonderful stories to explore. As it says in the book, "It is through the sharing of stories that our collective understanding grows." This book gives us insights and inspirations, and it also jolts us out of our comfortable, habitual thinking and allows us to consider our work in new ways. It describes the journey that began with 114 participants at the first Working Forum for Teacher Educators and invites us all to take part in that journey.

Diane Trister Dodge
Founder and President
Teaching Strategies, Inc.

PREFACE

The inspiration for the Working Forum for Teacher Educators came from the increasing momentum that grew over many years as early childhood teacher educators, researchers, advocates, and policy makers came together in conversations at the World Forum on Early Care and Education. Heartful teacher educators coming together initially by chance engaging in opportune conversations together.

Seeds were sown as teacher educators took the opportunity at the World Forum to share, collaborate, and reflect on their work with student teachers. As interest and conversations gained depth and breadth, teacher education themes were built into the World Forum. The goal was to create a place where educators could come together in meaningful ways to enhance their own experiences, enrich their knowledge, and take time for themselves prior to heading home to resume their roles as teacher educators.

Each World Forum enabled a globally diverse group to meet with others who shared their commitment to teacher education. Here was a place where hearts with a passion for guiding and supporting student teachers around the world came together to gain insight into new and enhanced ways of educating teachers—heartful and hungry leaders reflecting, sharing, and growing together. As the years passed and voices continued to come together at the World Forum, the realization that a gathering specifically focused on teacher education was emerging—a Working Forum for Teacher Educators.

In May 2008 over one hundred passionate teacher educators from 10 nations, came together for professional conversations at the inaugural Working Forum for Teacher Educators in Auckland, New Zealand. The focus was clear... sharing conversations for early childhood teacher educators to reflect on themselves as educators to enhance their work with student teachers, sharing their passion to best impact on the lives of young children, parents, and families throughout the world. The focus was not on gaining answers to the many questions about teacher education in early childhood, but rather taking the time to contemplate and dwell in their fullness. This, we see, is the spirit of true professional conversations.

This book captures the spirit of the heartful teacher educators who came together for three inspiring, conversation-rich days. It shares the conversations of that time, but also ignites ongoing conversations. It shares effective practices to enhance teaching practices and improve children's learning, and it offers inspiration for teacher educators to continue to look for opportunities to come together in a sense of togetherness as heartful teacher educators.

Voices are but lone voices unless opportunities for them to come together are created and conversations are born. Sincere acknowledgment to Bonnie and Roger

Neugebauer for having the vision to bring together early childhood leaders from around the world, to enable a voice for teacher educators to emerge and conversations to begin.

Voices come, but may go, unless there is the opportunity to capture them in print. Heartfelt thanks to our coeditors for their commitment to sealing the inaugural Working Forum for Teacher Educators voices in the shape of this book. Colin and Andrew have now captured and released the voices of the Forum presenters and participants to evoke new conversations and inspire new thought and reflection. Their task was not simply to put together a book of proceedings—we and they wanted more than that. So they set about not just recording the papers presented at this gathering, but also to capture the voices of participants. You will see many of these voices are recorded in the commentaries of this book. Above all else, the aim was to promote the ongoing conversations—to live in the questions rather than force the answers.

The inaugural Working Forum for Teacher Educators is a rich memory for all who were able to attend. *Conversations on Early Childhood Teacher Education* re-ignites the conversations shared by all at the Forum and offers new opportunity for ongoing and evolving conversations to lead us to better practices for young children through our student teachers—so, let the conversations begin…

Selena Fox   Chip Donohue
Chief Executive   Director of Distance Learning
New Zealand Tertiary College   Erikson Institute

Thanks to our coeditor, Colin Gibbs, for the inspiration to consider the notion of the heartful leader—one that rests most gently and comfortably around the educators of the inaugural Working Forum for Teacher Educators.

Moment by moment, as teachers move
among their students, they are touching lives.
Teachers, too, are poets and prophets.
If they are wise, then they and their students
will learn to care for each other, bestow value,
and grow together. If teachers are foolish,
no one will flourish. Of this, though
we may be sure: we become what we love.

Garrison, J. (1997). *Dewey and Eros: wisdom and desire and the art of teaching.*
New York: Teachers College Press, p. 202

The following paper is the keynote address given to the Working Forum for Teacher Educators by Professor Lilian Katz. Lilian sets the scene for the conversations that will follow with teacher educators from around the world.

INTRODUCTION

Conversations on teacher education

A gathering of early childhood teacher educators is an inspiring and positive occasion. The seriousness of commitment towards children, families, and communities is evident in the conversations that flow through corridors, auditoriums, and in the hearts and minds. The conversations enjoin participants in a constructive process of thinking, listening, talking, and of being.

The Working Forum theme of 'conversations' then manifests a sense of nourishment that draws out an important etymology. To be engaged in conversation is to 'live with' and to 'conduct oneself' (Online Etymology Dictionary, 2008). Such conversations have a long history. Think, for instance, of *The Republic* (Plato, 1974) in which the purpose of education, and the role of the educator, is identified as an essential to a society's well-being.

Hence, conversations on early childhood teacher education are a vital component in the ongoing commitment to young children and families, to communities, and to the individual student teachers who make that all important decision to pursue a career as an early childhood teacher. Like theories of development and learning, they orient our thinking and practice. These conversations provide space and time to think about teacher education, what it is and might be in different cultural and social contexts. Conversations of early childhood teacher education are significant because talking, contrary to popular belief, is not the opposite of doing. Talking is a doing that enriches our lives and gives it new and enriched meaning—a conversation.

This should not come as a surprise to those passionate about early childhood education, in which communication is a highly valued and complexly understood strand of the curriculum. In Aotearoa/New Zealand, for instance, the national curriculum *Te Whāriki* (Ministry of Education, 2006) has guided teachers, teacher educators, policy writers, curriculum developers, and researchers in thinking about the role of language, understanding, and conversation in weaving together our relationships. The fullness and diversity of child-child, and adult-child conversations are linked to the importance of communication for the child's well-being.

Conversations are a matter of well-being for teachers too, in the sense of their teaching presence. By this we do not mean that you have to be some 'where' (to be present) in order to be in a conversation. By stating the importance of conversations for presence, we are highlighting the value, in our minds and hearts, of being a teacher educator who *has* presence. And we believe that the period of time in which student teachers engage in teacher education is a time to reflect upon and build this presence. The conversations in this book explore many ways in which teacher educators can enrich this time of teacher education.

They begin with the working forum's opening address by Lilian Katz, in which some dilemmas of early childhood teacher education are examined. These dilemmas define our thinking about the practice(s) of nurturing young children and impacts upon our expectations of what teacher education is all about. For instance, the very question of whether we are engaged in a caring and/or educating profession receives considerable attention within the scope of 'professional conversations'. Teacher education is then a time in which student teachers can engage with the meaning and consequences of educational dilemmas.

The first chapter explores the development of early childhood programs, considering what it is that should be taught to student teachers, how it should be taught, by whom, and for what reason. These complex considerations link to questions of the difference between teacher training and teacher education. Conversations engage with both what theories guide our programs and how those theories inform the curriculum in its entirety, from who gets 'selected' to study in a program, to how their study is assessed.

Whilst many of us live in increasingly diverse communities, how often do we afford ourselves the time and space to think about the meaning and implications of living in a diverse community? Teacher education provides student teachers with that time and space. In Chapter 2 the authors welcome this challenge with their views on the valuing of difference. Teacher education conversations turn to the topic of responsibility. Whose responsibility is it to mold, prepare, guide, mentor, educate and/or train student teachers, and how do those responsible engage in these practices 'responsibly'?

Attention turns, in Chapter 3, to the hotly debated conversations on teacher education curriculum. We might fill an entire series of books on the 'things' that teachers should be 'taught'. In the four presentations selected there is a sense of content being something more than just knowledge and/or information, content is relational. The papers give a sense of teacher education curriculum as being a time to do more than simply download the blueprints for a quality curriculum into a 'teaching machine'.

Mentoring and leadership form a strong platform for the conversations in Chapter 4. This is an important space to think about the 'triadic' relationship between associate tutor, student teacher, and teacher educator. Lilian Katz suggests, in her opening address, that this relationship can sometimes resemble a battlefield. This chapter then highlights some ways to think about adult relationships that draw upon an ethic of collegiality, support, and openness. With increasing onus for teacher education being placed upon academic institutions in 'preparing' early childhood teachers comes increasing responsibility for ensuring a strong voice is heard from those working 'in the field' of our interests.

Chapter 5 engages with questions concerning online learning in early childhood teacher education. Practices of blended learning, flexible delivery, web-enhanced, and online learning are discussed, with particular attention to the use of web-based technologies for designing an environment in which student teachers experience their education as practical and collaborative. Central to the chapter is the voice of the student teacher, in effective utilisation of the learning environment, and in the very development of effective online programs.

Finally, Chapter 6 synthesises the conversations and itemises ten concerns and ten principles that might facilitate further conversations on teacher education. Drawing on the essence of these conversations which began with Lilian Katz's address, this chapter suggests that it is the person who is the teacher who will ensure that teaching and learning is wholehearted and grounded on principles. To achieve this, we are encouraged as teachers to nourish not only our minds and feelings towards children, but also the whole person—the thinking, feeling, believing, spiritual person who is the teacher.

The conversations on what it might be to be such a teacher educator could, and should go on long into our collective and individual futures. However, we would like to highlight some emerging themes that frequent this collection of conversations. These themes are not quality indicators or standards. They create new spaces to engage with the purposes and practices of teacher education (or as Lilian Katz describes in the first paper, the dilemmas of early childhood teacher education), and to re-explore many old and familiar spaces to nourish and invigorate them.

Emerging themes

The Working Forum provided opportunities for participants to share conversations on a range of issues concerning early childhood teacher education. As we reflected on these conversations, we identified five major themes based on relationality, nurturance, responsiveness, inclusiveness, and innovativeness.

1. Relationality

Central to early childhood teacher education is relationality. While it might be a truism to suggest that education is by its very nature, a matter of relationships, what do we expect of our relationships? We believe that early childhood teacher education has historically been provided by teacher educators who understand and value the importance of modelling nurturing educational relationships with student teachers. Increasingly, participation in early childhood teacher education is a matter of obligation or compulsion. Many student teachers will be studying in order to stay in the profession, others will be seeking career changes, while still others will be school leavers who have yet to be sure of their career aspirations and expectations. What impact will such policy developments have on the relationality of early childhood teacher education? The conversations in this book emphasise the role of the teacher educator in establishing and modelling 'relational-connectedness' (Gibbs, 2006). Such connectedness is observed in the emphasis on understanding and valuing each student teacher, and in being open to continuity between adult-adult and adult-child relationships.

2. Nurturance

Early childhood teacher education ought to be concerned with the nurturance of the individual. The theme of nurturance resonates throughout these collected conversations. Nurturance is considered in both an individual and a collective sense. With regards the former, each teacher educator is constantly engaged in providing a space of 'sanctuary' (Nugent, cited in Gibbs, forthcoming) for student teachers. Such spaces encourage student teachers to reflect upon their own experiences, values and beliefs, and their knowledge of, and passion for, working with young children. Collective nurturing refers to the collegial nature of teacher education. Think for instance of the nurturing of the very programs in which teacher educators work. These programs are constructed with care, and need nurturing for both the current and future students and for the students who have graduated and are working in their communities. The conversations in this book explore many aspects of nurturance, with specific attention to the notions of leadership and mentoring. These are aspects of teacher education programs that have a significant influence on graduating teachers, who are often expected to take senior roles in their chosen early childhood education pathways.

3. Responsiveness

Early childhood teacher education is informed by many interests and needs to be wisely responsive to all—to the individuals and communities involved in teaching and learning, through to society as a whole. Responsiveness resonates closely with nurturance and relationality. To be responsive in teacher education, as a teacher educator, incorporates advocacy, pastoral care, and knowledge of the wider social, cultural, economic and historical influences that impact on early childhood education. For instance, early childhood teacher educators are required to be responsive to the wider societal expectations regarding the nature and purpose of quality early childhood education; responsive to the needs of local communities with idiosyncratic experiences and aspirations; responsive to the needs of families who experience the highs and lows of familial life characteristic of the 21st century; and responsive to the needs of children, who are generally articulated as the reason that teacher educators are doing what they do. Hence there are both competing and harmonising demands and expectations of early childhood teacher education. It is not just the competing ones that need to be continually tested. Rather we also need to question those views which seem to harmonise, for this is the place of intersection for critical reflection, informed commentary, and philosophical acuity—all aspects of what it means to be a professional. And that might mean being able to professionally and academically affirm viewpoints, or to inform new directions. The Working Forum conversations focus upon responsiveness to the needs of student teachers, emphasising the importance of a student teacher experiencing responsive relationships, in order to gain a sense of how they might be responsive to the needs of others, and to their own.

4. Inclusiveness

Early childhood education demonstrates through its actions, commitments, and aspirations that it is inclusive. Being inclusive underpins of a philosophy of welcoming (Berikoff, 2008) that is a central concern for early childhood education. Teachers are in a constant state of welcoming, with children, families, regulatory bodies, advocates, interest groups, health and social service professionals, and educational resource companies. The ways in which these various groups are welcomed into the centre impacts significantly on the culture and the curriculum of the centre. In a sense it forms part of what is often termed the hidden curriculum. The onus is then upon teacher educators to promote deep levels of understanding what it means to be inclusive. In the first instance this is an expectation that teacher education is a journey in understanding one's self or selves. Such a journey throws light upon the ways in which we often distinguish between self and other, us and them, and how these distinctions are constantly impacting on educational settings.

5. Innovativeness

In meeting the local, national, and international demands, early childhood teacher education ought to encourage ongoing innovativeness and risk-taking in teacher education curriculum and program design and implementation. Globally, the trend has been one of standards setting. Standard setting and standardisation are two different concepts. It is seductive to think that establishing demonstrable standards is made easier when programs are standardised—when we share similar curriculum context and curriculum, then the belief is that standards will be more manageable. The key consideration here, though, is that such a model is incompatible with meeting the needs of teacher education—the one shoe doesn't fit all approaches to teacher education. In particular, we need to consider the implications of localised circumstances of teaching and learning in early childhood care and education, and how we might best prepare teachers to meet these needs. Being innovative, we believe, is a key quality. Innovative teacher education programs encourage innovative early childhood education which encourages innovative learning for children. Often encouraging means, more than directly guiding, simply allowing for innovation by remaining permanently open—an exciting prospect for all teachers.

Structure of the book

The process of developing this text began with expressions of interest in participation at the Working Forum from around the globe. As co-editors we were looking for proposed papers that would resonate with the theme of conversation, and make the essential connection between teacher education theory and teacher education practice. Accepted papers then went through various phases of support and editing as they were developed firstly for 20-minute presentations that were aligned with similarly themed conversations, and became the basis for Working Forum participant group discussions through which the conversations were continued. The participants remained in their assigned groups over the three days. Their discussions were recorded in order to add further conversational dimensions to this text. This innovation was regarded as an appreciation of the immense value of creating collegial spaces through which ideas, and papers, can be developed. Such spaces are seen as a 'reinvestment' in the potential of collaboration.

As co-editors we did not wish simply to edit then transmit the papers as a set of proceedings. Hence each chapter has a 'beginning the conversations' and a 'continuing the conversations' that reflects a synthesis of our views on early childhood teacher education and their relationship to the views of the participants. We provide editorial comments throughout the text in the spirit of critical reflection. These comments reflect our personal commitments to conversations on early childhood teacher education, and to the provocations that we regard as essential to the profession of early childhood teaching. We have not attempted to weave the conversations too tight—to suggest a unity in interpretation and vision. It is important to see conversational seams. The space in between our thoughts and expressions is often the space from which new ideas spring.

'in each paper we have highlighted interesting conversational points in the sidebars'

As co-editors we would like to acknowledge each of the presenters and participants for their contributions and commitment to early childhood teacher education. Many thanks also must go to Catherine Brown and Zoe White for their support with the administration of the text. We would additionally like to acknowledge Selena Fox, Chip Donohue, Glennie Oborn, Bonnie and Roger Neugebauer for their bringing together of early childhood teacher educators.

We provide editorial comments throughout the text in the spirit of critical reflection. These comments are formatted in a sidebar like this.

Editors

We're building a new institution, and it's not clear what its borders are yet.

Larry Schweinhart

Look for the potential for development that comes from a conversation.

Barbara Duffy

References

Berikoff, A. (2007, June). *Im/possibility of hospitality in early childhood spaces: Negotiating tension between the unconditional and conditional.* Paper presented to the 16th Reconceptualizing Early Childhood Education Conference. University of Victoria, BC.

Conversation. (n.d.). *Online Etymology Dictionary.* Retrieved from Dictionary.com website: http://dictionary.reference.com/browse/conversation

Gibbs, C. (2006). *To be a teacher: Journeys towards authenticity.* Auckland, New Zealand: Pearson Education.

Gibbs, C. (forthcoming). *A heart to teach: Moments of abundant teacher presence.*

Ministry of Education. (1996). *Te Whāriki: He whāriki mātauranga mō ngā mokopuna o Aotearoa—Early childhood curriculum.* Wellington: Learning Media.

Plato (1974). *The Republic.* (D. Lee, Trans.). Harmondsworth: Penguin Books.

THE CHALLENGES AND DILEMMAS OF EDUCATING EARLY CHILDHOOD TEACHERS

Lilian G. Katz
United States

Lilian G. Katz is Professor Emerita of Early Childhood Education at the University of Illinois (Urbana-Champaign) and Co-Director of the Clearinghouse on Early Education and Parenting. She is a Past President of the National Association for the Education of Young Children, and is Editor of the first online peer reviewed bilingual early childhood journal, Early Childhood Research and Practice. Professor Katz is author of more than one hundred publications about early childhood education, teacher education, child development, and parenting of young children, and wrote a monthly column for Parents Magazine *for 13 years. Lilian was founding editor of the* Early Childhood Research Quarterly. *Her most recent book (co-authored with J. H. Helm) is* Young Investigators: The Project Approach in the Early Years. *She has lectured in all 50 states in the United States and in 50 other countries and has held visiting professorships in Australia, Canada, England, Germany, India, Israel, and the West Indies (Barbados campus). Lilian is the recipient of two Fulbright Awards (India and New Zealand), an Honorary Doctor of Letters degree from Whittier College, and an honorary Doctor of Philosophy from the University of Göteborg in Sweden. Professor Katz was born and raised in England and became a U.S. citizen in 1953. She received her BA degree from San Francisco State University (1964) and her PhD in Psychological Studies from Stanford University, California in 1968. She and her late husband Boris Katz have three grown children, five grandsons, and one granddaughter.*

At the outset of this discussion I must acknowledge that there are many countries represented at the Working Forum about which I know far too little to be sure that my comments will be useful. So I must caution you that the ideas and suggestions outlined below are based on many years of experience and study mainly in North America, although I have worked with our colleagues in more than 50 other countries and have served as a visiting professor in five different countries.

I must, therefore, leave it to you to decide what is relevant and useful in your country with its own trends, constraints, and traditions with which I am not familiar.

Introduction

In most countries there are several different groups which have a stake in the education of teachers: national government authorities, provincial or state agencies, local school authorities, professors, instructors, and lecturers who are responsible for training teachers, the students themselves as well as practicing teachers, and of course, ultimately the children and their families as well.

In the United States today, the education of teachers is a topic of constant public and professional discussion, argument, and criticism. Not long ago one of the nation's premier pontificators suggested that the country's educational problems could be solved by closing down teacher education programs (George Will, 2007; http://msnbc.msn.com/id/10753446/site/newsweek/). More generally, in the United States there is a widespread view that whatever is wrong with our society, particularly our economy, is the fault of our schools, and schools are not as effective as they should be because of the teachers who need more and better training.

'one of the nation's premier pontificators suggested that the country's educational problems could be solved by closing down teacher education programs'

The constant criticism of education is focused primarily on elementary and secondary school teachers rather than on children (that is, before the beginning of elementary school) there seems to be a common belief that anybody, or I should say—any woman—can teach the little ones, based largely on maternal instinct. Furthermore, in the United States, the teachers of our youngest children are poorly paid and in far too many cases have very little professional preparation. But, poor working conditions, and low levels of teacher education at the preschool level are common problems in many other countries as well.

All of this current discussion about teacher education—at least in the United States—is occurring at a time when economists have become very vocal about the long-term benefits of high quality preschool education. Economists have shown that high quality early childhood, that is, preschool education, saves a lot of money in the long run (see, for instance, The Early Childhood Longitudinal Program ECLS, 2007). This strong belief that good quality preschool education can have long-term economic as well as educational benefits has raised the issue of how to define good quality (Katz, 1992). A number of studies have shown that the quality of preschool programs is related to the amount of training and the qualifications of the teachers. For example, in reviewing studies on the quality of preschool programs, Kontos and Wilcox-Herzog (2002) reported that the amount of professional preparation of the teacher or caregiver was related to the amount of encouragement they gave to the children. It was also related to the extent to which they promoted children's verbal skills. Another study produced similar results in showing that the more education teachers had, the more likely they were to engage in social interaction and conversation with children. We now know that extended interactions between adults and young children, such as conversations, can have strong positive effects on children's cognitive and intellectual growth (Blair, 2002).

'studies have shown that the quality of preschool programs is related to the amount of training and the qualifications of the teachers'

However, it should be kept in mind that the factors that contribute to the kinds of interactions teachers have with young children are very complex. Many young children are shy in the presence of adults who are new to them, or are not accustomed to extended conversations with adults, and it often takes time for them to get used to interacting with those who are not members of their family or their familiar neighborhood, or their own cultural or ethnic group. Helping young children to overcome these difficulties requires great skill, social as well as intellectual, on the part of the teacher.

Here I want to raise my concern about the distinctions between *academic* and *intellectual* goals of the education of young children that seem to be relevant to the education of their teachers as well. During the last few decades in several countries there has been increasing pressure on preschool programs to introduce children to basic literacy and numeracy skills, commonly referred to as academic instruction. Furthermore, increasing emphasis on testing children has intensified the pressure on preschool programs to prepare children for subsequent schooling, *pushing down* earlier and earlier what probably should not even be done later. In other words,

Historically, as women's roles have undergone critique, so too has the role of early childhood education. And yet perhaps assumptions about caring for and educating children still prevail.

Editors

Lilian creates an important distinction between academic and intellectual goals. This creates interesting challenges and possibilities concerning teaching.

Editors

academic goals are those focused on getting children ready for formal school-related skills and exercises. These are the kinds of things that can be correct, or incorrect. The children must attend to the teacher to memorize the correct answers and correct behaviors and skills. These are also activities and skills that must be practiced with exercises, for example, learning the alphabet, capital or lower case letters, or handwriting, or the rules of punctuation.

'increasing emphasis on testing children has intensified the pressure on preschool programs to prepare children for subsequent schooling'

Nobody argues against such learning—ultimately. But there are many arguments, at least in some countries, about *at what ages* such instruction should be introduced. There are several important things to consider about when is the best time to learn them, as well as about the best ways to learn them. The evidence that we do have— and we certainly need more—is that earlier mastery of academic skills is not necessarily better, especially for boys. It would be very helpful if our national or local authorities would support research to find out whether children who start formal lessons in reading and writing earlier are better off three or four years later than children who begin those lessons later.

'the evidence that we do have—and we certainly need more—is that earlier mastery of academic skills is not necessarily better, especially for boys'

On the other hand, *intellectual* goals refer to children's inborn dispositions to make sense of their experience, to theorize, analyze, synthesize, predict, to hypothesize, and to try to understand cause-effect relationships, and other similar activities of the mind. It is for this reason that I suggest that young children should be involved in investigations in which their growing active minds can be fully engaged.

In other words, offering opportunities for spontaneous play, while it is important and valuable, is not sufficient for supporting their intellectual (versus academic) growth. I have observed over and over again that young children who are intellectually engaged in worthwhile investigations begin to ask for help in using academic skills—for example, writing and counting, *in the service of their intellectual goals*.

As children grow older, we must consider both the intellectual and academic aspects of the curriculum. However, *in principle*, the younger the children are, the more important it is to support and strengthen their inborn intellectual dispositions (see Katz & Chard, 2000). Helping teachers to learn how to provide such support to young children seems to me to be a major challenge for teacher educators in most of our countries.

'the younger the children are, the more important it is to support and strengthen their inborn intellectual dispositions'

I raise these issues because of what I believe to be their relevance to the professional education of teachers. Specifically, if the intellectual goals of early education are to be addressed, then our students and practicing teachers will benefit from education and encouragement that will better enable them to support the development of young children's intellectual dispositions.

Issues in the education of teachers

I propose to discuss some of the issues involved in the education of teachers and teaching practice in two parts. First, I will share some ideas concerning four dilemmas involved in deciding which pedagogical approaches to emphasize during teacher education. Then, in the second part I will share some ideas about a developmental approach to becoming a professional teacher.

Part I. Dilemmas in teacher education

There are many dilemmas facing teacher educators (Katz & Raths, 1992). I use the term *dilemma* here to refer to a situation in which those who prepare teachers must make a choice between two problematic courses of action—traditionally referred to as the two *horns* of a dilemma. By definition, a dilemma is a predicament in which there are advantages as well as disadvantages to the choices of each of the two possible actions. In other words, a dilemma is a situation in which perfect alternatives are not available, and each of the two choices that are available can have both negative and positive effects. As such, a dilemma is not a matter of choosing between right or wrong, but between two different kinds of rights and wrongs. My argument here is also that these dilemmas help to account for both the apparent low level of impact and for the frequent dissatisfaction attributed by many to teacher education.

> 'a dilemma is a predicament in which there are advantages as well as disadvantages to the choices of each of the two possible actions'

Dilemma 1: Emphasis on current versus innovative practices

One of the major dilemmas for teacher educators is whether to train students to teach according to the current, typical, or standard pedagogical practices in preschools and schools or to use up-dated innovative practices. If we do the former, we would be in a situation in which we would be teaching students to use methods they themselves (teacher educators) often do not agree with. On the other hand, however, we could choose to prepare our students to use more modern recently developed or innovative pedagogical approaches that we have good reason to believe would be more beneficial to the children. Each of the two choices of this dilemma has advantages as well as disadvantages.

There are advantages to teaching our college students to use current pedagogical practices that most local teachers use or that the authorities require but with which the professors, lecturers, or instructors in teacher education programs disagree. I am not aware of the situation in all other countries; but in the United States and some other countries, those who prepare teachers are more in favor of what we call *developmentally appropriate practices*—which needs no elaboration here, I think—than are veteran teachers and school authorities, as well as most parents. These groups tend to prefer more formal traditional teaching methods, even for young children.

If student teachers are trained to use traditional formal methods of teaching then, they are likely to adjust more easily to their jobs as teachers than if they are taught to use more innovative developmentally appropriate methods. Such student teachers would quickly feel comfortable and confident in their new role in the classroom. They could

Even though you create community in your teacher education program, student teachers still go out to a wide variety of environments
Chris Naughton

If we accept that tradition and progress are of value, how might we as teacher educators draw from the strengths of both?
Editors

Teachers who are innovative generally show strong self-efficacy and therefore are able to exercise resilience. These can somehow be addressed in our programs.
Editors

also seek advice and suggestions from their more experienced colleagues who use these traditional methods and who will be sympathetic with the new teacher who is just starting to learn what they themselves already know. Indeed, there is some evidence that beginning teachers, at least, teach the way they themselves remember being taught when they were about 6-years-old, even though they are now teaching preschoolers!

Furthermore, when teacher educators emphasize current standard practices they are usually more readily accepted by teachers in the schools and preschools. There is also some evidence to suggest that experienced teachers in the schools tell students and new teachers that they are now *in the real world*, which they say teacher educators do not know enough about and therefore their points of view should not be taken seriously. In addition, there is some evidence that if teacher educators emphasize innovative developmentally appropriate rather than traditional practices, the student teachers often form a kind of *united front* with the teachers in the schools where they are having their practicum experiences and see them as their allies against the professors and lecturers, and give less importance to what the latter have to offer.

'developmentally appropriate teaching methods are more difficult to learn than formal traditional instructional methods'

On the other side of the dilemma, however, is the idea that those who educate teachers are expected to find ways to improve typical practices in the schools based on new knowledge and research about children's development and learning. If the professors, lecturers, and instructors simply encourage their student teachers to use traditional formal pedagogical practices currently in use, then student teachers would not really need a few years of training; in fact, teacher education colleges would not be necessary. Those wishing to become teachers could just spend some time—perhaps a half a year or more—in a classroom with a teacher who uses traditional pedagogical practices, and learn from observing and copying her behaviors and activities, and learn all that will be needed from such direct experience and observation.

If student teachers are trained by their instructors to use innovative practices they might become very discouraged when they begin their in-school experience, and they may feel totally unprepared for what they encounter in the *real world*. When it comes to teaching young children, developmentally appropriate teaching methods are more difficult to learn than formal traditional instructional methods. Such developmentally appropriate practices require careful observation and listening to the children and great sensitivity in responding to them.

Dilemma 2: Coverage versus mastery

All teachers at every level of every subject confront conflicting pressures concerning the extent to which to emphasize *coverage* of the topics in the field versus *mastery* of the knowledge and skills to be learned. In this sense, all teachers at every level are pulled in opposite directions: the more information, concepts, ideas, theories, and so forth that are *covered*, the less of them that are mastered. The wider the scope of the content and skills, the less mastery of them can be achieved, and vice versa. We cannot do equal justice to both coverage and mastery in any field of education.

'we cannot do equal justice to both coverage and mastery in any field of education'

In teacher education there is constant pressure to expand the curriculum so as to cover more content. In recent years we have added in studies concerning diverse cultures, second language learning, extensive elaboration of special needs topics, teacher-parent relationships, and so on. Rarely is it proposed that an element in a course be dropped. In the United States, recent teacher education reform papers urge us to reduce coverage of classes about teaching methods in favor of greater mastery of the content student teachers will ultimately be teaching. In the early childhood field, special attention to relationships between teachers and parents, parent education, and parent involvement are topics that should be included in teacher preparation courses.

One of the significant features of teaching young children is that, rather than being subject-matter oriented, it requires an integration of the curriculum. Thus, our student teachers need to be generalists with a wide range of knowledge. Even though it is unlikely that student teachers will *master* the wide range of knowledge that may form the basis of their teaching young children, the greater coverage will help them when the curriculum and children's interests require them to do so. Furthermore, our teacher education students who are learning to teach young children might be employed in widely diverse types of settings and institutions. It is, therefore, difficult to predict in advance what knowledge will be most useful. So, it would seem to be a good safety measure to expose them to as much information and knowledge as possible about the diversity of children and the communities in which they may become employed.

'our student teachers need to be generalists with a wide range of knowledge'

The main problem in choosing the coverage side of the dilemma is that it offers a teacher education course that might be called the *smattering approach*. Under these conditions, our student teachers are likely to feel under fairly constant pressure to *cram* lots of information into their minds, just in order to get through the required assignments and examinations. Such experience over the period of the course is unlikely to strengthen the disposition to delve into problems and to take responsibility for one's own learning. Furthermore, while the wide range of information, ideas, and skills covered may be relevant and useful, lack of sufficient mastery implies that they are not very likely to be retrieved and employed under the pressure of the real world of action in a classroom. It would, therefore, not be surprising to find that student satisfaction with such courses is low and their impact is low.

All of the suggested additional content to be covered has some merit. On the other hand, given a finite period of time for teacher preparation, would it not be wiser to opt for greater mastery of a narrower range of content and techniques? Are there some techniques that should be designated as having such high priority that their mastery should be emphasized at the expense of the greater coverage?

Another way to look at the choices at hand is to consider which alternative might be related to the acquisition of desirable dispositions. Dispositions have been defined as *habits of mind* or tendencies to respond in certain characteristic ways to classes of situations (Katz & Raths, 1992). It seems to me that mastery rather than coverage is more likely to support the development of the disposition to seek mastery and further knowledge as part of one's professional career which, in turn, can be assumed to impact professional competence and development.

'dispositions have been defined as habits of mind or tendencies to respond in certain characteristic ways to classes of situations'

Another aspect of this dilemma is the question: Can the early childhood profession agree on what knowledge and skills are essential and must be covered? Does the specific content really matter? How much child development knowledge, and of what kind, is really necessary? How much of the history of early childhood education is necessary? How much philosophy of education is essential? Furthermore, it is not clear to what extent there is repetition in the content of teacher education classes, a not uncommon complaint among student teachers.

The decision to emphasize mastery (versus coverage) would require some agreement concerning which knowledge, skills, and techniques are most worth learning and which can be omitted. Can we come to some consensus on this question? It may be that, of the two alternatives in this dilemma, mastery of content worthy of high priority is the preferred choice, primarily because it is likely to allow for greater attention to the cultivation and strengthening of professional dispositions that can be expected to serve the teacher training students *in the long term*.

For example, the dispositions to be resourceful, experimental, and to consider and try alternative approaches to working with children and parents, to be accepting, nurturing, thoughtful, open to fresh ideas, and so forth, can be more easily addressed when the teacher education program is less preoccupied with knowledge and topic coverage, and allows time to delve deeply into a smaller range of topics and techniques and to consider issues of appropriateness, context, situational constraints, and the pros and cons of various practices.

In-depth examination of a few central topics could be offered so as to encourage our students to manifest the disposition to be reflective, to *look up* sources and resources, and to consult others, for example. Emphasis on coverage of a wide range of topics and techniques may engender distaste for study, a feeling of having to *cram* one's mind with collections of vaguely related facts, a laundry list of techniques, and in the process develop an aversion to studying. Such a program may weaken the disposition to go on learning, or to use the skills acquired under such pressure. Indeed, it may not be so important what specific content is offered, but rather whether the content of courses provided is relevant and rich.

'emphasis on coverage of a wide range of topics and techniques may engender distaste for study'

Dilemma 3: Thematic versus eclectic approach
Another dilemma concerns whether a teacher education program should adopt a particular pedagogical model (such as Montessori, HighScope, and others), a philosophy (for example, constructivism, post-modernism, Steiner philosophy, and so on), or theme toward which all the content and skills covered and mastered in the component courses are oriented. It seems reasonable to assume that when messages from all their instructors are in harmony or consistent, the program will have a greater and longer impact on students' professional practices. Or should our student teachers be exposed to an eclectic and diverse array of competing approaches to early childhood teaching? Is not the exposure to competing ideas and methods one of the major values of a higher education? Furthermore, if a single theme or pedagogical approach is

---

These questions spark deeper questions such as what is the place of beliefs in teacher education, and what does it mean to master?

Editors

going to be adopted by a program, how would it be selected? What criteria should be used as a basis for selection? Which of the two alternatives of this dilemma will have greatest impact on our students? Which will be most satisfying to them?

A teacher education program organized around a coherent theme or philosophy would have to be offered by a team that takes a common or united position on what constitute appropriate practices, and in a sense indoctrinates students into that view. As suggested above, there are many examples of such an approach (for instance, Montessori training) that seem to have a lasting impact on graduates. However, such a doctrinaire approach is antithetical to the ethos of a university or institution that proposes openness to all alternative points of view. Furthermore, in a scholarly setting, which typically prizes and rewards individual scholarship often cultivating competition among faculty for star status, teamwork among faculty members is often difficult to achieve.

The eclectic approach also presents problems for student teachers. Student teachers are typically likely to be at a stage of development in which clear unambiguous guidelines and *tips for teaching* are sought. The exposure to competing approaches to teaching could become a source of confusion and anxiety, and hence dissatisfaction. Under these circumstances it would not be surprising for teacher education students to dismiss the college staff as unable to *get their act together* (as some undergraduates have put it) and to form a united front with cooperating or practicum teachers against the influence of university instructors (see Zeichner & Liston, 1987).

The eclectic approach also affects relations between colleagues. How can advocacy of a preferred approach to teaching by one member of the teaching staff occur without casting aspersions upon the judgment of colleagues who espouse other views? Such a situation presents difficult ethical as well as pedagogical conflicts. How is it possible to assert that approach A is developmentally appropriate without suggesting that approach B is not? To suggest to student teachers that they study the array of alternative approaches and select for themselves the one most compatible with their own predilections while they are typically at the stage in their own development when they coerce instructors into providing clear prescriptive *tips for teaching* seems impractical.

In addition, student teachers often press for clear guidelines concerning specific course requirements such as the length of term papers, points awarded for each assignment, and exam questions and explicit criteria by which to obtain an A in their courses. Student teachers' concerns with these kinds of academic procedures are a result of their previous educational experiences—the procedures by which they achieved their current status—and their current developmental stage.

There is reason to believe that a program organized around a coherent single theme or unified approach to teaching will have a deeper and more enduring impact on graduates than a teacher education that offers students a wide range of alternative approaches. However, as yet, no evidence to support this proposition is available.

'a program organized around a coherent single theme or unified approach to teaching will have a deeper and more enduring impact on graduates'

In considering this aspect of the dilemma, we find it useful to apply the *feed forward* hypotheses, namely, that preservice teacher education consists largely of providing

This point is thought-provoking—to some our teaching may appear to be indoctrination while to others it may seem to be emancipatory.
Editors

We think it is vital that teacher educators reflect on how they feel about the content of teacher education programs.
Editors

our students with answers to questions not yet asked. On the other hand, when student teachers' questions are answered, they may feel satisfied at the time, but when they evaluate their preservice education *retrospectively*—perhaps five years later, when they are on the job—their evaluations become more negative. Similarly, preservice experiences evaluated negatively at the time may, in retrospect be re-evaluated positively. In other words, the experiences student teachers have in their preservice course do not change, but the meaning and benefits attributed to them may change with increasing professional service.

Dilemma 4: Affective versus evaluative emphasis

Part of a teacher's role at every level is to address learners' needs for support and encouragement. The affective aspects of teaching refer to this important part of our work in which we express and convey feelings of support, understanding, and acceptance of the learner. Some teacher education programs emphasize the supportive and pastoral functions of the staff more than others. On the other hand, it is also part of every teacher's role to evaluate the progress of learners. Evaluation refers to the regular features such as testing, assigning grades or marks to student teachers' papers, and also deciding whether to approve or disapprove their teaching practices. These evaluative strategies are intended to help us to exclude weak or inept recruits from entering the profession.

Advantages of an emphasis on the affective aspects of the teacher educators' role is that most students in teacher education programs need some emotional support and encouragement to help them through the rough spots. In our field in particular, we have many mature students who have heavy family responsibilities other than being students. Teacher educators, especially in their roles as supervisors of teaching practice, are sometimes subjected to strong pressure from students for nurturance and support. Student teachers frequently seek encouragement to *keep them going*, and to *try again*, to continue in spite of fumbling first efforts. The major advantage to emphasizing the helping and nurturing aspects of the education and supervision of student teachers is that they are likely to feel fairly satisfied with their training experiences.

> 'teacher educators are sometimes subjected to strong pressure from students for nurturance and support'

The disadvantages of emphasizing the affective horn of the dilemma is that the provisions of strong support and encouragement may inhibit the development of student teachers' independence and self-reliance, thereby slowing the processes involved in maturing. Furthermore, the tutor or lecturer often has to choose between continuing to offer support in the hope that a weak student teacher will ultimately improve, versus counseling the student out of the program. If the supervisor or teacher educator waits too long to give critical feedback to the student teacher, it may become too late to deny certification to a student who has already invested much in his or her professional preparation and education.

There is a sense in which strong emphasis on the affective aspects of relationships between teacher educators and student teachers distinguish the ethos of the early childhood education department from other departments in the tertiary or university institution. While some may see this as a desirable distinction, many will take the view that early childhood educators are fuzzy minded, softheaded, and sentimental. They may be seen as less exacting than colleagues in other branches of higher education, as squeamish about applying high standards and making tough decisions about student achievement.

This dilemma invites thinking about a fresh approach to evaluation that is affectively sensitive.

Editors

'an optimal level of stress or pressure for accomplishment such that participants believe that they are being prepared for a profession for which the learning requires real effort and even some optimal stress'

The teacher educator's gate-keeping role requires realistic evaluation of student teachers' progress and counselling poor students out of programs, when necessary. Furthermore, when concern with standards and evaluation is optimally salient to students, a sense that the ethos of the teacher education program is a serious one is conveyed to students. I suggest that a teacher education program should impose an *optimal* level of stress or pressure for accomplishment such that participants believe that they are being prepared for a profession for which the learning requires real effort and even some (optimal) stress and also, that they are preparing for a profession into which not everyone is admitted.

Realistic evaluation requires an *optimal distance* between the teacher educator and the student teachers (Katz, 1995). Student teachers may interpret the distance as a lack of caring and be discouraged by it. One kind of student teacher response may be to form close emotional bonds with their cooperating or practicum teachers and together they may form an alliance against the college staff.

In sum, when teacher educators emphasize their supportive functions, they may admit to the teaching profession some students who might become poor teachers. If, on the other hand, they choose to emphasize their evaluative duties, some student teachers who might have become good teachers may be excluded. After all, some student teachers will improve with the nurturance and support of a supervisor, but some will not. Which error is preferable? How can both responsibilities—to be nurturing and to be evaluative—be optimized? Critical feedback can be more helpful and less debilitating when it is offered in the context of a genuine and trusting relationship.

'when teacher educators emphasize their supportive functions, they may admit to the teaching profession some students who might become poor teachers'

The development of such relationships is highly labor-intensive. They require constant informal contact between staff and student teachers and it would be necessary for the teacher educator to be easily and readily available to students for frequent and constant consultation, not just at times of crisis, but on a regular basis. This ready availability is difficult if staff members are expected to be productive scholars and researchers as well as leaders in their professional organizations.

'the Forum is one space in which teacher education can exchange views about which might be the least worst errors!'

It is most likely the case in all professions that the training and education required to enter into it presents us with many dilemmas and few clearly right or wrong answers to basic questions about our work. The Working Forum is one space in which teacher education can exchange views about which might be the *least worst errors!*

Part 2: A developmental approach to learning to teach

Many years ago I was invited to give a lecture to all the elementary school teachers in a small city. When I asked the district authority what I should talk about, she suggested that I just talk about good teaching. I then said that what might be of interest to the senior experienced teachers would probably not be helpful to the brand new teachers, and if I focus on being helpful to the new teachers, the experienced teachers would most likely be bored. That conversation got me started on thinking about learning to teach, and that having a career as a teacher can be thought about as a developmental process.

'beginners are beginners in every job!'

The concept of development and associated developmental stages has a long history in the field of early childhood education, although several postmodern scholars have argued against the concept of development. I use the term in its modern sense to mean that much learning occurs in some kinds of sequences so that thoughts and behaviors improve in adaptiveness to the environment in which the individual lives and works. In other words, no one can begin a social role, such as that of a teacher or a priest or a banker or prime minister or a physician—as a veteran. Beginners are beginners in every job! In most cases competence in any job improves with experience and the practice that comes with it. Most experienced teachers believe or feel that they were less competent during their first month or first year of teaching than during their fifth one, all other things being equal. Therefore, it seems to me meaningful as well as useful to think of teachers themselves as having developmental sequences or stages in the growth of their professional competence. Furthermore, I suggest that the challenges or tasks at each developmental stage of a teacher's career have particular training needs, so that the support that can help teachers with their work should change as they develop.

The first stage of professional development: Survival stage

During this stage, which may last for the first three months or first year of teaching, their main concern is whether or not they can survive the daily challenges of carrying responsibility for a whole group of young children and their learning. This preoccupation with survival may be expressed to the self in terms such as: *Can I get through the day in one piece? Without losing a child? Can I manage until the end of the week, or until Christmas holiday? Can I really do this kind of work day after day after day? Will I be accepted by my colleagues?* Teachers in their early teaching experiences have frequently reported such questions and doubts.

'the first full impact of responsibility for a group of immature but vigorous young children (to say nothing of encounters with their parents) inevitably provokes anxiety in many beginning teachers'

The first full impact of responsibility for a group of immature but vigorous young children (to say nothing of encounters with their parents) inevitably provokes anxiety in many beginning teachers. The discrepancies between anticipated successes and classroom realities might very well intensify feelings of inadequacy and un-preparedness.

What kind of support would be helpful?

During this survival period teachers are most likely to need support, understanding, encouragement, reassurance, comfort, and guidance. They need direct help with specific skills, and insight into the complex causes of behaviour, all of which are probably best if provided in the classroom. On site supervisors may be principals, senior staff members, advisers, consultants, directors, or other specialized and experienced program assistants often referred to as mentors.

Training must be constantly and readily available from someone who knows the novice teacher and is also familiar with the context in which she is trying to teach. The trainers or mentors should have enough time and flexibility to be available as needed by beginning teachers. Schedules of periodic visits, which have been arranged in advance, cannot be counted on to coincide with trainees' crises, though they may frequently be helpful.

The second stage of professional development: Consolidation

By the end of the first year, though for some teachers even sooner, the teacher has usually acquired some confidence in his or her ability to survive immediate daily crises. In this second stage teachers usually begin to focus on individual children and problem situations. Teachers begin looking for answers to questions like: *How can I help a clinging child or a disruptive child? How can I help a particular child who does not seem to be learning?* These kinds of questions are now differentiated from the general survival issues of keeping the whole class running smoothly.

During the first stage, the new teacher acquires a baseline of information about what young children are like and what to expect of them. By the second stage the teacher begins to identify individual children whose behavior departs from the pattern of most of the children she knows. Thus, she identifies specific individual patterns of behavior that have to be addressed to ensure the steady progress of the whole class.

What kind of support would be helpful?

During this stage, on-site training continues to be valuable. A trainer or mentor can help the teacher by joint exploration of an individual problem case. Take, for example, the case of a young preschool teacher eager to get help who expressed her problem in the question: *How should I deal with a clinging child?* An on-site trainer can, of course, observe the teacher and child in situ and arrive at suggestions of strategies to try fairly quickly.

In other words, an extended give-and-take conversation between teachers and trainers or *mentors* may be the best way to provide help for teachers to interpret their experiences and move toward a solution of the problems faced.

> 'an extended give-and-take conversation between teacher and trainer or mentor may be the best ways to provide help for the teacher to interpret her experience'

The trainers might ask the teachers such questions as: *What have you tried so far? How did the child respond when you did that? Can you give an example of some experiences with this particular child during this week?* The trainers can then respond to teachers' descriptions of their experience with new suggestions and encouragement.

Also, in this stage, psychologists, social and health workers, and other specialists can strengthen the teachers' skills and knowledge. Exchanges of information and ideas with more experienced colleagues may help teachers master developmental tasks of this period. Opportunities to share feelings with other teachers in the same stage of development may help to reduce some sense of personal inadequacy and frustration.

The third stage of professional development: Renewal stage

Often, during the third or fourth year of teaching, teachers begin to get tired of doing the same old things, offering the same activities, and celebrating the same sequence of holidays. They start to ask more questions about new developments in the field: *What are some new approaches to helping children's language development? Who is doing what? Where can I get some new ideas? What are some of the new materials, techniques, approaches, and ideas being developed these days?*

> 'often, during the third or fourth year of teaching, teachers begin to get tired of doing the same old things, offering the same activities, and celebrating the same sequence of holidays'

It may be that what teachers have been doing with children has been quite adequate for them, but they begin to feel that the annual Valentine cards, Easter bunnies, and Christmas trees are not sufficiently interesting! Their own need for renewal and refreshment should be taken seriously.

What kind of support would be helpful?

During this stage, teachers are likely to find it especially helpful to meet colleagues from different programs on both formal and informal occasions. Teachers in this developmental stage are particularly receptive to experiences in local, regional, and national conferences and workshops, and benefit from membership in professional associations and participation in their meetings. They also benefit from reading professional magazines and journals, and viewing films and videotapes. This is also a time when teachers welcome opportunities to visit other classes, programs, and demonstration projects. Concerns about how best to assess young children's learning, and how to report and document it are also likely to blossom during this period.

The fourth stage of professional development: Maturity

Some teachers may reach maturity within three years, while others need five or perhaps even more. Teachers at this stage have come to terms with themselves as teachers and have reached a comfortable level of confidence in their own competence. They now have enough perspective to begin to ask deeper and more theoretical or philosophical questions, such as: *What are my historical and philosophical roots? What is the nature of growth and learning? How are educational decisions made? Can schools change societies?* Perhaps they have asked these questions before. But with a few years of experience, the questions represent a more meaningful search for insight and perspective.

What kind of support would be helpful?

Throughout maturity, teachers benefit from opportunities to participate in conferences

As noted earlier, innovativeness is also associated with resilience. This can be true for teachers regardless of their experience.

Editors

How can we move practitioners from doing 'weather reports' to valuing the purpose of reflection?

Victoria Farguhar-Ayson

and seminars and perhaps to work toward an advanced degree. Mature teachers welcome the chance to read widely and to interact with educators working on many problem areas on many different levels. Training sessions and conference events, which teachers in the second stage enjoy, may not be of interest to the mature fourth stage teachers. Similarly, introspective and philosophical seminars enjoyed by teachers in the mature stage may lead to restlessness and frustration among teachers in their first survival stage.

'Mature teachers welcome the chance to read widely and to interact with educators working on many problem areas on many different levels'

Conclusion

And now, a few suggestions:

- I suggest that for all of us as teachers it is a good idea to cultivate our own intellects and nourish the mind. For teachers, the cultivation of the mind is as important as the cultivation of our capacities for understanding, compassion, and caring—not less important, not more important—but equally so. In other words, we must come to see ourselves as developing professionals—whether we teach adults or children. So I suggest: become a student of your own teaching—a career-long student of your own teaching.

'for all of us as teachers it is a good idea to cultivate our own intellects and nourish the mind'

- Never take someone else's views or opinions of you or your work more seriously than you take your own! Take others' views seriously—there may be much to learn from them—but not more seriously than you take your own; for that is the essence of self-respect, and I believe that children benefit from being around self-respecting adults.

- As teachers, all we have at a given moment in a given situation is our own very best judgment. Throughout our professional lives we study and reflect in order to refine that judgment; we exchange with colleagues, consider others' solutions to the problems we face; we come together at meetings like the Working Forum; we examine the available evidence—all in order to improve our judgment. But in the last analysis, our very best judgment is all there is.

- Finally, remember that whoever might be the leader of our country in 40 or 50 years from now is likely to be in someone's early childhood program today—maybe in your class. I hope she is having a good experience!

'whoever might be the leader of our country in 40 or 50 years from now is likely to be in someone's early childhood program today'

Critical reflection is now regarded as an essential component of teacher education. How do we ensure that beginning teachers engage in collegial reflection with more experienced teachers?

Editors

References

Blair, C. (2002). School readiness: Integration of cognition and emotion in a neurobiological conceptualization of child functioning at school entry. *American Psychologist*, 57(2), 111-127.

Katz, L. G., & Chard, S. C. (2000). *Engaging children's minds: The project approach (3rd ed.)*. Stamford, CT: Ablex Publishing Corporation.

Katz, L. G., & Raths, J. D. (1992). Six dilemmas in teacher education. *Journal of Teacher Education,* 43(5), 376-385.

Katz, L. G. (1972). The developmental stages of preschool teachers. *Elementary School Journal*, 73(1), 50-54.

Katz, L. G. (1992). Multiple perspectives on the quality of early childhood programs. *Childhood Education*, 69(2), 67-71.

Katz, L. G. (1995). Helping others with their teaching. In L. G. Katz (Ed.), *Talks with teachers of young children*. Norwood, NJ: Ablex Publishing Corporation.

Kontos, S., & Wilcox-Herzog, A. (2002). *Teacher preparation and teacher-child interaction in preschools*. ERIC Digest EDO-PS-02-11. University of Illinois, Urbana-Champaign: ERIC Clearinghouse on Elementary and Early Childhood Education.

The Early Childhood Longitudinal Program ECLS (2007). *Institute of Educational Sciences: National Center for Educational Statistics*. Retrieved from http://nces.ed.gov/ecls

Zeichner, K., & Liston, D. P. (1987). Teaching student teachers to reflect. *Harvard Education Review,* 57(1), 23-48.

CHAPTER 1
Policy, programs and practice:
Pathways of early childhood teacher education

In his classic essays, Alfred Whitehead reminded us that:

Humpty Dumpty was a good egg so long as he was on the top of the wall, but you can never set him up again. Whitehead, 1962, p. 94

In recent times, especially, it has become the pasttime of many—including politicians, economists, even educationalists—to reconceptualise education, and especially the preparation of teachers.

Alfred Whitehead's reminder is timely—for the desire to radically change programs of teacher education, and all that is valued in these, must not be at the cost of compromising that which is already established as being good. This, in turn, means that we must know with some confidence what is 'good' in education. Our conversations may help us in such a quest to understand.

Education is an intensely philosophical and political human practice that has increasingly been a public concern. The rapid emergence of political interest in regulating and standardizing early childhood education provides sound evidence of such public interest in education. German political philosopher Hannah Arendt warns that such transformations may have a negative effect on the development of children. She argues:

The more completely modern society discards the distinction between what is private and what is public, between what can thrive only in concealment and what needs to be shown to all in the full light of the public world, the more, that is, it introduces between the private and the public a social sphere in which the private is made public and vice versa, the harder it makes things for its children, who by nature require the security of concealment in order to mature undisturbed. Arendt, 1954, p. 188

Hannah Arendt's challenge to teacher educators is, then, to develop early childhood teacher education programs that are sensitive to the delicate balance between the private and public worlds—between the needs of society, and the needs of individuals and families. In this first chapter the conversations orient around such a balance through exploration of what early childhood teacher education should be about.

Now, in an international publication exploring early childhood teacher education, there is the problem of defining the very term 'teacher education'. Just as there are many forms of early childhood education around the world in which adults engage in educating children before compulsory schooling, so too are there many variations and contexts of early childhood teacher education. In this chapter some of these forms and contexts are explored with particular attention to key philosophical and political underpinnings of teacher education programs. Put simply, this chapter provides some international perspectives on what teacher education has been, is now, and ought to be in the future.

With this broader perspective in mind, this first chapter attends to current and future developments in teacher education in New Zealand, Great Britain, and the United States. The chapter begins with a conversation entitled Cherishing Children. This paper on child advocacy highlights the necessary, but difficult and complex role of protecting children. Roger McClay, former commissioner for children in New Zealand, provides arguments of both the general need to advocate for children, and the role that teacher education might play in inspiring teachers as professionals whose work is very much situated between the private world of family and the public world of society. This challenge is made more complex in a world of such social and cultural diversity, where family and society, private and public, can have very different meanings and manifestations. As such, his paper is not just of relevance to New Zealand, but has important insights for the international context.

Alison Lutton is the NAEYC teacher education program accreditation director. In her paper, NAEYC early childhood professional preparation standards: A vision for tomorrow's early childhood teachers, she discusses the importance of diversity when guiding teacher education programs within boundaries of accepted standards for quality early childhood teacher education. Alison highlights many important contributions of teacher education as exemplars of the potential for community leadership by teacher educators.

Ros Littledyke's paper then asks: *What are our priorities for preparing teachers to work in the early childhood care and education sector?* Her discussion highlights the diversity of teacher education pathways which have different program structures, contents, and participants in Great Britain. Her conversation highlights a key dilemma for teacher educators and student teachers regarding the choice of a suitable teacher education program. Ros summarises the benefits and challenges of different teacher education pathways, with particular attention to the development of shared principles and philosophies.

Finally, Larry Schweinhart's paper, Designing a curriculum for early childhood teachers and caregivers, provides detailed evidence of the benefits of teacher education and argues that such benefits should be universally available. Importantly, Larry invites attention to the ways in which secondary schooling might be regarded as a key site for early childhood teacher education, in which all teenagers might benefit from guidance in the educative nature of being an adult.

These papers provide multiple perspectives on international teacher education programs. We are reminded of wisdom of old which states that:

life [and teacher education programs]: *cannot be made to conform to a system, it cannot be forced into a framework, however nobly conceived… but that the highest function of education is to bring about an integrated individual who is capable of dealing with life as a whole.* Kristnamurti, 1953, p. 24

This chapter opens such a conversation.

Beginning the conversations

The international growth of teacher education in the early childhood sector must be understood within the context of the growth of early childhood programs. Arguably, a nation will construct its teacher education guided by what it wants for its children. And this must surely begin with an understanding of early childhood education.

For instance, assumptions regarding the very purpose of education have a significant impact on the role of the teacher, and hence on the role of teacher education to the extent that even the necessity of having teacher education becomes a point of difference for different national contexts.

Therefore, we suggest that before engaging in the Working Forum conversations on the development of teacher education programs around the world, it is worthwhile to reflect on the following questions:

- What is the history of early childhood education in your country?

- Who is educated to be an early childhood teacher, and how is their teacher education provided?

- What is the relationship, in your country, between the private and public spheres, especially as it relates to early childhood education?

- What are the expectations that are on early childhood teachers, where are these sourced, and how might teacher education respond to these?

CHERISHING CHILDREN

Roger McClay
New Zealand

Roger McClay has worked professionally in education, politics, child advocacy, business, and advising. He is currently the government education liaison person for World Vision New Zealand and Heart Children New Zealand, having come from a term as a political advisor in Parliament and five years as New Zealand's Commissioner for Children. As Commissioner, Roger was outspoken on issues concerning children and young people, and raised the public profile of the office in order to bring improvement to the way in which New Zealand treated its youngest and most vulnerable citizens. Roger was raised on a dairy farm on the Manukau Peninsula before training at Ardmore Teachers College for a career in teaching. He was a teacher and school principal for 15 years. In 1981 he became a Member of Parliament. He was also a Minister of the Crown from 1990-1996 with responsibilities in Youth Affairs, Education and Social Welfare. He was an Associate Minister of Pacific Island Affairs and the Minister responsible for the National Library. He and his wife Dawn live in Auckland and have three adult sons and nine grandchildren. Roger is a Director of R & D McClay Ltd., which specialises in child advocacy and government and education liaison. He is the Chair of the Keep New Zealand Beautiful Board. He is a funeral celebrant and occasionally teaches in local schools as a reliever. Roger is a board member of Variety: The Children's Charity, and a patron of a number of child-based children's charities. In 2005, he was made a member of the Queens Service Order (QSO) in recognition of his public service and contribution to children, and their rights and welfare.

Introduction

Every year on ANZAC Day on April the 25th, we Australians and New Zealanders celebrate and honour those of our brave sons and daughters, who have stood and fought for freedom and democracy and a life of opportunity and the rights of individuals. We remember particularly those who even died for such things. The servicemen and women of our nations died defending the ways we should treat our children. Within this context of remembering those who advocated for us, I would like to speak today about advocating for our children.

> 'within this context of remembering those who advocated for us, I would like to speak today about advocating for our children'

Children are about the last to be recognised officially as having rights. That is in the opinion of the United Nations anyway. We had the rights of almost everyone and everything else before the United Nations Convention on the Rights of the Child (UNCROC) was finally passed in the 1980s. The good news is that it has become the most signed Rights Convention ever. Get a copy of it into the hands of every student teacher. Talk about it often with those students. The rights of children are so basic and sensible. Every society has a responsibility to actually cherish its children. *To cherish* means *to care for tenderly, to nurture, to hold dear*. And that is not too much to ask for in my opinion.

> 'to cherish means to care for tenderly, to nurture, to hold dear'

Our role as a leader is to make children more visible
Catherine Hamill

In the epic New Zealand film, *Once Were Warriors* (Tamahori, 1994) is depicted the mayhem of abuse which can be inflicted within a family when dysfunction and anger are allowed to prevail. In one memorable scene, the father Jake Heke proceeds to beat and punish his wife, even in the presence and hearing of their young children. The children are depicted cowering and whimpering in a bedroom. Everyone leaves when the violence starts. I still have emotional difficulty when watching the four little children cowering on the bottom bunk as dad once again beats their mother to a pulp.

I will never forget, either, my little friend the late great James Whakaruru. I made him almost a household name in New Zealand in the early days of my time as Commissioner for Children, and for good reason. James was born to his 15-year-old mother in the mid '90s.

I call him *late*, as he sadly died just short of his fifth birthday. He was killed by a huge strong, cruel man. At least the size of Jake Heke in that film, *Once Were Warriors*. James's killer was in his mid-twenties and was the bed partner of James's mother… when he was not in prison for having beaten and goaded and injured little James previously. He was not James's birth father.

I call James great, because this little 4-year-old withstood beatings and kicking and beltings and punches and scratches and kneeing and being hurled against walls for most of his short life. He was great because he lasted so long… more than forty visits to hospitals and emergency centres, before we heard anything of him… and then of course it was too late. Imagine that. Any early childhood teacher would have noticed something wrong, I think. On his small tombstone on his grave on a hill top in Hawkes Bay, it says this of my little tormented friend: *James Whakaruru, the inspiration for a nation to cherish its children*. And so we should!—cherish them that is.

Perhaps you have children like James in your country, too? Maybe there are adults like Jake Heke in your societies as well. It might be that teachers trained to work with your children have Jameses in their sights or children whose mothers and fathers are virtually at war with each other. Child abuse and neglect are not always easily noticed. Violence is still so often hidden and not talked about. Forty doctors visits were not even enough for someone to push an alarm bell and rescue this boy.

Encourage teachers to know about abuse and neglect and sound an alarm. The child usually cannot. Encourage student teachers to know what child advocacy is about.

> 'encourage student teachers to know what child advocacy is about'

Speak when the victims cannot. Take action when no one else is likely to. If societies are to cherish children they have to be aware of what can and does happen or not happen to children. Child advocacy is about knowing the UNCROC and it is about professional people like teachers, doctors and nurses, and you and me being advocates for children. Child advocacy is about delving into the uncomfortable zones of family life.

It is easier to not interfere. Some children do not even realise they are living in a world of abuse, neglect, and cruelty. Jake Heke's children and James Whakaruru did not know any other world but the one they were in. Young children cannot understand why the man or woman they love (a mum or dad) is abusing them, emotionally or

Whichever way you look at it, Jake's behaviour is unacceptable. One's immediate reaction may be to blame Jake; but such blame may not really account for the complexity of the circumstances.

Editors

How do we teach respect?

Nanisi Nabbs

As teacher educators, we have a responsibility to protect student teachers by equipping them with the resources to make informed decisions in instances of child advocacy, including protecting themselves.

Editors

We need to help student teachers have the skills to articulate and stand up for their beliefs.

Hui Meng Chen

Teaching is not just a job. It is a work for a larger purpose.

Rachel Tong

physically, and for some poor children even sexually. They know they do not like it, but they do not always know that it is not the way life is supposed to be. And if they do, they do not know who or how to ring for help. Teachers are often the first to be able to do that for them. Get your teachers to be the Commissioner for Children in their places of work. Get them to look out for the ways we might be letting our youngest and greatest assets—our children—down.

But neglect and abuse is not just about physical, emotional, and sexual stuff. Children have a right to be educated well and that goes for our disabled children too, of course. They have a right to medicine and medical care, just as good as that which a King or Prime Minister might expect and even demand to get. They, too, have a right to a place they can call home and some adults who will care for… even love them. They should be safe at home and when not at home. They have a right to not be bullied. We must not abuse them by not listening to their point of view. They cannot be expected to work in order to eat and sleep and feel wanted. They need relaxation and recreation.

It really is all about common sense. It really is all about whether we think we should cherish our children. The early childhood teachers of the world could collectively do so much to see that children like James Whakaruru do not die in vain. They could sound the alarm bells to ensure that children like Jake Heke get the care they need.

Just imagine the impact if every early childhood establishment in your country said *Enough is enough. We want to cherish children* and deliver to them not only the early social and educational welfare they are entitled too… but better still, the very living and life they have a right to.

'just imagine the impact if every early childhood establishment in your country said *Enough is enough. We want to cherish children*.'

Child advocacy is not always easy. Many will try to tear down your ideals about what the rights of children are. *Children should be seen and not heard… smacking never did me any harm… parents know best…* and so on and so forth. These views are still alive and thriving in most communities. James's mother did not know how to be an effective parent. She could not protect or save her son. Neither her parents nor Jake Heke's parents, were good at it. Their parents had not been either. It was intergenerational bad parenting. Why should early childhood teachers not lead their community in running parenting seminars or even full-fledged parenting courses? WOW! What an impact that would have on how we might better cherish our children.

'I mean nurture and value and hold them dear.'

It is certainly time to honour the memory of our lost men and women in times of war. It is time to use our skills as teachers to show our respective societies how to really cherish our children. Please be sure your students know of these things.

Reference

Scholes, R. (Producer), & Tamahori, L. (Director) (1994). *Once were warriors* [motion picture]. New Zealand: Communicado.

NAEYC EARLY CHILDHOOD PROFESSIONAL PREPARATION STANDARDS: A VISION FOR TOMORROW'S EARLY CHILDHOOD TEACHERS

Alison Lutton
United States

 *Alison Lutton began her career with children and families in the 1970s and has worked with children in residential, center and home-based programs. She was an early childhood faculty member at the Community College of Philadelphia and at Northampton Community College where she helped to develop an online associate degree. Alison is a past president of ACCESS, the association of early childhood faculty in associate degree granting institutions. She is currently Director of the Early Childhood Associate Degree Accreditation system for the National Association for the Education of Young Children [NAEYC].*

Introduction

Early childhood teacher education in the United States faces both great opportunities and great challenges. In particular demographic shifts in the United States' population are changing the landscape in early childhood, elementary, secondary, and higher education. This changed demographic landscape can only strengthen our professional commitment to building high quality early childhood programs for all children.

This conversation argues that shared professional standards for early childhood teacher education can serve as a vision and a solid framework for the new approaches and innovation that will be required to build a profession of teachers who hold college degrees, and are culturally competent and diverse in ways that reflect the children and families served. The conversation explores some of the big questions that face early childhood teacher educators in the United States today, intending to engage in discussion and learn from the international perspectives gathered during the Working Forum for Teacher Educators.

> 'shared professional standards for early childhood teacher education can serve as a vision and a solid framework for the new approaches and innovation that will be required to build a profession of teachers'

A changing profession

Cochran (2007) suggests that the United States may be undergoing a paradigm shift that offers an opportunity to shape an approach to early childhood education that is both uniquely American *and* that values and benefits from a global perspective. The early childhood professional landscape has changed over the past decade in ways that have already impacted teacher education in the United States. These changes include:

- the 1999 and 2007 Head Start reauthorizations, which first mandated associate's degrees and then bachelor's degrees for Head Start teachers

> To make a difference, we need to address where the greatest need exists.
>
> Glennie Oborn

- the work of the NAEYC and others to strengthen existing program accreditation systems and to build new ones

- state and community public-private partnerships that brought new voices and new debates to the table

- dramatic demographic changes in the population of the United States, and

- a federal policy emphasis on accountability and assessment across the education system as a whole.

The NAEYC publication *The Children of 2010* (Washington & Andrews, 1998) highlighted demographic shifts indicating that children of color would be the majority in four states by the year 2010. In 2008, 40% of all children in the United States are children of color—Latino, Asian, African American, or African in descent. By 2020, that number will have risen to 47% (Child Trends Data Bank, 2005). One out of five children in the United States lives in an immigrant family. The largest increases in immigrant children are now occurring in southern and mid-western states (United States Census Bureau, 2004).

> 'one out of five children in the United States lives in an immigrant family'

Changes in the United States early childhood infrastructure present both opportunities and challenges. Public support and funding for prekindergarten is growing. But we do not have a federal commitment to the goal of providing all children with the early development and learning experiences that support success in school and beyond. The expectation that all early childhood teachers should have college degrees is rising. We have national professional standards for the programs that serve young children and for the programs that prepare teachers of young children (NAEYC, 2005; Hyson, 2003). But the current child care workforce appears to be losing ground in both education levels and compensation (Bellm & Whitebook, 2006).

> 'the current child care workforce appears to be losing ground in both education levels and compensation'

NAEYC's vision is:

of a well financed, high-quality system… all early childhood professionals have excellent preparation, ongoing professional development, and compensation commensurate with their qualifications and experience. NAEYC, 2007, p. 2

Teacher educators have a critical role to play if we are to make that vision a reality.

Do your teachers need to be qualified?

Over the four days of work together at the Working Forum I have heard participants from different nations asking each other: *Do your teachers need to be qualified*? This question clearly means different things in different national contexts, but it seems to always imply:

- the teachers we are most concerned about are teaching children ages birth through five years outside of established school systems, and

- to be recognized as qualified requires some sort of specialized college degree; depending on our home tertiary or higher education systems that may be a 2-, 3-, 4-, or 5-year degree program specializing in early childhood.

Behind this question are more questions. Is it really a good thing to require that all teachers be degreed teachers? Will requiring college degrees in fact result in better teachers? Will degrees bring more public esteem and better pay? Can this goal be reached outside of the formal school systems, in child care settings? Will we lose some very good teachers? Who will be left behind? Will we have the teacher diversity that we need to serve children and families well?

This paper proposes that, yes, we do need qualified early childhood teachers who have college degrees with early childhood specialization. And, yes, we do need teachers who reflect the diversity of the children and families served. Accomplishing both of these things is no easy task.

We need to take an honest look at teacher education in the real world, as it is experienced by our student teachers. We need to think not just about how to prepare our student teachers to become leaders and advocates, but at how to become leaders and advocates inside our own colleges and universities. We need to learn more about how our higher education systems work in our home countries and states. I would suggest that we all need to ask ourselves two sets of questions as early childhood teacher educators.

1. Does any, and every, degree program prepare qualified teachers?

How should we evaluate the quality of our own programs? Do we know what our shared program goals are for all of our student teachers? Does the faculty share a set of expectations for acceptable student performance on each of these goals? We would all say child development is critical content in any early childhood degree program. But which theorists should all of our graduates learn about? What aspects of those theories are most important? How should student teachers apply these in practice with young children? How do we know what our graduates really know, understand, and can do?

> 'how do we know what our graduates really know, understand, and can do?'

2. How well do our higher education institutions and degree programs work for different kinds of student teachers?

Who do they work well for? Who do they not work well for? What are the current demographics of our tertiary education students?

> 'what are the most salient aspects of diversity that we need to monitor if we are to have the teacher workforce that we will need ten years from now?'

Are there emerging trends in enrolment, retention and successful graduation that need attention? What are the most salient aspects of diversity that we need to monitor if we are to have the teacher workforce that we will need ten years from now? What needs to change about the ways that we currently structure or do early childhood teacher education? What do we need to do now to begin that change?

Our answers to these questions will be informed by our collective understanding of our identity.

Editors

In order to understand how accreditation impacts on quality, it is important to understand how accreditation bodies engage in determining quality.

Editors

Standards as a vision and framework for change

How will we increase the number of qualified teachers with specialized college degrees and build a profession of teachers who reflect the diversity of children and families served? Certainly not by simply doing teacher education as we have always done it. In the United States we have been working to build a shared vision that expresses our vision of a qualified early childhood teacher.

In the United States, accreditation systems are used by government agencies, scholarship programs, and the public to assure the quality of higher education programs. Accreditation is granted based on institution and program standards as demonstrated in written reports, peer reviews and site visits. One of the challenges in this context is to build and use accreditation standards that can serve as a framework for creativity and innovation in teacher education. The NAEYC has had guidelines for early childhood professional preparation programs since 1985. These were revised in 1996 and again in 2001. The most recent revisions made a conceptual change away from guidelines on inputs such as content, field experiences and faculty qualifications toward standards that express our shared professional vision of what tomorrow's early childhood teachers should know and be able to do.

Our national consensus building is reflected in the five current NAEYC standards for preparation of early childhood professionals. As noted in the introduction to the standards, the very word standards makes some people nervous, and with good reason. If poorly developed and inappropriately implemented, standards can be rigid and incompatible with innovative practices. But at their best, standards—whether for children, for programs, or for practitioners— reflect a shared vision based on evidence and professional consensus. Hyson, 2003, p. 5

The five NAEYC standards describe what early childhood professionals should know and be able to do:

- promote child development and learning

- build positive relationships with families and communities

- observe, document and assess young children

- teach and learn using developmentally effective methods and sound knowledge of academic disciplines

- become a professional who is guided by ethical and other professional standards.

Can these standards work as a framework that supports innovation, creativity and faculty leadership? We are exploring that question now. These NAEYC standards are used to review baccalaureate and graduate early childhood programs that seek accreditation from the National Council for Accreditation of Teacher Education. The NAEYC Commission on Early Childhood Associate Degree Accreditation, a new accreditation system that was launched in 2006, also uses these standards.

Both accreditation systems require that teacher education programs demonstrate that they offer learning opportunities and implement student assessment systems aligned with these five standards. In order to maintain accreditation and be successfully reaccredited, the programs must demonstrate ongoing collection and monitoring of student performance data, using it in meaningful ways, reflecting on where their student teachers—or subgroups of student teachers—need greater challenges, different supports, or new opportunities. The rubric used to evaluate teacher education programs requires demonstrated alignment with core standards, and rates as strongest those programs that demonstrate responsiveness to the needs of their unique students and communities.

Preparing the teachers we need

Building a professionally prepared early childhood workforce is a part of the solution to the compensation crisis facing the field. Earnings for people without college degrees are falling precipitously (Barton, 2008). But achieving a college degree does not come easily. Among 25- to 29-year-olds in the United States today, only 31% of Whites, 19% of Blacks, and 10% of Hispanics have attained bachelor degrees (National Center for Education Statistics, 2008).

'building a professionally prepared early childhood workforce is a part of the solution to the compensation crisis facing the field'

This reality is reflected in the demographics of the current early childhood workforce. The most ethnic and linguistic diversity in the United States' education workforce is currently in our child care staff. The percentage of White teachers rises as degree requirements and salaries rise, from 63% of child care workers to 78% of preschool teachers and 82% of elementary and secondary teachers. The figures are most striking for Latino teachers. Child care teachers are 16.5% Latino, but just 6% of preschool, elementary, and secondary teachers are Latino (Chang, 2006).

Current research in the United States is exploring the ways that education, training and credentials are linked to improved quality in programs or improved academic gains for children. Results to date are mixed (Early et al., 2006), but some meta-analyses find more positive outcomes for children when teachers have bachelor degrees (Kelly & Camilli, 2007). Research does not yet enable us to compare associate and baccalaureate level teachers with specialized early childhood degrees (Bellm & Whitebook, 2006). But we know that teacher interactions can predict children's academic, language and social skills (Mashburn, 2008). The field does seem to have consensus that early childhood teachers need specialized early childhood training and general education foundations in the curriculum areas taught in an early childhood program. In most children's programs, the composition will include a structure of differentiated staffing-teaching teams working together with members that have different roles, responsibilities, and qualifications.

'the field does seem to have consensus that early childhood teachers need specialized early childhood training and general education foundations in the curriculum areas taught in an early childhood program'

An indicator that is not yet integrated into most of our systems is the composition of the early childhood teachers as a group—the early childhood workforce in a nation or community, or the team in a program. We know that we want a workforce of teachers who are culturally and linguistically competent and who can work effectively with children and families from backgrounds that are not their own. We also know that we

This situation invites us to consider the conditions that lead to ethnic and linguistic diversity in the early childhood workforce.

Editors

want a workforce of teachers who reflect the diversity of the children and families that they serve.

'we want teachers who reflect the diversity of the children and families that they serve'

Supporting diversity in teacher education programs: Innovation and articulation

The increased diversity in the United States population is changing the education landscape in higher education. Between 1996 and 2006, higher education enrollment in the United States increased by 19%. Much of that growth has been in publicly-funded community colleges, which were founded with the mission of making higher education more accessible to low-income and community-bound students. These colleges typically offer 2-year or associate degree programs designed to build competence to enter a profession and foundations for transfer on to higher level degrees (Government Accountability Office, 2007).

Today, 46% of all undergraduate students in the United States are enrolled in community colleges including almost half of all African American, Pacific Island, and Asian college students. The majority of all Native American and Hispanic college students in the United States are in community colleges (American Association of Community Colleges, 2008).

Many of these students want to be teachers. Some are already working as teachers of young children in child care, Head Start, prekindergarten programs, and as teacher aides in kindergarten, first and second grades. In order to build a qualified and diverse workforce, we need to welcome and support these students. We need to intentionally design teacher education programs that support their successful enrollment, retention, and graduation at both associate and baccalaureate degree levels. We need to deliberately design aligned associate and baccalaureate programs.

'we need to intentionally design teacher education programs that support their successful enrolment, retention and graduation at both associate and baccalaureate degree levels'

These students deserve programs that will meet their interests and needs that are designed with substantive early childhood coursework in the first two years, and that begin field work early and repeat it often so that students have the opportunity to apply new knowledge immediately and to develop reflective practice over time.

Teacher educators as leaders

In my work I have the opportunity to meet teacher educators from all over the United States. In many programs, teacher educators are experimenting with innovative strategies to increase access, retention, and graduation rates for non-traditional students. I will share just a few examples from the United States:

'teacher educators are experimenting with innovative strategies to increase access, retention, and graduation rates for non-traditional students'

- Community colleges typically have a high percentage of students who need to master high school English before they can take college level courses. In one college, the English and early childhood faculty worked together so that early childhood student teachers used early childhood content in the reading and writing assignments in the developmental English course. Enrolment and retention went up, as did the rate of successful course completion for early childhood majors.

- A college in Pennsylvania developed online courses that child care staff in remote rural areas could access state scholarships. They allowed student teachers to do field experiences in their worksites using technology to observe them and to communicate closely with the child care directors, supervising teachers and student teachers. Initial data from common key assessments indicate comparable student performance in the on-campus and online student teacher groups.

- A community college in North Carolina developed a program to recruit and train substitute teachers so child care staff can attend college courses during the day.

- An early childhood faculty member at a tribal college was awarded a fellowship from the American Indian College Fund to study ways that non-native faculty can better understand and support Native American college students.

- A community college in Wisconsin responded to data indicating that Hispanic students were dropping out of the early childhood program at high rates. They now offer first year courses in Spanish and an introductory course at worksites.

- A Texas university includes a community college internship as part of its graduate early childhood program, hoping to build a more qualified and diverse pool of future teacher educator faculty.

Lastly, a news item published during the Working Forum emphasized the opportunities and challenges for both early childhood educators and teacher educators. Monday's *New Zealand Herald* included the headline, *Gran defies barriers to win degree*. Maile Loloa is a preschool teacher who will graduate at age 67 from Manukau Institute of Technology with a Bachelor of Education, specializing in early childhood. Mrs Loloa said, *I believe I can **still** do it* (emphasis added). One of her instructors was a participant in the Working Forum and an author in this publication.

'we have the opportunity to help shape the future for our student teachers, for our profession, and for the broader work of education in and for a democratic society'

Here is what I learned from this story: A few of us in the room were in our twenties, some in our thirties, and many in our forties, fifties, sixties, and beyond. But as teacher educators, we all have a lot of work still to do. If we do this well, we have the opportunity to help shape the future for our student teachers, for our profession, and for the broader work of education in and for a democratic society.

References

American Association of Community Colleges. (2008). American Association of Community Colleges statistics homepage. Retrieved from http://www2.aacc.nche.edu/research/index.htm

Barton, P. E. (2008). How many college graduates does the United States labor force really need? *Change,* January-February 2008. Washington, DC: Heldref Publications.

Bellm, D., & Whitebook, M. (2006). *Roots of decline: How Government policy has de-educated teachers of young children.* Center for the Study of Child Care Employment, Institute of Industrial Relations, Berkeley, CA: University of California at Berkeley.

Chang, H. (2006). *Getting ready for quality: The critical importance of developing and supporting a skilled, ethnically and linguistically diverse early childhood workforce.* Oakland, CA: California Tomorrow.

Child Trends Data Bank. (2005). *Racial and ethnic composition of the child population.* Retrieved from http://www.childtrendsdatabank.org/pdf/60_PDF.pdf

Cochran, M. (2007). *Finding our way: The future of American early care and education.* Washington, DC: Zero to Three National Center for Infants, Toddlers, and Families.

Early, D. M., Bryant, D. M., Pianta, R. C., Clifford, R. M., Burchinal, M. R., Ritchie, S., Howes, C., & Barbarin, O. (2006). Are teachers' education, major, and credentials related to classroom quality and children's academic gains in pre-kindergarten? *Early Childhood Research Quarterly,* 21(2), 174-195.

Government Accountability Office Report to the Chairman, Committee on Education and Labor, House of Representatives. (2007). *Higher education tuition continues to rise, but patterns vary by institution type, enrollment and educational expenditures.* Washington, DC: U.S. Government Accountability Office.

Hyson, M. (2003). Preparing early childhood professionals: *NAEYC's Standards for Programs.* Washington, DC: NAEYC.

Kelly, P., & Camilli, G. (2007). *The impact of teacher education on outcomes in center-based early childhood education programs: A meta-analysis.* New Brunswick, NJ: National Institute for Early Education Research.

Mashburn, A. J., Pianta, R. C., Hamre, B. K., Downer, J. T., Barbarin, O. A., Bryant, D., Burchinal, M., Early, D. M., & Howes, C. (2008). Measures of classroom quality in pre-kindergarten and children's development of academic, language and social skills. *Child Development,* 79(3), 732-749.

National Association for the Education of Young Children. (2005). *NAEYC Early childhood program standards and accreditation criteria: The mark of quality in early childhood education.* Washington, DC: NAEYC.

National Association for the Education of Young Children. (2007). *Making a difference: Excellence in early childhood education. A call to action—Recommendations to the 110th United States Congress.* Washington, DC: NAEYC.

National Center for Education Statistics. (2008). *Digest of Education Statistics 2007.* Washington, DC: National Center for Education Statistics.

Washington, V., & Andrews, J. D. (1998). *Children of 2010.* Washington, DC: NAEYC.

United States Census Bureau. (2004). *The foreign born population in the United States, 2003.* Retrieved from http://www.census.gov/prod/2004pubs/p20-551.pdf.

WHAT ARE OUR PRIORITIES FOR PREPARING STUDENT TEACHERS TO WORK IN THE EARLY CHILDHOOD CARE AND EDUCATION SECTOR?

Ros Littledyke
Australia

Ros Littledyke has had a long and varied career in early childhood education, both as a classroom teacher and teacher educator in the United Kingdom, Canada, Australia, the United States of America, and Finland. Formerly senior lecturer and Field Chair of the BA (Hons) Early Childhood Studies degree at the University of Gloucestershire, she is now a lecturer in early childhood education at the University of New England, New South Wales, Australia. Her research interests include the impact of the affective domain on cognitive development in young children and the professional development of early childhood educators. She has also written and published on environmental education, music education, and early learning.

Introduction

This present conversation is set within the context of the recent developments in the United Kingdom to raise the profile of early years practitioners. The status of Early Years Professional can now be awarded to those working within the private preschool sector who have gained a non-related degree and do not possess Qualified Teacher Status. Early childhood settings in the United Kingdom include family centers, children's centers, play groups, nurseries, long day care, and reception classes in primary schools which cater for children from 4- to 5-year-old. Children normally begin their primary education at 5 years of age. The conferring of Early Years Professional status is in response to the desire of the current United Kingdom Government to improve the quality of provision for families and children within the early childhood education sector. One way of achieving this is to have a degree-qualified practitioner in every early childhood setting by 2015. The pilot phase of the government initiative scheme involved the preparation of a group of highly skilled and experienced practitioners on a fast-tracked program to gain Early Years Professional Status. Ten Government-selected providers supported the candidates in a three month process of demonstrating their skills, knowledge and practice against a set of 39 criteria. This process included practical tasks and a site visit from a qualified assessor. Phases two and three include longer periods of preparation which involve some additional study on the part of the candidates.

In addition to recent Government initiatives, the Early Childhood Studies (ECS) degrees in the United Kingdom are also becoming increasingly popular as a route into early childhood care and education and are frequently accessed in the third year by graduates from 2-year Foundation Degrees in Early Years.

The focus of this conversation is on a critical analysis of the differing educational and training cultures for early childhood practitioners and a consideration of what might be the most effective form of preparation. This is explored both in terms of the curriculum and programs of study offered to students, and the characteristics of student teachers accessing the increasing variety of routes into the sector.

From the perspectives of a teacher educator on a number of Bachelor of Education programs, a Program Leader for two ECS degrees, and a lecturer on two Foundation Degree programs, the relative strengths and weaknesses of four different entry routes into early years care and education have become an increasing preoccupation. The tensions between the tightly controlled curricula offered to early years students on Bachelor of Education programs in the United Kingdom and the broader programs of study offered on degree courses such as ECS are becoming more evident and are potentially divisive within the sector. It is my contention that the provision of high quality care and education for our youngest children should be based on shared principles and a greater philosophical cohesion between early primary and preschool contexts.

Expanding teacher education in the United Kingdom

EN BRA FRÖKEN:
• Inte avbryta leken
• Vara snäll mot barnen
• När barnen gör fel, ska fröken säga till i vanlig röst.

An appropriate starting point for this discussion on teacher preparation is to reflect on the needs of the children in our care as they perceive them. This picture was taken in a preschool in Täby, Sweden. The illustration is of three school rules devised by a group of 4- and 5-year-old children for their teacher:

• Don't interfere with our play
• Be kind to the little children
• We children want to know when we get things wrong, but please tell us in a normal voice.

The origins of this paper, however, date back to 2000. At this time the author was a course leader for an ECS degree in the United Kingdom and also lecturing on an Early Childhood Specialist strand in a Bachelor of Education degree. Early Childhood Education (or Early Years Education) in the United Kingdom, is referred to as the Foundation Stage and covers the 3- to 5-years-olds. It has recently been broadened to include birth to 8-years-old range and is now referred to as the Early Years Foundation Stage. A colleague and I thought it might be useful for our specialist third year Bachelor of Education (Foundation Stage) and ECS student teacher groups to organize a forum for a mutual sharing of information. What became clear through this exercise was that although these student teachers might ultimately work in the same sector, their perspectives on appropriate practice were very different.

ECS degrees are a developing route of entry into teaching for those wishing to teach in the Foundation Stage and are broadly based degrees. Student teachers exiting this degree do not have Qualified Teacher Status and may enter a variety of careers within the early years sector including Foundation Stage teaching. On the other hand, Bachelor of Education student teachers generally plan to follow a career in primary schools and are subjected to a narrower, centrally controlled curriculum focusing far more on content and pedagogy. The result, at the time, appeared to be a more rigid approach to understanding practice than that of the ECS students. It was almost as if these two groups of student teachers inhabited two different cultures.

Although both groups of student teachers were able to agree on certain principles of effective practice, such as the central role of play, it was clear that the ECS student teachers were better able to articulate their philosophy and base this on a better understood, broader theoretical framework. While this was encouraging with respect to the ECS student teachers' professional development, it was worrying that the Bachelor of Education student teachers seem to have a more limited understanding of the broader issues underpinning good practice.

The outcome of this forum led a colleague and me to make some fundamental changes to the Bachelor of Education course in order to address this issue. We were, however, constrained by the context of the Government standards which drove course design for all Bachelor of Education degrees. The focus on content and pedagogy left a limited amount of time for the exploration of the broader context of early childhood.

Since then we have seen a rapid expansion in the early years sector in the United Kingdom with the development of the Sure Start initiative in 1998, and the introduction of *Every Child Matters* (2003), *Birth to Three Matters* (2004), and the *Early Years Foundation Stage* (2007) documents. Early years care and education in the United Kingdom has since become a somewhat crowded policy space, much of it highly positive however.

'early years care and education in the United Kingdom has since become a somewhat crowded policy space'

The *Every Child Matters* (2003) document and related *Sure Start* (1998) initiative was in response to the tragic death of a young child, Victoria Climbie. It identified a need for health, social care, and education to work together and communicate effectively. The interagency focus has not been without its glitches, and as an example of change in practice, has been challenging for some practitioners to embrace (Easen, Atkins, & Dyson, 2000; Milbourne, 2005; Robinson, Anning, & Frost, 2005).

However, there has been a recognition that this is a necessary way forward in supporting young children (Webb & Vulliamy, 2001). In addition, the development of Family and Children's Centers as integrated service hubs incorporating education, health, and social care as a support to families, has been a positive outcome of the Government's commitment to early childhood services in the United Kingdom.

Predicated on these sector developments is the increasing popularity of ECS degrees as an appropriate preparation for practitioners planning to work both in the Foundation Stage and the care and education sector. The degrees are multidisciplinary and provide a sound academic and professional base for a variety of careers working with young children and their families. On graduating, these student teachers will often access a Post Graduate Certificate in Education (PGCE) program and they enter the teaching profession.

The creation of the Children's Workforce and Development Council (CWDC) in 2007, which was conceived with a clear agenda to support the well-being and development of young children, has resulted in a whole new category for the early childhood worker, that of the Early Years Professional. This development of the CWDC is part of the Government's commitment to ensuring that there is a practitioner qualified to degree level in every early years setting by 2015. These identified professionals do not need Qualified Teacher Status in order to take on positions of responsibility in children's centers and early childhood settings. They are not, however, qualified to teach in primary schools.

Another positive development that has taken place is the introduction of the two year Foundation Degrees in the United Kingdom. These provide another route into teaching for mature students already working in an early childhood setting, who may have valuable experience but sometimes few formal qualifications. The model adopted by the University of Gloucestershire was that of students undertaking their first year in designated further education or TAFE colleges and then completing their second year at the University. Once graduated from their second year with a Foundation Degree, these students then had the opportunity to access a level three program of an ECS degree and thence to a full graduate degree and a PGCE. This development has been particularly welcome as a means of attracting mature and experienced practitioners into the teaching profession who might otherwise have been prevented from doing so for a number of reasons such as economic constraints or lack of confidence.

This surge in development and interest in early childhood care and education has, of course, not just taken place in the United Kingdom and is certainly reflected both in New Zealand and Australia. The model of teacher preparation in the United Kingdom is distinctive, however, in that Bachelor of Education student teachers may undertake an early years strand as a specialism within a primary course rather than having, what appears to be, a rigid division between the Bachelor of Teaching and Bachelor of Education, such is the case in New South Wales, Australia.

> 'the United Kingdom is moving closer to the New Zealand and Australian model with the introduction of the Early Years Professional as a distinct career path'

There are both positive and negative aspects to this model, however (Elliott, 2006), and it could be argued that the United Kingdom is moving closer to the New Zealand and Australian model with the introduction of the Early Years Professional as a distinct career path. While the Government's acknowledgement of the significant work of the Early Years Professional in the United Kingdom is highly positive, this could result in an increased divide between preschool and primary school practice in the United Kingdom. Not only would a more rigid divide between the two sectors result in greater transitional issues for young children, it could in fact work counter to the Government's intentions. Those working as Early Years Professionals could become associated purely with the care sector while practitioners with Qualified Teacher Status working in primary schools would have a perceived higher status as school teachers. Such a variety of routes into care and education will attract a very different type of student teacher with different needs and different perspectives on early childhood care and education. The traditional model of the Bachelor of Education, and more recently the ECS degrees, tend to attract the younger school leavers; and the Foundation Degrees and Early Years Professional routes, by the nature of their entry criteria (that candidates must have at least five years work experience in the sector), will attract more mature and highly experienced student teachers.

> 'a variety of routes into care and education will attract a very different type of student teacher with different needs and different perspectives on early childhood care and education'

The benefit of the Bachelor of Education degree is that student teachers experience a broader view of education because they will be working with students across the primary age range. This means they will have the opportunity to discuss issues of

It is important to identify the significance of the divide between primary and early childhood education. This might be simply historical idiosyncrasy, or may serve economic, social, political, or other purposes.

Editors

good practice throughout the primary age phase, appropriate content and pedagogy, and develop good understanding of continuity and progression within the National Curriculum. A further advantage is that a large percentage of their degree course is devoted to school experience or the practicum for which they are given very detailed (though some would suggest constraining) guidelines for practice and focused tutor support. They have a clear career path and are able to exercise some flexibility within this since they are not tied to one age phase in school. There is often a strong sense of cohesion within these groups with shared perspectives and developing experiences.

The less positive aspects are a standards-driven curriculum, resulting in a rather narrower focus on content, with less opportunity to explore the issues underpinning early care and education. The use of the term 'teacher training' rather than 'teacher education' for such programs also suggests a rather more limited vision for Bachelor of Education student teachers. In addition, Foundation Stage specialist students within these Bachelor of Education programs have reported a sense of being marginalised within the larger primary group.

The ECS degrees will often attract young school leavers. These student teachers often have a strong sense of cohesion and shared perspectives. Their strengths lie in their ability to work across health, social care, and education. They are also well prepared to enter the teaching profession in the Foundation Stage, especially with the recent focus in interagency work. What these student teachers do not have, however, is a working knowledge of the National Curriculum and the Foundation Stage Guidance. They are, though, able to work from principles of good practice and a clearly articulated philosophy, based on a sound theoretical framework rather than legislation, when planning learning experiences and environments for young children. School and placement experience can, however, be somewhat inconsistent within these degrees. They are not controlled by a Government agency, the Teacher Development Agency (TDA), and some ECS programs have little or no placement experience in the course. Access to placements can also be an issue. In the TDA controlled Bachelor of Education programs, schools are paid for supporting students. In the ECS sector most of these placements are based on goodwill. Quality assurance issues can also undermine some of the student experience, though with the development of Early Years Professional role it is hoped this situation will improve over time.

By nature of the degree entry requirements for the *Sure Start* endorsed foundation degree, student teachers' placement experience or practicum is not an issue since they will already be working in an early years context. This is a great advantage for teaching and learning strategies in that work-based assignments can be meaningfully embedded into the course and will encourage student teachers to undertake deep reflection and evaluation of their practice. In my experience, much of the best work that these student teachers have produced are their work-based reflections and portfolios that include records of their practical work, evaluations and reflections on journals, book chapters, relevant newspaper articles, and their own learning.

These student teachers are mature, experienced, sometimes challenging, and highly rewarding to work with. Their issues tend to be centered on their own confidence in being able to undertake academic work. The concept of the whole first year in higher education being an induction year is one that is very real for them. They often need a great deal of support in their academic endeavours, not always because they are unable to write academically, but because they do not believe they can. Measures need to be included in the first year that both encourage and extend these student teachers' thinking. Once they have broken through this perceived barrier, many of them go on

> The term 'training' may imply that teaching is a technical act which, maybe unintentionally, devalues the professional complexity of teaching.
>
> Editors

> Moral and ethical education needs to be introduced in the first year to set a foundation.
>
> Donna Wrack

As teacher educators, a challenge is to enable student teachers to explore their own visions, and to appreciate both its sharedness and distinctiveness.

Editors

to demonstrate an ability to reflect and analyze theory and practice at a very advanced level and potentially progress to becoming outstanding practitioners.

'these student teachers often need a great deal of support in their academic endeavours'

These different routes into early years education take place in different cultures, contexts and with different entering characteristics of learners. Many of the ECS and Bachelor of Education student teachers are very young and may still be developing socially and emotionally as well as intellectually. Mature student teachers entering the *Sure Start* endorsed foundation degrees, often with growing families, seem more able to reflect confidently on links between theory and practice, though they are sometimes less confident about their academic skills. Institutions designing early years programs have to respond to both the needs of their students and the professional demands that their students will meet on graduation. My experience is that these differing routes into early years care and education result in a very different type of professional, especially between the Bachelor of Education and ECS student teachers.

The development of the sector, the increasing proliferation of different routes into early years care and education, and the introduction of the new Early Years Professional raise a number of issues:

- Which model best prepares student teachers for the rapidly developing early years care and education sector? It may be necessary for our student teachers to undertake a variety of roles as practitioners within the sector, especially with the development of interagency working. Student teachers will need a much broader understanding of the issues underpinning care and education.

- The different cultures experienced in student teacher preparation may mean that practitioners working in the same workplace and fulfilling the same role may not have a shared vision—how would this impact on children?

'different cultures experienced in student teacher preparation may mean that practitioners working in the same workplace and fulfilling the same role may not have a shared vision'

- The pay, conditions of work, and status may well be unequal for those fulfilling the same pedagogical role— this is particularly a concern with the Early Years Professional status. An issue has also arisen in United Kingdom of the difference in status between care and education. Teachers have felt their status has been undermined by association with a carer role rather than that of an educator role.

- What is the most successful model for preparing early years practitioners to have a robust professional identity and who will be confident advocates for young children? What does it mean to be an early years professional? What do we see as a professional role in early years care and education?

'what do we see as a professional role in early years care and education?'

- How do we best prepare our student teachers to care for, and educate, children for an unknown future? Is a tightly constrained, centrally controlled, standards-driven curriculum appropriate or should we be needs-led and focusing on flexibility and creativity?

- The divide between philosophies and practices of early childhood educators and primary school teachers is an issue. How does the transition between preschool and primary school impact on young children?

The non-integrated, differentiated routes between preschool practice and primary practice are one model of early childhood teacher preparation which has many supporters. However, non-integrated routes raise the issue of transition between the two sectors. Transition is recognized as one of the *flashpoints* in a young child's educational experience and it can often have a negative impact (Yeboah, 2002). It is based on an assumption that children seemingly metamorphose over the summer between preschool and primary school into different beings with a different set of needs.

There are, of course, strategies that schools and early childhood settings employ to ease this transition, but should we not organize our education and practitioner preparation in such a way that transition is seamless? The 'them' and 'us' culture between the two sectors that is currently prevalent is both unhelpful to educators and potentially damaging to children.

> 'should we not organize our education and practitioner preparation in such a way that transition is seamless?'

A recent survey that I undertook with my distance learning student teachers revealed no clear preference in current opinion as to whether having two separate degrees in New South Wales, Australia, is divisive. While this survey attracted only 40 responses from a pool of 250 student teachers, the feedback was interesting. These student teachers were asked two questions:

- Do you feel that the differentiation in teacher education between early childhood education and primary school is obstructive in any way? and

- Do you think of yourself as a professional and, if so, why?

In all, 45% of these student teachers believed that the non-integration between the two sectors is divisive and 55% believed that it is positive. The reasons that they gave were interesting. Those who believed that the differentiation is positive gave answers which focused mainly on the children's needs and experiences. One student teacher said:

The training given for 4-8 years is very relevant to the requirements of this age group to be nurtured and challenged in ways that follow their interests as a lead to meaningful learning.

Another commented:

Early childhood is meant to focus on how children's brains develop and is structured for future learning. I think that early childhood teachers need this specific knowledge to ensure that their classrooms are designed to allow for a variety of learning styles and experimentation... I see primary years as solely teaching children knowledge. So they need skills in understanding specific areas of the curriculum and finding a variety of ways to deliver and explain this

> In organizing for seamless transitions, there are interesting issues that may arise. For example, what happens to pedagogical distinctiveness when transitions are made seamless?
> Editors

information. I think they could still do with some basic knowledge on how children develop to help them solely as a professional.

The above quotations perhaps identify some misconceptions about primary practice but also highlight the significance of the division to the participants. The view of many of these experienced student teachers is that primary teaching is all about content rather than process.

Those who responded with a negative view of the differentiation between the sectors tended to focus more on the impact on career development and status. For instance, one wrote:

In some respects I believe the divide between primary and early childhood has a negative impact on the way we are viewed as early childhood educators. I think the differentiation in pay and conditions suggests the work we do is less important. I think we could work together to bridge the gap between how learning is approached in early childhood settings and the rigidity of the school system.

The following student teacher, who worked as a nursery nurse in school in the United Kingdom, highlights some of the issues very clearly:

When you are working in child care centers, you are not treated as a professional. While in school my opinions about child development and education were considered and not only that, were valued. Why is it that being the same person in child care as I am in school I get valued so much more for my knowledge and experience? When I am in what is considered an 'educational position' rather than a child care position, it is considered by many to be a baby sitting service… People like me who have very good skills with children feel undervalued when the pay does not reflect the position's responsibilities.

> 'people like me who have very good skills with children feel undervalued when the pay does not reflect the position's responsibilities'

Some 90% of the participants replied to the second question that they had a positive sense of their professionalism, identifying their skills rather than the theoretical framework on which they based their practice. For instance, one commented:

In my career I do feel like a professional, but this is a personal choice I make on a daily basis. I use the skills I have and the ones I am gaining through my degree to educate the children, parents, and people I come into contact with on a daily basis. I work in a long day care center so it is easy to fall into the 'just a babysitter' tag that is sometimes attached to our job. I use my expertise to grow as a teaching professional and put these skills into daily practice when I am working with children.

The responses of these early childhood education student teachers reflect some of the issues raised above:

- the perceived differences in practice

- the impact of transition on children coping with very different philosophies of education as they move from early childhood settings to primary school, and

- the perception of status for practitioners, especially those working in long day care as highlighted by the student teacher who worked in the United Kingdom.

The issues surrounding transition, I believe, could be avoided by a clearer articulation between early childhood education practice and philosophy and the practice and philosophy of primary education. Like Elliott (2006), I would not wish to see the disappearance of the dedicated early childhood programs currently in existence, but would suggest that perhaps we need to be more proactive in the tertiary sector and provide more contexts in which the two phases of education can study, work, and develop together to overcome what appears to be a mutual lack of trust. For instance, in the 'pedagogical meeting places' (Korpi, 2005; Moss & Bennett, 2006) it is seen as desirable that *the preschool should influence at least the early years of compulsory school* (Moss & Bennett, 2006, p. 2).

> 'we can no longer count on an army of young women with limited education to take up low status, poorly paid work in the child care sector'

With regard to the status of early childhood practitioners, I am reminded of a comment made by Peter Moss at a Foundation Stage conference in London a few years ago. He suggested that in the United Kingdom especially, we can no longer count on an army of young women with limited education to take up low status, poorly paid work in the child care sector. Young women will no longer be willing to do this kind of work when access to more highly paid work is available.

The introduction of the EYPS in some measure is a response to Peter Moss's comment, though this initiative has highlighted some considerable tensions in the system. Government states that it recognizes the need for well qualified staff in the sector; well qualified staff will demand increased pay and better conditions which, in turn, will raise the cost of child care which then impacts on the opportunities for women to access the workforce.

All of us working in the early childhood sector recognize the fundamental significance of high quality care and education staffed by well qualified and reflective practitioners and our respective governments (Australia, New Zealand, and the United Kingdom) appear to reflect that understanding in their endeavors to increase the proportion of well qualified graduates in early childhood settings (Elliott, 2006), though not all in these countries, it would seem, share that perception.

In response to a question in Parliament about early childhood educator qualifications, the Education Minister (NZ) referred to 'unqualified early childhood teachers' adding that life experience, warmth, and age should be sufficient to confer qualified teacher status on experienced and competent people already working in childhood services. Elliot, 2006 p. 37

As Elliott points out, the notion of conferring qualified teacher status on unqualified teachers is a contradiction in terms and does little to enhance the status of those working in the sector. One has to question what it is that governments really want. Hopefully, though, we have moved on since 1905:

> 'the notion of conferring qualified teacher status on unqualified teachers is a contradiction in terms and does little to enhance the status of those working in the sector'

There is general agreement that the best informed is not necessarily the best baby minder. It is desirable that there should be special training for infant teachers, but under present circumstances might not two supplementary teachers of good motherly instincts be as good for

This comment resonates with Lilian Katz's concerns about general perceptions of early childhood care and education as a gendered profession.

Editors

60 babies between three and five years of age as one clever ex-collegian? These girls, who would stay for a few years before marriage, would not expect or need so high a salary as the teacher trained for a life profession. Board of Education, 1905

Plus ça change?

References

Department for Education and Skills. (2004). *Birth to Three Matters*. Sudbury, UK: DfES Publications.

Board of Education. (1905). *Report of Children Under Five Years of Age in Public Elementary Schools*. London, HMSO, United Kingdom.

Easen, P., Atkins, M., & Dyson, A. (2000). Inter-professional collaboration and conceptualisations of practice. *Children and Society*, 14(5), 355-367.

Department for Education and Skills. (2007). *Early Years Foundation Stage.* (2007). Sudbury, UK: DfES Publications.

Elliot, A. (2006). Early Childhood Education, *Australian Education Review, Special Report*. Camberwell, ACER.

Department for Children, Schools, and Families. (2003). *Every Child Matters, Executive Summary*. Norwich, UK: The Stationery Office.

Korpi, B. M. (2005). The foundation of lifelong learning. *Children in Europe*, 9, 10-11.

Milbourne, M. (2005). Children, families, and inter-agency work: experiences of partnership work in primary education settings. *British Educational Research Journal*, 31(6), 675- 695.

Moss, P., & Bennett, J. (2006). *Toward a new pedagogical meeting place? Bringing early childhood into the education system*. Briefing Paper, Nuffield Educational Seminar. Retrieved from http://www.nuffieldfoundation.org/go/grants/education

Robinson, M., Anning, A., & Frost, N. (2005). When is a teacher not a teacher?: Knowledge creation and the professional identity of teachers within multi-agency teams. *Studies in Continuing Education*, 27(2), 175-191.

Webb, R & Vulliamy, G. (2001). Joining up the solutions: The rhetoric and practice of inter-agency cooperation. *Children and Society, 15*(5), 315-332.

Yeboah, D. A. (2002). Enhancing transition from early childhood phase to primary education, *Early Years*, 22(1), 51-68

DESIGNING A CURRICULUM FOR EARLY CHILDHOOD TEACHERS AND CAREGIVERS

Lawrence J. Schweinhart
United States

Larry Schweinhart is an early childhood program researcher and speaker throughout the United States and in other countries. He has conducted research at the HighScope Educational Research Foundation in Ypsilanti, Michigan, since 1975 and served as its president since 2003. Larry has directed the HighScope Perry Preschool Study through age 40, the Michigan School Readiness Program Evaluation, HighScope's Head Start Quality Research Center, and the development and validation of the HighScope Child Observation Record. Larry received his PhD in Education from Indiana University in 1975. He and his wife have two children and three grandchildren.

Introduction

Early childhood programs in the United States are not institutionalized like educational programs for children and youth. Instead, they operate in four types of early childhood settings: schools, community agencies, other people's homes, and parents' own homes. Three long-term studies show that the quality of these preschool programs can have long-term effects and strong return on investment. However, three other, short-term studies show that not all preschool programs have such powerful effects, and indeed most existing preschool programs in schools and community agencies have only modest effects on children's development.

> 'three long-term studies show that the quality of these preschool programs can have long-term effects and strong return on investment'

A central task of some early childhood teacher educators is to provide prospective early childhood teachers with coursework towards bachelor degrees and certification. But these apply mainly to school teachers and are not required of most teachers and caregivers in community agencies, private homes, or parents in their own homes.

> 'such education should begin in high school courses on child development, parenting, and caregiving'

Early childhood teacher educators in community colleges and preservice and inservice training programs of all sorts must train adults for these roles as well. Such education should begin in high school courses on child development, parenting, and caregiving. Thus, an early childhood curriculum must be accessible at two levels—school teachers and caregivers or parents. At both levels, it should specify basic principles and practices of teaching and learning. For school teachers, it has a fully articulated structure that specifies content objectives consistently with the lifelong curriculum and is supported by an assessment system. The HighScope Curriculum, for example, is accessible not only to school teachers, but also to caregivers and parents.

In employing people to work with us, I have seen those who have been in training regurgitate what they have learnt. On the other hand, the words written or spoken by untrained people came from the heart. What do we do to them when they go through our programs?

Julie Treweek

Education in early childhood versus childhood and youth

Early childhood programs are not institutionalized like educational programs for children and youth. Throughout the world, children and youth attend public schools that are publicly funded and available to virtually everyone. While some early childhood programs are publicly funded, many are not. If they operate within public schools or are otherwise publicly funded, they may be available to virtually everyone. Otherwise, they are only available to children who meet the entrance criteria, which always include age.

Instead, some early childhood programs operate within public schools, others operate within community agencies, and still others are established in people's homes by relatives or non-relatives who take care of other people's children. In addition, one might say that some parents operate their own early childhood programs by rearing their children themselves exclusively. These four types of early childhood settings— schools, community agencies, other people's homes, and parents' own homes—might be further subdivided, but alone constitute sufficient differentiation to make the point that the basic types of early childhood settings vary greatly in governance, available resources, and reasonable expectations for how much they contribute to children's development.

In fact, longitudinal research on the effects of early childhood programs shows that they vary greatly in what they can achieve. Three studies show that high quality preschool programs in schools and community agencies can have long-term effects and strong return on investment. However, three other studies show that not all preschool programs have such powerful effects, and indeed most existing preschool programs in schools and community agencies have only modest effects on children's development.

> 'longitudinal research on the effects of early childhood programs shows that they vary greatly in what they can achieve'

Three longitudinal studies

Three long-term early childhood program follow-up studies stand out for their duration and methodological quality—the HighScope Perry Preschool Study, the Carolina Abecedarian Project Study, and the Chicago Child-Parent Centers Study. These three studies offer the best recent evidence of the long-term effects of good preschool programs.

The HighScope Perry Preschool Study

The HighScope Perry Preschool Study is a scientific experiment that has identified the short- and long-term effects of a high quality preschool education program for young children living in poverty (Schweinhart, Montie, Xiang, Barnett, Belfield, & Nores, 2005). Teachers of this program had degrees and certification in education specialized in early childhood. They also engaged in continuing self-study and curriculum development.

> 'results revealed that the program group outperformed the no-program group'

Importantly, results revealed that the program group outperformed the no-program group on various intellectual and language tests from their preschool years up to age 7; school achievement tests at 9, 10, and 14; and literacy tests at 19 and 27. During their schooling, fewer program than no-program females were treated for mental impairment or retained in grade. More of the program group than the no-program group graduated from high school, specifically, more program females than no-program females. As teens, the program group had better attitudes toward school than the no-program group. More of the program group than the no-program group were employed as adults, and the program group had higher median annual earnings than the no-program group. More of the program group than the no-program group owned their own homes. By 40, fewer of the program group than the no-program group were arrested five or more times, and fewer were arrested for violent crimes, property crimes, and drug crimes. Fewer of the program group than the no-program group were sentenced to prison or jail. In constant 2000 dollars discounted at 3%, the economic return to society for the program was $244,812 per participant on an investment of $15,166 per participant—$16.14 per dollar invested.

Carolina Abecedarian Study

Ramey and his colleagues at the University of North Carolina at Chapel Hill began the Carolina Abecedarian Study in 1972 (Campbell, Ramey, Pungello, Sparling, & Miller-Johnson, 2002). They randomly assigned 111 infants from poor families either to a special program group or a typical child care group. The special program was a full-day, full-year day care program for children that lasted the five years from birth to elementary school. The special program's goal was to enhance children's cognitive and personal characteristics so they would achieve greater school success. It offered infants and toddlers good physical care, optimal adult-child interaction, and a variety of playthings and opportunities to explore them. It offered preschoolers a developmentally appropriate preschool learning environment.

> 'this was the first study to find preschool program benefits on participants' intellectual performance and academic achievement throughout their schooling'

This was the first study to find preschool program benefits on participants' intellectual performance and academic achievement throughout their schooling. Mean IQs of program and no-program groups, which were the same at study entry, were significantly higher from ages 3 to 21, as were achievement scores at age 15. Fewer of the program group than the no-program group had been retained in grade, and fewer had received special services. More of the program group than the no-program group graduated from high school or received a General Educational Development certificate, and more had attended a four-year college. Fewer of the program group than the no-program group became teen parents. However, the program and no-program groups did not differ significantly in arrests by age 19 (Clarke & Campbell, 1998). In 2000 dollars discounted at 3% annually (converted from the 2002 dollars reported), the program cost $34,476 per child ($13,362 per child per year) and yielded benefits to society of $130,300–$3.78 return per dollar invested (Barnett & Masse, 2007).

Chicago Longitudinal Study

Beginning in 1985, the Chicago Longitudinal Study, conducted by Arthur Reynolds and colleagues examined the effects of the Chicago Child-Parent Centers (CPC) program offered by the nation's third largest public school district (Reynolds, Temple, Robertson, & Mann, 2001). The part-day preschool program was citywide and the

This observation is interesting. However, we feel cautioned by the Māori proverb, which translates in English as 'the inside of the house is indeed inside the house; the outside is certainly outside'.

Editors

sample consisted of 1,539 low-income children at 25 schools—989 who had been in the program and 550 who had not. Families in this study went to their neighborhood schools, and children were not randomly assigned to groups. The program emphasized attainment of academic skills through relatively structured learning experiences presented by teachers.

The preschool program group did significantly better than the no-preschool program group in educational performance and social behavior, with lower rates of grade retention and special education placement followed by a higher rate of high school completion and a lower rate of juvenile arrests. In 2000 dollars discounted at 3% annually (converted from the 1998 dollars reported), the program cost $6,956 per child participating 1.5 years on average and yielded benefits of $49,564 per participant, $7.10 return per dollar invested (Reynolds, Temple, Robertson, & Mann, 2002).

At least two of these three studies found positive effects on children's intellectual performance in childhood, school achievement in adolescence, reduced placements in special education, reduced retentions in grade, improved high school graduation rate, reduced arrest rates, and reduced teen pregnancies. All three studies found economic returns were at least several times as great as the initial program investment. Economists have viewed this evidence as stronger than that for most other public investments (Heckman, 2006; Rolnick & Grunwald, 2003).

'all three studies found economic returns that were at least several times as great as the initial program investment'

Not all early childhood programs have these effects

In contrast, three recent studies of government-sponsored preschool programs in the United States show that not all early childhood programs, not even all early childhood programs in schools or community agencies, have such powerful results. Typical early childhood programs in schools and community agencies appear to have modest effects on children's development—worthwhile, but not extraordinary.

'typical early childhood programs in schools and community agencies appear to have modest effects on children's development—worthwhile, but not extraordinary'

The Head Start Family and Child Experiences Survey (FACES)

This is a study of a nationally representative sample of Head Start programs for low-income 3- and 4-year-olds in the United States (Zill et al., 2003). The first cohort of 3,200 children entered Head Start in fall 1997; the second cohort of 2,800 children entered Head Start in fall 2000. In Head Start, children improved on important aspects of school readiness, narrowing the gap between them and the general population, but still lagging behind. Relative to national norms, children made significant gains during their Head Start year, particularly in vocabulary and early writing skills. Children in Head Start grew in social skills and reduced hyperactive behavior, especially if they started out more shy, aggressive, or hyperactive. The study found that Head Start classrooms were rated to have good quality. Most programs used a specific integrated curriculum, particularly Creative Curriculum™ and HighScope.

Use of these curricula and higher teacher salaries were predictive of positive child outcomes. Teachers' educational credentials were linked to greater gains in early writing skills. In addition, provision of preschool services for a longer period each day was tied to greater cognitive gains by children.

Based on follow-up of the 1997 cohort, Head Start graduates showed further progress toward national averages during kindergarten, with substantial gains in vocabulary, early mathematics, and early writing skills. Most Head Start graduates could identify most or all of the letters of the alphabet by the end of kindergarten, and more than half could recognize beginning sounds of words.

> 'most Head Start graduates could identify most or all of the letters of the alphabet by the end of kindergarten, and more than half could recognize beginning sounds of words'

The Head Start Impact Study

Now under way, this study involves a nationally representative sample of Head Start programs for low income 3- and 4-year-olds and random assignment of about 5,000 children to Head Start or no Head Start. This study has so far provided results for entering 3-year-olds and entering 4-year-olds after one year in Head Start and will follow them through the end of kindergarten and first grade (Administration for Children and Families, 2005). It has found evidence of small to moderate Head Start effects on children's literacy skills (pre-reading, pre-writing, parent-reported literacy skills, 3-year-olds' vocabulary), reduced problem behaviors of 3-year-olds, children's access to health care, parents' reading to their children, and reduced use of physical discipline of 3-year-olds.

Study of the effects of five state-funded preschool programs

Barnett, Lamy, and Jung (2005) led a study of the effects of five state-funded preschool programs on the academic skills of entering kindergartners. In the past couple decades, most of the 50 states in the United States have invested state money in preschool programs mostly for children at risk of school failure. This study involved 5,071 children from Michigan, New Jersey, Oklahoma, South Carolina, and West Virginia. Children who did and did not make the age cut off for program entry were compared using a regression discontinuity design. The programs were found to have statistically significant, meaningful effects on children's vocabulary, print awareness skills, and early mathematics skills.

The long-term studies identified larger short-term effects than recent short-term studies have. For example, in the Head Start Impact Study, the difference between the Head Start and no Head Start groups for the Peabody Picture Vocabulary Test (version III) scores of entering 3-year-olds after one year of Head Start was 1.5 points. Children gained 4 points on this measure during their program year in the Head Start FACES study and in the 5-state preschool study. In contrast, children in the HighScope Perry Preschool program gained 8 points in their first year on the PPVT (original version), and a total of 14 points in two years.

Effects have been found for these various programs in schools and community agencies in contrast to parents raising children at home or child care in other settings. The other category of early childhood settings, early childhood programs in people's homes, has been seldom studied, and few effects have been identified. Yet this category is a major source of child care. Further, the studies finding effects have almost all focused on children living in poverty. Few studies have been conducted, hence few effects found, for programs serving children in middle-income families, except for one conducted in Tulsa, Oklahoma, by Gormley, Gayer, Phillips, and Dawson (2005), which found strong program effects on achievement test scores for letter and word identification, spelling, and applied mathematics problems. Clearly, more research is needed on early childhood programs in people's homes and programs that serve young children living in middle-income families.

'few studies have been conducted, hence few effects found, for programs serving children in middle-income families'

Generalizing findings

Until more research is conducted, how should early childhood teacher educators conceptualize their task? Narrowly defined, it is to provide prospective early childhood teachers with coursework towards whatever degree or certification they are seeking. Even then, the match between these degrees and available jobs must shape the content of the coursework. Teachers with bachelor's or master's degrees will probably focus on school teacher certification and be eligible for jobs in schools not only in prekindergarten but also in the elementary grades. Some of them will find teaching jobs in community agencies.

Head Start, the federal program for young children living in poverty in the United States, offers a case study regarding early childhood teacher certification. When the program was originally designed in 1964, Head Start teachers were not required to have school teacher certification and emphasis was placed on hiring people from the community being served. The Federal Government developed and supported programs for Child Development Associate (CDA) credentials starting in 1975 to improve the quality of Head Start teaching staff and child caregivers. In recent years, Congress has required an increasing percentage of Head Start teachers to have degrees, with bachelor degrees for 50% of Head Start teachers targeted for 2011. In May, 2003, 29% of Head Start teachers nationwide had a bachelor's or graduate degree in early childhood education or a related field, 23% had an associate's degree, and 34% had a CDA credential or equivalent (U.S. General Accounting Office, 2003). About half of the Head Start teachers in public and private schools had bachelor or graduate degrees, while the percentage in other types of agencies ranged from 7% to 39%.

How do early childhood teacher educators address the challenge of preparing students for child care and, indeed, for parenthood? A national survey in the United States found that in 2001, the country had 20.2 million children under 6-years-old who had not yet entered kindergarten (Mulligan, Brimhall, West, & Chapman, 2005). Three-fifths of these children had some type of non-parental care and education arrangement at least weekly: 33% received care and education in a center under various auspices (a proportion that grew steadily from 8% of infants to 65% of 4-year-olds); 16% received care and education from a non-relative in a home; and 22% received care and education from a relative in a home. The proportions are probably typical of what would be found in other countries. If early childhood teacher educators focus only on certifying school teachers, the teachers they educate are serving only a small fraction of young children.

'how do early childhood teacher educators address the challenge of preparing students for child care and, indeed, for parenthood?'

The gap between professional recommendations and government regulations regarding child care in the United States is very wide. The National Association of Child Care Resource and Referral Agencies (NACCRRA) in the United States (2007) recommends that child care center directors have at least a bachelor's degree, but only one state does so; and that child care center teachers have at least a Child Development Associate credential, but 21 states require no education and 28 require only a high school diploma or the equivalent.

> 'the gap between professional recommendations and government regulations regarding child care in the United States is very wide'

Only five states require orientation, first aid, and other health and safety training. NACCRRA recommends that states require that child care center teachers have 40 hours of training initially and 24 hours a year. As long as the government expects so little of child care teachers, it is difficult for child care advocates to argue that more training and professional development is necessary.

> 'as long as the government expects so little of child care teachers, it is difficult for child care advocates to argue that more training and professional development is necessary'

In addressing the question of how early childhood teacher educators should prepare students for child care and parenthood, it is helpful to have an expansive, inclusive definition of early childhood teacher education, one that goes well beyond coursework in universities to include community colleges and preservice and inservice training programs of all sorts. It is clear that the United States states do not require much training or education for child caregivers. Some might be tempted to write off the training that they are required to receive as hopelessly inadequate to the task. Put in terms of the longitudinal studies cited above, high quality early childhood programs with well-trained teachers have the capacity to make an extraordinary contribution to the development of young children. One reasonable response is to work hard to secure high quality early childhood programs for as many young children as possible.

At the same time, it is important to educate people who become home and center caregivers and parents to do the best job possible. Such education should begin in high school if not earlier, because high school is the way to reach as many future caregivers and parents as possible. Courses in child development, parenting, and caregiving should be common in high schools, even required.

> 'courses in child development, parenting, and caregiving should be common in high schools, even required'

Epstein (1993) identified ingredients of effective early childhood teacher training in a sequence of studies of HighScope training of trainers programs. These studies found that the training of trainers programs had the desired effects on trainers, of trainers on teachers, and of teachers on young children. Inservice training has the advantage over preservice training that the teachers being trained know what their job demands are, and the situation compels them to apply the lessons of the inservice training to their jobs. For inservice training to be effective, it needs to be taken seriously. That is, it needs to have consistent trainers; distributive, cumulative learning rather than one-shot workshops; a coherent curriculum that guides practice; hands-on learning rather than just lectures; and opportunities for sharing and reflection among practitioners.

'inservice training has the advantage over preservice training that the teachers being trained know what their job demands are, and the situation compels them to apply the lessons of the inservice training to their jobs'

Implications for early childhood curriculum

Early childhood curriculum is what early childhood teachers and caregivers do and is the content of early childhood teacher training. It describes what teachers actually do and prescribes what they ought to do. The research findings that model early childhood programs have long-term effects on participants' lives and strong economic return on investment, while typical programs have only moderate short-term effects, combine to present a strong rationale that early childhood curriculum should prescribe the teaching practices of these model programs. But the analysis of early childhood teacher training has direct implications for the nature of early childhood curriculum, specifically that it has two distinguishable audiences—school teachers, on the one hand, and caregivers and parents, on the other. Certainly, these two audiences overlap and some parents and caregivers are much more competent at contributing to children's development than are some teachers. The point is that the two audiences have different needs and perceptions of what early childhood curriculum is for.

To meet the needs of school teachers, an early childhood curriculum needs a fully articulated structure that fits with, and indeed serves as the foundation of, the lifelong educational curriculum. This means it has content objectives in language, literacy, mathematics, science, the arts, socio-emotional development, and physical education. It must be supported by psychometrically adequate tools for the assessment of children's learning and curriculum implementation. It must specify basic principles of teaching and learning, and teaching practices consistent with these principles.

'to meet the needs of caregivers and parents, programs must be accessible to them regardless of their educational backgrounds'

To meet the needs of caregivers and parents, it must be accessible to them regardless of their educational backgrounds. It must still identify basic principles of teaching and learning, and teaching practices consistent with these principles, but it must do so in a way that can be clearly communicated in a matter of days, through instruction and coached practice. These principles and practices should apply in homes as well as classrooms, to parents as well as caregivers. They should be accessible to students in high schools and community colleges, to caregivers receiving inservice training, and to parents taking a parenting course.

This is not a proposal for two early childhood curricula, but rather for one early childhood curriculum that meets the needs of two different audiences. An early childhood curriculum needs to fit into the educational system and the parenting or caregiving system. The educational system looks ahead to what children must do as they get older. The parenting or caregiving system addresses the present needs of children and families.

One of the most interesting debates in early childhood education is how the notion of curriculum is used to construct a teacher identity. Where student teachers perceive curriculum as something described and prescribed, how might this impact on their professional autonomy?

Editors

As we explore this idea of parenting courses in schools, we wonder how teachers will assess student performance, and subsequently how the community will regard students who may fail to meet parenting learning outcomes.

Editors

'an early childhood curriculum needs to fit into the educational system and the parenting or caregiving system'

Let us take the HighScope Curriculum as an example. It was originally designed by public school teachers and administrators to fit the needs of a public school setting. In the home visits of the HighScope Perry Preschool program, it was adapted for parents. From its beginnings, it was adapted to fit well into Head Start programs. It was extended from infancy to elementary school through various projects funded by foundations and the federal government. It has all the components of a fully articulated early childhood curriculum.

It has also been framed for child caregivers as well as parents. HighScope Press publications and HighScope workshops address family child care and caregiving practices for infants and toddlers as well as preschoolers. The curriculum's central focus, on adult-child interaction in which adults respect children and their thinking abilities, is accessible to parents and caregivers as well as teachers. Its emphases on room arrangement and daily routine are also accessible to everyone.

Many people who take care of, and raise, children will never get a degree in child development or early education. Our continuing challenge is to make the basic principles of good child development and early education available to them within the educational opportunities available.

'many people who take care of, and raise, children will never get a degree in child development or early education. Our continuing challenge is to make the basic principles of good child development and early education available to them within the educational opportunities available'

References

Administration for Children and Families, U.S. Department of Health and Human Services. (2005). *Head Start impact study: First year findings.* Washington, DC: Author. Retrieved from www.acf.hhs.gov/programs/opre/hs/impact_study/reports/first_yr_finds/first_yr_finds.pdf

Barnett, W. S., Lamy, C., & Jung, K. (2005). *The effects of state prekindergarten programs on young children's school readiness in five states.* New Brunswick, NJ: National Institute for Early Education Research, Rutgers University. Retrieved from nieer.org/docs/index.php?DocID=129

Barnett, W. S., & Masse, L. N. (2007). A comparative benefit-cost analysis of the Abecedarian program and its policy implications. *Economics of Education Review, 26*(2), 113-125.

Campbell, F. A., Ramey, C. T., Pungello, E. P., Sparling, J., & Miller-Johnson, S. (2002). Early childhood education: Young adult outcomes from the Abecedarian project. *Applied Developmental Science, 6*(1), 42-57.

Clarke, S. H., & Campbell, F. A. (1998). Can intervention early prevent crime later? The Abecedarian Project compared with other programs. *Early Childhood Research Quarterly, 13*(2), 319-343.

Epstein, A. S. (1993). *Training for quality: Improving early childhood programs through systematic inservice training. Monographs of the High/Scope Educational Research Foundation, 9.* Ypsilanti, MI: HighScope Press.

Gormley, Jr., W. T., Gayer, T., Phillips, D., & Dawson, B. (2005). The effects of universal pre-k on cognitive development. *Developmental Psychology, 41*(6), 872-884. Retrieved from http://www.crocus.georgetown.edu/reports/oklahoma9z.pdf

Heckman, J. (2006, January 10). Catch 'em young. *Wall Street Journal,* p. A14. Retrieved from www.tompaine.com/articles/2006/01/11/catch_em_young.php.

Mulligan, G., Brimhall, D., West, J., & Chapman, C. (2005). *Child care and early education arrangements of infants, toddlers, and preschoolers: 2001.* (NCES 2006-039). Washington, DC: National Center for Education Statistics, US Department of Education. Retrieved from http://nces.ed.gov/pubs2006/2006039.pdf

National Association of Child Care Resource and Referral Agencies. (2007). *We can do better: NACCRRA's ranking of state child care center standards and oversight.* Washington, DC: Author. Retrieved from http://www.naccrra.org/policy/recent_reports/scorecard. php

Reynolds, A. J., Temple, J. A., Robertson, D. L., & Mann, E. A. (2001). Long-term effects of an early childhood intervention on educational achievement and juvenile arrest: A 15-year follow-up of low-income children in public schools. *Journal of the American Medical Association, 285*(18), 2339-2346.

Reynolds, A. J., Temple, J. A., Robertson, D. L., & Mann, E. A. (2002). Age 21 cost-benefit analysis of the Title I Chicago child-parent centers. *Educational Evaluation and Policy Analysis, 24*(4), 267-303. Retrieved from http://www.irp.wisc.edu/publications/dps/pdfs/dp12450 2.pdf

Rolnick, A., & Grunewald, R. (2003). *Early childhood development: Economic development with a high public return.* Fedgazette (Federal Reserve Bank of Minneapolis). Retrieved from http://www.minneapolisfed.org/research/studies/earlych ild/abc-part2.pdf

Schweinhart, L. J., Montie, J., Xiang, Z., Barnett, W. S., Belfield, C. R., & Nores, M. (2005). *Lifetime effects: The HighScope Perry Preschool Study through age 40.* Ypsilanti, MI: HighScope Press.

U.S. General Accounting Office. (2003, October). *Increased percentage of teachers nationwide have required degrees, but better information on classroom teachers' qualifications needed.* GAO-04-5. Retrieved from http://www.gao.gov/new.items/d045.pdf

Zill, N., Resnick, G., Kim, K., O'Donnell, K., Sorongon, A., McKey, R. H., Pai-Samant, S., Clark, C., O'Brien, R., & D'Elio, M. A. (May 2003). *Head Start FACES (2000): A whole child perspective on program performance — Fourth progress report.* Prepared for the Administration for Children and Families, U.S. Department of Health and Human Services (DHHS) under contract HHS-105-96- 1912, Head Start Quality Research Consortium's Performance Measures Center. Retrieved from www.acf.hhs.gov/programs/opre/hs/faces/reports/faces0 0_4thprogress/faces00_4thprogress.pdf

Table 1

Findings of Six Recent Short-Term and Long-Term Early Childhood Program Studies in the U.S.

Study	Design	Findings
High/Scope Perry Preschool Study (Schweinhart, et al., 2005)	Random assignment of 123 low-income children; original sample of 123 children, low attrition; part-day program for 3- and 4-year-olds.	Program effects on intellectual performance and language up to age 7; school achievement and literacy from 9 to 27; reduced mental impairment, grade retention; more high school graduates; fewer teen pregnancies; better attitude towards school; more adult employment; higher annual earnings; more home owners; fewer adult arrests for violent, property and drug crimes; fewer prison sentences; 1614% return on investment
Carolina Abecedarian Project Study (Campbell, et al., 2002)	Random assignment of 111 infants from poor families either to a special program group or a typical childcare group. The special program was a full-day, full-year day care program for children that lasted the 5 years from birth to elementary school.	Program benefits on intellectual performance and achievement up to age 21; reduced grade retention and special services; more high school graduates and college attendees; fewer teen pregnancies; 378% return on investment.
Chicago Child – Parent Centers Study Reynolds, et al., 2001, 2002).	Sample of 989 part-day preschool program participants and 550 similar children who did not attend the program.	Program effects of reduced grade retention and special education placement, more high school graduates; fewer juvenile arrests; 710% return on investment
Head Start Impact Study (Administration for Children and Families, 2005)	Nationally representative sample of Head Start programs; random assignment of about 5,000 low-income 3- and 4-year-olds to Head Start or no Head Start.	Modest effects on children's literacy skills, reduced problem behavior, parent reading to children
Head Start Family and Child Experiences Survey (Zill et al., 2003)	Nationally representative sample of Head Start programs; cohorts of 3,200 children and 2,800 children; no comparison group	Modest gains in children's literacy and social skills in Head Start and kindergarten years
Five-State Preschool Study (Barnett, et al., 2005)	Regression discontinuity design, samples of 5,071 children from five state preschool programs	Improvements in children's literacy and mathematics skills

Continuing the conversations

The conversations in this first chapter highlighted both the strengths of early childhood teacher education around the world, and the immense challenges that are faced by governments and higher education institutions in developing quality teacher education programs. Many strategies have been suggested to promote higher levels of quality teaching, and there is some convincing evidence to support these strategies.

Many of us live, however, in increasingly diverse social and cultural communities where making decisions about quality teacher education requires complex knowledge about a wide range of values, beliefs, and practices.

- How do teacher educators ensure the diverse voices in their communities are given volume in their teacher education programs, and how do they go about maintaining responsiveness to these communities?

- What responsibility should local, regional, national and international institutions and authorities play in guiding teacher education?

These conversations are important, for what we value will be what becomes emphasised. Our challenge is to ensure what we set in place does not dismantle what we want to remain in place.

While the conversations in this chapter argue strongly for government intervention, others argue that the maintenance of diversity has historically been, at best, ineffective. At worst, governments are charged with maintaining privileged educational relationships through the marginalisation of diverse views and practices, and the standardisation of early childhood teaching practices.

- How might certified knowledge in teacher education impact upon community knowledge where, and when, communities have little input?

- In what ways do governments consult with communities in developing early childhood education policy?

- How do teacher education programs ensure that the community voice is heard in their curriculum?

Perhaps then, before a teacher education program considers how it meets the needs of the community, it must reflect upon how it understands difference and diversity, and the tensions that may exist between sharing common ground, and allowing for difference. Such reflections will be productive in considering the ways in which teacher education does not simply maintain culture, it both deconstructs and produces culture.

These conversations about the nature and purpose of early childhood teacher education are important and they need to remain open. Society is not going to remain static; therefore, an answer to an educational problem today may no longer be relevant tomorrow. Teacher educators who heed the many voices in their community are living examples of the potential of early childhood education to celebrate difference.

Chapter two continues this conversation through exploring the impact of culture on early childhood teacher education.

References

Arendt, H. (1961). *Between past and future: Six exercises in political thought.* London: Faber & Faber.
Kristnamurti, J. (1953). *Education and the significance of life.* New York: Kristnamurti Foundation Trust Ltd.
Whitehead, A. N. (1962). *The aims of education and other essays.* London: Ernest Benn Ltd.

CHAPTER 2

Conversations on multiculturalism in teacher education

Students depend on teachers who have its best interests at heart and to make sound educational decisions. Teachers have the moral obligation to do all they can to fulfil these expectations and to do so for all children, not just for some. Villegas & Lucas, 2002, p. 53

Every country has its own story to tell about their changing demographic statistics. For instance, since World War Two in Aotearoa/New Zealand, the population of Māori (the indigenous people of Aotearoa-New Zealand) has rapidly become urbanised. Furthermore, by 2040, immigration and population growth patterns will mean that the majority of peoples in Aotearoa/New Zealand will be of non-European backgrounds (Ministry of Education, 2002). In the United States, more than one in three students enrolled in schools is of an ethnic minority background (National Center for Education Statistics, 2000). Yet, at the same time, Ana Maria Villegas (1998) notes that the teaching profession is becoming more homogenous rather than ethnically diverse.

Early childhood centers have the potential to both model and celebrate what it means to live in a multicultural world. But to achieve this, we need to consider what it means to be teachers in multicultural contexts. Inevitably, this begins with knowing who we are—our beliefs, assumptions, motivations, and practices. As we come to know more about ourselves as people and as teachers, then we are better positioned to understand and appreciate more about others.

Marilyn Cochran-Smith puts it this way:
In order to learn to teach in a society that is increasingly culturally and linguistically diverse, prospective teachers... need opportunities to examine much of what is usually unexamined in the tightly braided relationships of language, culture, and power in schools and schooling. This kind of examination inevitably begins with our own histories as human beings and as educators—our own cultural, racial, and linguistic backgrounds and our own experiences as raced, classed, and gendered children, parents, and teachers in the world. It also includes a close look at the tacit assumptions we make about the motivations and behaviors of other children, other parents, and other teachers and about the pedagogies we deem most appropriate for learners who are like us and who are not like us. Cochran-Smith, 1995, p. 500

This chapter positions our conversations around what it means to be a teacher in multicultural contexts, and what this might mean for teacher education. Marilyn Cochran-Smith challenges us to examine our underlying assumptions as well as our motivations and behaviors. Such a view is important, for how we come to teach reflects the persons we are.

Our culture shapes who we are as teachers. What we think, what we believe, how we perceive the world, and how we behave, are influenced by the cultures to which we belong. Our thinking, beliefs, attitudes, and actions reveal our sensitivities, appreciation, respect, and responsiveness to cultures other than our own. Gibbs, 2006, p. 180

If we are to be culturally responsive as teachers, then we need to show deep, genuine, and on-going learning about the relationships between social life and human activity. We need to appreciate the instrumental power of beliefs in explaining how teachers and students are motivated to behave and learn. And furthermore, to be culturally responsive as teachers means showing genuine preparedness to allow one's personal self to be shaped and reshaped in ways that help us understand our own cultural positioning, the cultures of others, and the intimate interconnections between these. This chapter presents four interesting perspectives, all of which challenge us to examine our assumptions, beliefs, and practices as teachers and as teacher educators, especially as these relate to multiculturalism.

The paper by Sonja Zoellner, Marek Tesar, and Ra Keelan, *Our roots—our teaching*, presents the view that our cultural stories, including myth, provide us with important connections in time, space, and with peoples. Sonja, Marek, and Ra refer to beliefs of Māori society that *Ma tou rourou, ma takurourou, ka ora ai nga iwi: through the sharing of stories, collective understandings grow*. They challenge us, therefore, to draw from the wisdom of cultural stories and, in doing so, to be willing to 'dig deep within ourselves' so that we may form connections to empower both ourselves as teachers and teacher educators, and our teaching.

The paper by Lavinia Tiko and Unaisi Nabobo-Baba is titled *Indigenous Fijian conceptions of mentoring and related capacity building: Implications for teacher education*. Lavinia and Unaisi explain the importance of 'Sautu'—the good, bountiful, and peaceful life—as the conceptual basis or goal upon which to appreciate Fijian education. They also suggest that to truly accommodate this goal means to acknowledge the interconnectedness of the land, place, time, and genealogy—and, as well, that all things are intimately interconnected physically, emotionally, psychologically, and spiritually. We might well ask—how do our teacher education programmes reflect the essence of this goal? Such a cultural positioning creates exciting possibilities for the (re)conceptualisation of early childhood teacher education.

Bessie Rios has experience working in teaching and teacher education with many cultures. In this interview with the editors, Bessie tells about her journey and aspirations in early childhood and teacher education, particularly in the Philippines. In a country where there are over 2.2 million infants and 11.3 million preschool children, there are pressing concerns as to how to meet the needs of learners, including preparing sufficient quality teachers to staff these programs. The Center for Early Childhood Care and Development (CECCD), Bessie explains, is guided by a philosophy which centers on *molding the molders*. This philosophical approach, which has its roots in an American missionary agency, aims to prepare teachers with a distinctive difference. This interview invites conversations about different philosophical approaches in early childhood education, and how these may meet diverse multicultural contexts and expectations, especially in teacher education.

Andrew Gibbons' paper, *The limits of biculturalism: Ka Hikitia and early childhood teacher education in Aotearoa* begins by briefly exploring the colonisation of Aotearoa/New Zealand and Māori, by the British. Andrew then introduces the New Zealand Ministry of Education's new initiative to restore Māori culture through education, namely, *Ka Hikitia*. He examines some strengths and weaknesses in this document, and importantly, he exposes some thinking which he suggests symbolises *the government's good intentions while obscuring the maintenance of the status quo*. This is an important conversation for it draws us back to the central concern of understanding, respecting, and acting in ways that honour the world view of Māori. His argument is based in the New Zealand context. But it resonates with the international situation concerning education and teacher education for, and by, indigenous peoples.

Beginning the conversations

How we construct early childhood teacher education programmes often reflects the aspirations and world views of dominant cultures. The following papers present different perspectives on multiculturalism in early childhood teacher education. As you read, consider what the implications may be for programmes with which you are familiar. Here are some questions which may help your conversations:

- How might different philosophically-based early childhood teacher education programs meet the needs of cultural inclusiveness?
- *Our thinking, beliefs, attitudes, and actions reveal our sensitivities, appreciation, respect, and responsiveness to cultures other than our own.* (Gibbs, 2006, p. 180). What might this mean for preparing teachers?
- To what extent do the early childhood programs you are familiar with draw from indigenous peoples' knowledge? How is this reflected in the structure of the program, the content, the pedagogy, and the preparation of teachers?
- What is the place of in-service teacher education to ensure preparedness and capability in catering for cultural diversity?

These papers also imply that teachers and teacher educators have a moral responsibility to be concerned with social justice.

- How do you see this as being evidenced in an authentic way in teacher education, and in teaching in early childhood centres?

Given these conversations, what might be the implications for (re)conceptualising teacher education? And how might the nature of teaching in early childhood also be (re)conceptualised to accommodate such diversity?

OUR ROOTS—OUR TEACHING

Marek Tesar
New Zealand

Sonja Zoellner
New Zealand

Ra Keelan
New Zealand

Marek Tesar is a lecturer at New Zealand Tertiary College. His main areas of interest are myths, social and emotional problems of gifted children, inclusion, methodology, and test construction. Marek previously worked as a child psychologist, researcher, and lecturer at the Research Institute of Child Psychology and Patopsychology in Bratislava, Slovakia.

Sonja Zoellner is a senior lecturer at New Zealand Tertiary College. Her professional interests include the impact of culture and relationships on teaching and learning, the development of educational philosophy, and promoting bicultural and multicultural understandings. Sonja has taught in various early childhood settings in Aotearoa/New Zealand and in Germany. She is currently studying to complete a Bachelor of Education.

Ra Keelan is a senior lecturer at New Zealand Tertiary College, with a focus on bicultural and multicultural development. His primary areas of interest are Māori myth as blueprints to life, gender roles within traditional Māori society, and Māori development (beyond 2008). Ra began his EC career in Kohanga Reo (Māori Immersion Programme). He then moved to primary school, polytechnic, and then universities. Prior to joining New Zealand Tertiary College he worked for The Office of the Vice Chancellor (The University of Auckland), and as a School Manager, Faculty of Education, University of Auckland, New Zealand.

Ehara taku tu i te tu taki-tahi
Engari ko taku tu, mo oku tupuna
(No Tainui, me Ngati Maniapoto)

I do not stand before you as an individual
But a representation of the multitudes that came before

If you stand as an individual, you don't progress
If you stand as a tribe, as one, you can move forward

Our stories in this paper represent connecting points for conversations about early childhood teacher education. They weave together our own peoples' stories, ancient cultural wisdom, transmitted through the generations. From central Europe, Australia, and Aotearoa/New Zealand these are our cultural roots, our strengths and certainties— connections spanning time, space, and cultures. As we share these stories, we gain new understandings. These enable us to reflect on our roots, our philosophies, and our practices as early childhood educators.

In this conversation we explore the nature of myth and its extension to legends and fairy tales as they support, stimulate, and animate our lives and those around us (Campbell, 1988). We suggest that understanding tribal legacies is crucial for enhancing cross-cultural awareness and connectedness (Gibbs, 2006). Through our peoples' stories we examine the evolution of intergenerational growth, learning, and teaching. Our narratives are aligned with the intentions of *Te Whāriki—the Early Childhood Curriculum of Aotearoa/New Zealand* (Ministry of Education, 1996), which honour Māori (indigenous peoples of New Zealand) and Pākehā (non-indigenous peoples of New Zealand). As teachers, we see ourselves as the collective guardians of our cultural stories. These take us on a transformative journey to help us know ourselves, our students, and our teaching through cultures, stories, and generations.

'through our peoples' stories we examine the evolution of intergenerational growth, learning and teaching'

Te kākano—The seed

To begin, it is important to make a distinction between myths, legends, and fairy tales for they are te kākano, the seeds, from which insights and understandings about life are gained. Myths, legends, and fairy tales are hard to define. No one single definition is ever going to satisfy all teachers (Dockal, 2005). For the purpose of this paper, however, we use the term myth to refer to raw, abstract, natural, genuine, inartificial, unpolished wisdom as a narrative of cultural understandings of life and the world. A legend is thought of as being derived from a myth, the societal retelling of the story's animation of life (Campbell, 1988). The retelling of a legend involves the variation of a myth in the form of concrete, real examples, with elements of historic truth and often involving supernatural characters. In extension to these genres, a fairy tale encompasses both fiction and supernatural characters to amplify the educational impact of the story, which can be intended to be either positive or negative (Burns, 2006).

'myth presents to us the supernatural in the natural—it brings two worlds together symbolically'

Berdyaev (1935) brings an important perspective to our understanding of myth when he defines it as *a reality immeasurably greater than concept. Myth presents to us the supernatural in the natural—it brings two worlds together symbolically* (p. 70). This understanding of myth is strongly connected to the Māori notion of myth, which connects the natural with the supernatural, the tangible with the intangible, and the implicit with the explicit. It is a way of passing down values, principles, beliefs, and history. Smith says that *the myth and its storyteller connect the land with the people, and the people with the story* (1999, p. 145), whilst Campbell (1988) sees myth as our connection with *the powers that animate our life* and that *animate the life in the world* (p. 22). Māori see all things in life as interconnecting the past, present, and future with people whose memories endure as living essences of all being and time. King highlights the importance of this belief when he states that *unless we know where we come from—as individuals and as a nation—we cannot know where we are. And if we don't know where we are, we cannot know in which direction we are heading* (cited in Starzecka, 1996, p. 52).

'unless we know where we come from—as individuals and as a nation—we cannot know where we are. And if we don't know where we are, we cannot know in which direction we are heading'

How we define 'myth' is central to how we perceive myths should influence our lives and our teaching.

Editors

Storytelling is the medium through which *knowledge with rich tacit dimensions (i.e., myth, legend, fairy tale), is transferred informally through processes of socialisation and internalisation* (Swap, Leonard, Shields, & Abrams, 2001, p. 96). Traditionally, in Hegel's philosophy, the Zeitgeist (spirit of an era) is associated with only one period of time. As the Zeitgeist evolves, the message changes according to both the era and the people who are the involuntary characters of the story (Storig, 2003). Understanding the Zeitgeist of storytelling is important. We believe that, in the case of myth, the Zeitgeist of storytelling is omnipresent and that the content of the myth itself does not change—only the form changes. We agree with Hegel that all people are involved (Storig, 2003); but in the case of the Zeitgeist of storytelling we argue that myth is historically stable and the content unchanging. It is, therefore, timeless and era-less. The interpretation of legends and fairy tales, however, circulates as knowledge within society. Legends and fairy tales change in accordance with an evolving society (encompassing all ethnic collectives, to which we refer here as tribes). Therefore myths, legends, and fairy tales, permeate society across generations, time and place. Myths, legends, and fairy tales, as seeds from which insights and understandings are gained, serve as a metaphor for early childhood teaching and learning.

Te pīhinga—The shoot

The understanding gained from the seeds, that is, from the myths, legends, and fairy tales, can be seen then as the shoot sprouting from the seeds. The stories develop, as the seed does too, revealing the content that nourishes and guides people, societies, and teaching. To illustrate, indigenous to Aotearoa-New Zealand, Māori myth is based on three realms.

Te Kore (The Nothingness/fullness of potential)
Te Kore is the first realm; devoid of life and light. Over the eons, Te Kore evolved to contain Ahorangi (female essence/potential) and Ihorangi (male essence/potential). Separately, they only *promised* life, but in joining they brought that promise to physical reality, thus the primal parents—*Papa*tuanuku (Earth Mother) and *Rangi*nui (Sky Father), were created *matua kore—without parents* (Simmons, 2001, p. 29), and in their creation, the second realm of Te Pō (The Night/awakening) began.

Te Pō (The Night/awakening)
It is within Te Pō that the Māori gods, the children of Papa and Rangi are conceived and born thus creating Ira Atua and Ira tangata (godly and human life) (Simmons, 2001). Trapped between their parents' embrace, the children desired space to move, grow, explore, experience, see, feel, and touch. Out of desire, they conspired to separate their parents. It is *Tane*mahuta (God of Forest life and people) who succeeds where others before him had failed. In placing his shoulders against his mother and his feet upon his father he was able to kick until the sinews with which they held each other together, tore and they cried out in pain (King, 1996). When the primal parents separated, light flooded into the space, and the third realm of Te Ao Mārama [World of understanding (life) and knowledge (light)] began.

Te Ao Mārama
Te Ao Mārama, the third realm, describes the empowerment of the Māori Gods to explore, multiply, and grow. This is a legacy that we all inherit from them, one that must be embraced by teachers and fostered by learners. Through the storyteller, this realm speaks of a time when the Māori gods sort their opposite and equal, and sort balance. Papa advised them to seek Kura Waka where the soil runs red with her fertility. At this place, they fashioned Hine Ahu One (Maiden formed from Earth), and

Our worldviews see the notion of 'nothingness' in different ways. In turn, this shapes the ways in which we see and educate children. For example, if nothingness is seen as zero or emptiness, then we would perceive children as being like clean slates. However, te kore refers to the fullness of potential—a positive understanding of 'nothingness'.

Editors

each male God gave of himself so she would be his equal and opposite. Their negligence lay in the fact that she, too, was also of their mother, thus already possessed an equal measure. Their collective contributions enhanced her beyond their understanding. Unlike the Gods, she was born to the world of light and knowledge, and therefore possessed the ability to understand her own potential; and realise the potential of their contributions. Māori mythology helps us to understand the journey from the state of fullness of potential (Te Kore), through development (Te Pō), to understanding and knowledge (Te Ao Mārama). It therefore connects for us a life of learning.

> 'Māori mythology helps us to understand the journey from the state of fullness of potential (Te Kore), through development (Te Pō), to understanding and knowledge (Te Ao Mārama). It therefore connects for us a life of learning'

Science, knowledge, cultural identity

Myths, legends, and fairy tales are found in all cultures and in some ways are shared by all peoples, irrespective of the geographical borders and political systems between them. Myths contribute to the formation of cultural identity and are aspects of the cultural collective unconscious (Jung, 1993) which we use voluntarily and involuntarily as our supply of raw tribal and ancestral knowledge. Interestingly, myths can be seen as an archetype of tribal knowledge connecting completely different tribes. We can see, for example, concepts about mythological creatures with special powers and characteristics featured in the stories of many cultures (Dobsinsky, 2006; Reeder & Christanto, 1997). For example, bunyips in Australian aboriginal stories (Onus, 1987) have a special significance. In Aotearoa/New Zealand the mythical taniwha similarly guides the Māori people from a deeply inspirational level (Ministry of Education, 1998). It is our personal perceptions of myths that differentiate us from each other—tribe from tribe and individual from individual.

These relationships are further complicated by the correlation between myth and science. Philosophical approaches towards this important notion are varied and even contradictory. For example, Claude Levi-Strauss (1983) in his book *Raw and Cooked* (where 'raw' refers to 'myth' and 'cooked' to 'culture') uses science in a structural approach towards myth; while Karl Popper (2000) claims that all theories (science) are initiated from myth. He further claims that it is not important whether myth is true or not, but whether it is testable. In reflecting on science and myth in relation to people and society, they may be seen as opposing genres. Frielich, Raybeck and Savishinsky (1991) argue that science and myth are almost like *natural enemies* (p. 7). They further state that while myth is playful and deals with fantasy, science is serious and searches for truth and reality. Therefore they conclude that *myth makes life more meaningful and less stressful* (p. 7) than science, because myth provides a certain clarity, while science offers multiple solutions.

> 'myth makes life more meaningful and less stressful'

Myth can be seen as historic knowledge that provides answers to universal questions. In this sense we agree with Piaček and Kravčik (1999), that:

> *myth means that one does not need to ask questions… because living in the myth is living in the world where answers are already given, before questions are even asked.*

Part of 'belonging' in Te Whāriki (The New Zealand early childhood curriculum) is celebrating our uniqueness and diversity—celebrating each family's roots.
Roseanne Saluni

Whilst the implication may be that science helps us to improve our lives while myth shows us how to live, myth can also, by its very fundamental nature, be seen to inspire science, inform questions, and complement inquiry.

In relation to early childhood education, both myth and science provide the content for the Aotearoa/New Zealand bicultural curriculum document, *Te Whāriki* (Ministry of Education, 1996). Myth provides an understanding of the underlying rationale of the curriculum, whilst science supports inquiry and exploration. In other words, while science helps us to pass on new knowledge to student teachers, myth also teaches us about the deep cultural wisdom on which it is based.

> 'while science helps us to pass on new knowledge to student teachers, myth also teaches us about the deep cultural wisdom on which it is based'

Out of the development of the seed, as it begins to grow, the tree begins to unfold. Stories, too, are unfolding in this stage to reveal their wisdom to the people, societies, and to us as early childhood teachers.

Te māhuri—The sapling

Where te kākano, the seed, holds the potential for life and is the foundation of understanding, te māhuri is that potential realised through the growth of the shoot and then the sapling, and the awakening of the mind to learning. If we dig deep enough we find the roots that sustain growth and carry life to every part of the sapling. Through the twists and turns of past cycles of dreams, events, and growth, they nourish all that is. Trunks rise from the roots and hold firm the past, present, and future. They are the solid, dependable foundations from which life paths, represented by the branches, leaves, and twigs, can reach and tangle, bend, break, be nurtured, and regenerate. All of these elements impact on the growth of the entire tree, and similarly the entire story; the tribal myth, is impacted by the paths of the people.

In Aotearoa/New Zealand, we see cross-cultural connections between our ancient cultural wisdom, and our tribal stories. It is a new cultural landscape continually evolving through the blending of peoples' stories and lives.

> 'in Aotearoa/New Zealand, we see cross-cultural connections between our ancient cultural wisdom, and our tribal stories'

From quite a different perspective within new cross-cultural landscapes, identity within German tribes is strengthened by their own myths, legends and fairy tales. Some tribes journeyed far from their homelands of forests and castles, as well as the homes of their mythological and legendary heroes, and of the make-believe in their fairy tales. Ideological dreams and commitments directed their paths, across borders and continents. In the accompanying intergenerational transmission of their stories lay the unwitting transmission of stable cultural knowledge and cultural identity. The stability of myths and supporting evolution of legends and fairy tales nourished them in the pursuit of their collective and individual dreams and identities (Temple Society of Australia, 2005).

For some German tribes, Australia became their new homeland where ancient aboriginal myths governed life for the indigenous people. Immigrant cultures carried with them their own stories. Philosophies, rituals, and cultural lives were stimulated, even so distant from their origins, by the underlying myth-based truths transported around the world (Mountford, 1970; Temple Society of Australia, 2005). Such a mingling of stories caused both strength and division, not only in Australia. Global diversity then, can lead to a great new richness of stories, but also to domination and loss, where sometimes indigenous stories are little understood (Mountford, 1970).

> 'global diversity can lead to a great new richness of stories, but also to domination and loss, where sometimes indigenous stories are little understood'

Other myths followed the paths of the central European Slavic tribes into a multicultural world. As a people often ruled by other nations, their identities were preserved in the coded messages of legends and fairy tales enabling the passing of identity from one generation to another. Children were educated about heroes—about those who should be their role models and about those who were the ever-tempting devils—through stories. To pass this information on from one person to another was difficult in a small country, crowded with peoples of different nationalities, cultures, and languages. Often one language was spoken to one's superiors or one's neighbours and another was spoken at home. In the past, the fireplace in the evenings was the safe haven where elders were able to pass on their stories. The legends and fairy tales of which this education consisted are now regarded as a national heritage (Ministerstvo Kultury, 2006).

In all cultures the origins of the physical universe and life are explained and explored through these ancient stories, however their real strength is inner. Universal concepts about how to lead one's life, of goodness, of decency, of the necessary and the desirable, the forbidden, and the acceptable, come startlingly alive. Through these narrations the dreams, lives, and events of past generations (Burns, 2006) stand as practical guides for current generations. As educators, knowing these stories helps us make a distinction between ourselves and other people; between past, present and future, between peoples and cultures worldwide. That is the true value of myths, legends, and fairy tales. And these values are as long as the stories that enclose them.

Te kōhure—Tree development

In the Māori world view, as dawn goes down to day, as Te Kore gave way to Te Pō, which in turn gave way to Te Ao Mārama, so too does te māhuri—the sapling give way to te kōhure—the development of the tree. Comparably, world views are shaped by life contexts (Varner & Beamer, 2005), including perspectives on childhood, knowledge and learning. These are the foundations of our beliefs and values on how, who, and what to teach.

> 'world views are shaped by life contexts including perspectives on childhood, knowledge, and learning'

What then can we learn in relation to teaching? The aspirations for teaching rest on the stories that emerge from and nurture every element of the journey that people make individually and collectively. First, there is an inherent implication that it is desirable for there to be strength, structure, and stability in a teacher's philosophy. Secondly, an understanding of stories raises questions about what is valuable to learn, to spend time doing, aiming for, and desiring (Woods & Barrow, 1975). If, as Aristotle

These reflections on cultural encoding highlight the challenge of maintaining cultural diversity in a society where heroes, myths, and symbols are primarily transmitted via television, merchandising, and the Internet.

Editors

claimed, myth is really *composed of wonders* (Burns, 2006), then does not this sense of wonderment and awe further lead us to an appreciation of mystery, uncertainty, and surprises? Content and inquiry then are derived from and explore the unknown, around each twist and turn in the new collective cultural landscape.

A firm connection between cultural knowledge and knowing ourselves becomes deeply evident as we share and come to know cultural stories. In educational contexts, however, developing such insight and understanding often becomes a complicated process. The motto 'know thyself', written in the Delphos Oracle (and rediscovered to the modern world by Socrates), is very important (Weischedel, 1995). Transferred to modern education, we recognise therefore, that apart from knowing ourselves as teachers, we should take a step further to deeply know our students. Unique, mutually beneficial learning experiences can result, transcending our own and our students' previous learning and fundamental understandings.

> 'transferred to modern education, we recognise that apart from knowing ourselves as teachers, we should take a step further to deeply know our students'

Student teachers' journeys in education begin in Te Kore, that is, they can be seen to be devoid of awareness and understanding, yet with the potential of fullness. Reflected in their eyes is either the potential of Ihorangi—the active learner who engages through seeking answers and challenging thought, or of Ahorangi—the passive learner, who engages through observation, consideration, and reflection.

Familiarity with Māori myth requires we honour student teachers for being the union of Ihorangi and Ahorangi. Ihorangi and Ahorangi are the potential spawned from the once childless womb, and are the living mirror that projects their lineage and identity; and the students are the reflection of our own creation story. It is upon this reflection that whanaungatanga (kinships, relationships, partnerships) can be exploited, and through this whanaungatanga our spiritual self is reawakened and enhanced as cooperating learners and teachers.

> 'through this whanaungatanga our spiritual self is reawakened and enhanced as cooperating learners and teachers'

As student teachers awaken their minds, extend their curiosity (Ahorangi), and enhance their stamina (Ihorangi) to learn, the inherent meaning of Te Pō is drawn to the forefront of our consciousness. This meaning parallels the stages of pregnancy. The name Te Pō acknowledges female and male activities in the night, while the stages that make it up describe the eight months that follow. These stages include: te rapunga (the sperm's search), te whaia (the chase on locating), te pupuri (the bonding/impregnation), te kukune (the swelling), te hihiri (the desire to grow), te hinengaro (brain development), te mahara (memory development), te huringa (the foetus turning in preparation for birth). The ninth stage is te whanautanga (the birth) into Te Ao Mārama (The World of Light).

When student teachers and educators acknowledge each others' whanau and personal identity, their own sense of self and being is enhanced. Again, it is upon this premise that whanaungatanga is central to enhancing student-teacher relationships. Student teachers' attainment of knowledge through learning mirrors Te Ao Mārama. Where the Māori gods sought council from Papa, the primacy of Tuakana—Teina (elder

That teacher educators present an inner strength of conviction may enable student teachers to feel more able to take on the unpredictable that mystery presents.

Editors

Know your parents and whanau [family] well, build family and whanau. This is whanaungatanga in action.

Kirsty Cuthers

teaching younger) was established, from which mentoring is derived. Where the gods gave of themselves to Hine Ahu One, the lesson that diverse knowledge offers greater understanding and perspective is gained, and through this growth self realisation, confidence, and pursuit of excellence is achieved.

> 'when student teachers and educators acknowledge each others' whanau and personal identity, their own sense of self and being is enhanced'

The three realms of Māori myth are interconnecting stories that link people, land, language, and all life. This notion can be applied to other cultures too, where connections become evident through their stories. Therefore, as the current representation of their culture, each student and teacher, regardless of ethnicity, has an inherent right to this knowledge, to carry into the future.

> 'each student and teacher, regardless of ethnicity, therefore, as the current representation of their culture, has an inherent right to this knowledge, to carry into the future'

Once more, a sense of whanaungatanga is enhanced, highlighting common ground between cultures to collectively and safely pursue bicultural and multicultural development, explore cultural diversity and cross-cultural wonderment. These connections provide the prism through which to continue developing our individual cultural identities.

> Ma te makuku o te pu, ka ora tonu te rakau —
> in watering the roots, the tree continues to thrive.

In the same way as we develop our own cultural identity, student teachers' identities are enhanced, as their whole sense of being within their culture develops. Student teachers' attainment of Te Ao Mārama illuminates the myth story. In seeking advice from Papa, the Māori gods set the primacy of Tuakana—Teina (mentoring) that student teachers are encouraged to foster. In the gods giving of themselves, they illustrate this concept of guiding and supporting the younger or less knowledgeable, nourishing their tree of knowledge. The three realms culminate into the enormous tree of Māori mythology, and each student is the child who inherits this knowledge, to carry into the future.

Te hua—The fruit

When te kōhure (the development of the tree) attains its growth potential it bears te hua (the fruit). Similarly, when we as teacher educators understand cultural myths, legends, and fairy tales, the fruit yielded is that of understanding student teachers' belief systems and tribal roots. In pursuit of this understanding the first concern is cultural self-knowledge (Walsh, 2007).

> 'when we as teacher educators understand cultural myths, legends, and fairy tales, the fruit yielded is that of understanding student teachers' belief systems and tribal roots'

Only when this personal layer is unpeeled, according to Walsh (2007), are we open to absorbing the stories of others; of our student teachers. How can we *plan, implement, and evaluate* (Ministry of Education, 1998, p. 40) curricula (Ministry of Education, 1996) without knowing who our student teachers are, in a real and fundamental way? How will we promote a way of teaching such curricula to children?

As snapped, gnarled branches, twigs, and leaves tell of deviations, tangents, new directions in the growth path, the life journey of a tree. So, too, the deeper cultural insights of people and their stories can reveal both a route of adventure and new beginnings, or of displacement, exile, and alienation from families, property, and their homelands. Myriad political, social, and economic reasons lie behind such new directions, inextricably linking all stories from the past, their inheritance, in the here and now (Clifford, 2007). We are the constantly evolving cultural identities, blending indigeneities, as they are confronted with incoming tribes, growing new lives, growing new stories, always from the foundation of our own roots.

As the branches reach greater heights and complexity, so too does our teaching. Stimulated by the power of myth, we honour our cultural obligations, our paths. First, we might dig deep within ourselves, to know our own past, present, and future, based on the fundamental wisdom of our cultural stories. We recognise the life determining impact of cultural stories on our teaching, and so we open ourselves to exploring and validating our students' stories. The cultural aspirations of teachers, students, and peoples live on in our teaching.

> *Ma tou rourou, ma taku rourou, ka ora ai nga iwi–*
> *through the sharing of stories, collective understandings grow*

In Aotearoa/New Zealand we strive to share Māori myths, legends, and fairy tales, side by side with those of other cultures. By adhering to this proverb, we fulfil our role as current guardians by passing on the inheritance to those who will follow, and those who are yet to awaken.

We are interested in this term 'indigeneities' and the idea that indigenous cultures might be blended. A challenge for teacher educators is to be sensitive to what it means to be indigenous.

Editors

References

Burns, P. (2006). *Mythology and folklore.* Retrieved from http://www.pibburns.com/mythfolk.htm

Berdyaev, N. (1935). *Freedom and the spirit.* London: Geoffrey Bles.

Campbell, J. (1988). *The power of myth.* New York: Doubleday.

Clifford, J. (2007). Varieties of indigenous experience: Diasporas, homelands, sovereignties. In M. de la Cadena & O. Starn (Eds.), *Indigenous experience today* (pp. 197-224). New York: Berg.

Dobsinsky, P. (2006). *Moje najkraysie rozpravky.* Bratislava: Perfekt.

Dockal, V. (2005). *Zamereno na talenty.* Praha: Nakladatelstvi Lidove noviny.

Freilich, M., Raybeck, D., & Savishinsky, J. (1991). *Deviance: Anthropological Perspectives.* New York: Bergin & Garvey. Retrieved from http://www.amazon.com/gp/reader/0897892046/ref=sib_dp_pt#

Gibbs, C. J. (2006). *To be a teacher: Journeys towards authenticity.* Auckland, New Zealand: Pearson Education

Jung, C. G. (1993). *Analyticka psychologie. Jeji teorie a praxe.* Praha: Academia.

King, M. (1996). *Māori. A photographic and social history.* Auckland: Reed Publishing.

Levi-Strauss, C. (1983). *The raw and the cooked: Mythologiques.* Chicago: University of Chicago Press.

Ministerstvo Kultury. (2006). *Pôsobnost' Ministerstva kultúry Slovenskej republiky v oblasti kultúrneho dedičstva.* Retrieved from http://www.culture.gov.sk/kulturne-dedicstvo

Ministry of Education. (1996). *Te Whāriki: He whāriki mātauranga mō ngā mokopuna o Aotearoa/ Early childhood curriculum.* Wellington, New Zealand: Learning Media.

Mountford, C. P. (1970). *The dreamtime: Australian aboriginal myths.* Adelaide: Rigby Limited.

Ministry of Education. (1998). *Quality in Action: Te Mahi Whai Hua.* Wellington, New Zealand: Learning Media.

Onus, L. (1987). *Bunyips – Living Lore.* Retrieved from http://www.nla.gov.au/exhibitions/bunyips/html-site/imagination/living.html

Piaček, J., & Kravčik, M., (1999). FILIT. Retrieved from http://ii.fmph.uniba.sk/~filit/fvm/mytus.html

Popper, K. (2000). Science as falsification. In T. Schick, (Ed.), *Readings in the philosophy of science* (pp. 9-13). Mountain View, CA: Mayfield Publishing Company.

Reeder, S. O., & Christanto, D. (1997). *Flaming witch.* Sydney, Australia: Random House.

Simmons, D. (2001). *The carved pare. A Māori mirror of the universe.* Wellington: Huia Publishers.

Smith, L. (1999). *Decolonizing methodologies: Research and indigenous peoples.* Dunedin: The University of Otago.

Starzecka, D. (Ed.). (1996). *Māori art and culture.* Auckland: David Bateman.

Storig, H. J. (2003). *Malé dejiny filosofie.* Praha: Karmelitánske nakladatelstvi.

Swap, W., Leonard, D., Shields., M., & Abrams, L. (2001). Using mentoring and storytelling to transfer knowledge in the workplace. *Journal of Management Information Systems,* (1)18, 95-114.

Temple Society of Australia. (2005). *Memories of Palestine: Narratives about life in the Templar communities 1869-1948.* Bentleigh: TSA Heritage Group.

Varner, I., & Beamer, L. (2005). *Intercultural communication in the global workplace.* New York: McGraw-Hill/ Irwin.

Walsh, D. (2007, September). *Who are 'we'? The many dimensions of culture.* Paper presented at Early Childhood Convention, Rotorua, New Zealand.

Weischedel, W. (1995). *Zadni schodiste filozofie.* Praha: Votobia.

Woods, R. G., & Barrow, R. St. C. (1975). *An introduction to philosophy of education.* London: Methuen & Co. Ltd.

INDIGENOUS FIJIAN CULTURAL CONCEPTIONS OF MENTORING AND RELATED CAPACITY BUILDING: IMPLICATIONS FOR TEACHER EDUCATION

Unaisi Nabobo-Baba
Fiji

Lavinia Tiko
Fiji

Unaisi Nabobo-Baba has a MAEd from the University of the South Pacific in Education and Development and a doctorate from the University of Auckland on indigenous knowledge and epistemology recognized as a significant contribution to indigenous knowledge, research, and scholarship at the AERA conference in Chicago, 2007. Unaisi has taught in secondary schools, College of Advanced Education, and University. She has published internationally and has a number of journal articles; book chapters; and five books: one authored, one co-authored, and three edited. Her research interests include teaching and learning in specific contexts, indigenous knowledge, education and development related discourse, Pacific Islands and small island states education, education and global change agendas, school and community relations and education, women and development, remoteness and islandness and implications of these on schooling, indigenous knowledge and epistemology and implications of these on modern day education and development, international aid and education.

Lavinia Tiko is a lecturer in early childhood education at the University of the South Pacific (USP), Suva, Fiji. She has a Bachelor's degree and a Graduate Diploma in Educational Leadership from the University of Waikato, New Zealand. She also has a Master of Arts degree in early childhood education from the Institute of Education, University of London. Her research interests are in transition from preschools into primary schools, early childhood teacher education, quality teachers and programs in early childhood education, and partnership in early childhood education.

Introduction

This paper documents aspects of Fijian knowledge, its conceptual basis, and its application in a contemporary context and draws implications of epistemology for Fijian education (Nabobo-Baba, 2004, 2005, 2007). This is in order to then situate how we philosophically embrace and define our relationships in terms of mentoring of the young, the student or the trainee by the mentor, who can be an elder sibling, clan elder, teacher, teacher educator, or trainer.

The paper begins by explicating the meaning of sautu and states that it is the ultimate or expected outcome of education and schooling in terms of indigenous Fijian thought. The paper then examines the Fijian world view and the role of knowledge and ways of knowing (epistemology) so as to highlight that values necessary for good mentoring are premised on indigenous knowledge and epistemology. Such values and principles include: the importance of clan or kin relationships, clan belongingness, culturally acceptable behaviours such as looking out for your kinsmen, living life and having a conduct that is dina, dodonu and savasava (truthful, straight/ethical, and clean), and the importance of the pursuit of yalomatua (spiritual wisdom). Mentoring, as well the mentor's and mentee's roles, are governed and based on such culturally-accepted principles, values, and ethics of relationships and knowledge impartation. The qualities of, or criteria for, mentors are then explored, and the paper rounds off with some implications for teacher education.

To develop Fijian cultural ideas of mentoring, the paper draws from some of the findings of Nabobo-Baba's (2005, 2007) research on indigenous Fijian knowledge and epistemology. It includes her lived experiences of indigenous Fijian veituberi (mentoring).

Fijian world view: Sautu—the desirable state of the good, bountiful, and peaceful life

This paper is premised on the belief that the goal of education and life itself is sautu—the desirable state of being which is exemplified through the good, bountiful, and peaceful life. It is the epitome of life and the ideal one strives for in life, research, education, and all other endeavors. All discourses on education, including those of nurturing or mentoring students, take place because we make the assumption that we are seeking the most beautiful quality of life. Amongst indigenous Fijians this quality of life is called sautu.

> 'all discourses on education, including those of nurturing or mentoring students, take place because we make the assumption that we are seeking the most beautiful quality of life'

Sautu also denotes good health and wealth. Good health is explained in terms of physical, emotional, psychological, and spiritual well-being. Fijian anthropologist Asesela Ravuvu (1976) noted:

A person is believed to be healthy and well if he [sic] behaves accordingly and appropriately to the expectations and demands of the traditional custom. If he is unwell, then he will be generally considered ill and non-existent or lifeless; dead, although physically present, if he acted inappropriately and ignored tradition. Ravuvu, 1976, p. 45

Wealthy people may have an abundance of material resources and wealth but, above all else, it is more important that they have wide and healthy networks of relationships. Healthy relationships means a person attends to the needs of relatives when they call for help. A wise, wealthy, and healthy person in terms of mentoring and its closely associated ideas of capacity building, is a person who shows credible leadership especially as a beacon or signpost that the young, the mentee, or the trainee can use as standard-setter. In this epistemology, then, mentoring and the mentor's personal life are one and the same. Among Fijians, lived life is itself mentoring.

> 'among Fijians, lived life is itself mentoring'

Fijian world view: Vanua and the natural environment are our home—past, present, future

Perhaps similar to other indigenous or aboriginal worldviews, the Fijian world view (Nabobo-Baba, 2005) has central elements that influence their beliefs and philosophies,

To live life is to be present. To be present is to positively nurture self, others, and the spaces in which we teach.

Editors

their epistemologies or ways of knowing and learning. This includes principles of engagement with the environment. The world view, more importantly, defines what is considered to be important knowledge and related values of wealth, people, environment, spirituality, and the classificatory kinship system—intra- and inter-Vanua (tribal).

In terms of indigenous Fijian epistemologies and wisdoms, the environment is part of one's inheritance, hence the tautology, The Vanua (environment included) is Us! The environment is a subset of what the Fijians called Vanua (tribal wisdoms) which includes the tribe, its chief, its people, their land, environment, seas, forests, their spiritualities, and all that things living and non-living that live within it. The natural environment is the Vanua—the two are not different—and hence when we submerge islands, fell forests through intensive logging, mining and agriculture, we are slowly killing off a people, their culture, wisdoms, and life. In the small islands of Fiji and the Pacific Islands generally, these processes can be irreversible or may take millennia to reinstate or redress. Mentoring in such Vanua become crucial then for survival. Thus, mentoring is happening all the time, paid only because one is nurturing one's blood so to speak. This means that mentors who do their work well are highly respected in society.

> 'the Vanua (environment included) is Us!'

From this standpoint, the environment, including young people (kawa) and people in general, is theorized as a tribe's wealth and inheritance, given by God for the tribe in the past for the people living today and for those yet to arrive. Given this, the natural environment and the people who own these both become non-negotiable entities. People need mentoring so that they may look after the other for longevity and continuity of survival. Although indigenous Fijian knowledge, like all other knowledge systems, is in a perpetual state of change, the Vanua is pivotal to indigenous Fijian life and identity.

> 'people need mentoring so that they may look after the other for longevity and continuity of survival'

A minority culture such as the indigenous Fijian, should safeguard their cultures and life ways, including their indigenous wisdom. This, too, may depend on the style of teaching and mentoring that takes place. In terms of education, therefore, the world view impacts on the selection of content (episteme) and process (epistemology) of teaching or mentoring. In terms of the Fijian world view, there are three related dimensions: lagi (the heavens), vuravura (the earth), and bulu (the underworld or spirit world). The three worlds are interconnected. Reference to the three worlds are made daily among Fijians and:

in things ceremonial, God in heaven, other God spirits or spirit figures, people on earth and na veika bula kece ga (all things alive), as well as the bulu (afterlife/underworld) are mentioned. Nabobo-Baba, 2005, p. 169

This demonstrates how Fijians do not separate the world, the heavens, and the Earth (vuravura).

In terms of mentoring or capacity development, such a world view places an ethical and moral responsibility on the nurturing of the young. It is a duty and an obligation to one's people or kinsmen, God or the spirit of the worlds to which we as people on earth continue to be held accountable.

These dimensions emphasise the centrality of inter-relational, intra-relational, and trans-relational connectedness in education (Gibbs, 2006).

Editors

'it is a duty and an obligation to one's people or kinsmen, God or the spirit of the worlds to which we as people on earth continue to be held accountable'

The essence of indigenous Fijian knowledge and epistemology

The centrality of Vanua (place), its history, genealogy, land or earth (qele), and people are important in Fijian epistemology. *Things cultural are seen in their relationship to the whole* (Nabobo-Baba, 2005, p. 166). Cultural knowledge which is deemed important is no different—it is seen in relationship to the whole which is the Vanua itself and the interconnectedness of Vanua (tribe), lotu (religion and or spirituality), veiwekani (clan relationships) and i tovo/vakarau vakaVanua (acceptable cultural behaviours and values) (Nabobo-Baba, 2005, p. 166).

'things cultural are seen in their relationship to the whole'

To begin to look at epistemology—how knowledge is processed, ways of knowing, knowledge philosophy, critique, and transmission—we must first examine Vugalei notions of important knowledge. Knowledge is couched within a distinct place and time, a language, and a people who are themselves undergoing change resulting from modernity or global influences. An awareness of indigenous epistemology is important because of its transformative possibilities as we come to understand knowledge production processes in a specific indigenous context.

Thaman (1997) refers to the need for cultural analysis in education (the same can be said of research), meaning the need for systematic analysis of indigenous cultures, knowledges (epistemologies), skills, values, languages, and environment when discussing the relationship of culture and the curriculum in the Pacific. This suggests that when it comes to understanding mentoring, there is a need for cultural analysis to examine how mentoring is perceived, theorised, and experienced in this specific indigenous context. What this means is veituberi (mentoring) needs to be read in the way it is locally framed—in this instance we suggest the Vanua (tribal context) as the frame. In other contexts, mentoring may be framed using local or indigenous ideas and principles of teaching and or mentoring and the more general or overarching ideas of knowledge and epistemology.

'when it comes to understanding mentoring, there is a need for cultural analysis to examine how mentoring is perceived, theorised and experienced in this specific indigenous context'

People are the most important consideration in indigenous ways of knowing. The learning and teaching of people, their histories, languages, and relationships are considered first and foremost. Such is the nature of the epistemology, as people are deemed the most important component of the Vanua. The most important of this people category is those to whom one relates or identifies with in genealogy or through new blood ties of marriages. This suggests that when mentoring is done by those who identify or belong together, the impartation of knowledge, skills, and values by the mentor is expected to be done well and holistically.

'when mentoring is done by those who identify or belong together, the impartation of knowledge, skills, and values by the mentor is expected to be done well and holistically'

What this means in a education context is that the development of a good relationship which engenders good values and endears mentors to mentees in productive ways to realize outcomes, may need to be encouraged. A question that may arise here is: How does the mentee reciprocate or win the commitment of the mentor in a situation where monetary incentives may not be forthcoming or adequate especially if they are not related by blood? What are other ways of recognizing the mentor in changing cultural situations?

Ai Vakarau vakavanua Vaka Viti—culturally accepted behaviours and standards of ethics

Another dimension to the same questions would be to examine the ways and types of incentives mentors are given in schools or institutions of formal education. Fijians point to the notions of na sala vakaVanua (the correct path), na sala e dodonu (the straight path), na I vakarau vakaVanua vaka Viti (the correct way, culturally Fijian) as they put an emphasis to cultural behaviors and manners as one of the pillars of Fijian epistemology. All these behaviors reflect an ethically defined existence and those who adhere to these behaviours are deemed suitable to be mentors. With regards to ethics, indigenous Fijians generally talk of a correct or straight path in doing everything in life, learning included (see Katz, 1993). What is known, or gets to be learnt in a learning trip, the shaping of the intellect, is dependent on such ideals of accepted behaviors which are based on culturally accepted values. Such values are defined by the Vanua processes, clan limits or boundaries in relation to the knowledge under discussion (Nabobo-Baba, 2005). This suggests that the mentor and mentee both share similar values and principles of nurturing and or veituberi (mentoring). When values underlying such experiences or processes are shared, then mentoring is enhanced.

'when values underlying such experiences or processes are shared, then mentoring is enhanced'

What this may mean is that the mentoring process in schools or teacher education programs may need to stipulate some desirable standards of behavior, values, and principles of giving and taking knowledge, offering support and receiving the same that is shared by the learning community involved. This does not necessarily mean that people or members involved in the process will not deflect from such values and principles.

Yalomatua (spiritual wisdom) as an essential gift and quality of mentors

Sautu in the Vanua exists when people have wisdom, yalomatua. Yalomatua is spiritual wisdom, the epitome of all knowledge categories. It entails a collection of knowledge used wisely to enhance one's life and those of one's relations or people and the Vanua. Yalomatua is wealth acquired and distributed in the service of one's people to ensure their welfare. In this scenario, hoarding of wealth is deemed a show of ill-upbringing and a sad life. It is unchiefly and considered the manner of the classless. What this means is that in terms of mentoring, the mentor has to display this as it is a crucial criteria, if the mentoring process is to have credibility.

Belongingness and Vanua (clan) responsibility

The essence of belongingness embraces, in part, the roles each clan member has for each other's welfare including their education, even if it means that this happens only at a theoretical level. In Nabobo-Baba's (2005) study of her native Vugalei, she noted the importance of people identifying their relationships to each other and to other tribes. Fijians situate themselves in relation to others all the time—this is the first thing one does when meeting a person for the first time. One asks the question: *O i kemuni beka mai vei? (may I please know your village/clan or where you're from?).* To ascertain one's relationship is the essence of Fijian communal life. It is also the essence of developing or nurturing clan kawa. Kawa translated literally means a clan's bridge to the other side. Figuratively, kawa suggests a link between the old and the young generation to ensure the clan has a future. This is provided through guidance and mentoring provided to the young by the adults or experts in different fields.

> 'to ascertain one's relationship is the essence of Fijian communal life'

Fijians have a predominantly oral culture—thus, knowledge construction is a communal activity and dialogic in character. It is also deeply embedded in ecology (social, cultural, physical, spiritual, and political environments) and has defined relationships with all things, secular and spiritual. It is taken for granted that all who belong to a given place will display cultural responsibility for all that they deem of value and belonging to them, including knowledge and epistemology. Within this understanding, empiricism is only one way to verify truth. The others—experimental, the supernatural, nature and the elements, elders, chiefs' mana (prestige or respect), the mana of the Vanua, the herald clan—are among other verifiers of truth.

Further in this epistemology, one's learning in the Vanua then becomes everyone's responsibility. So practically, when we talk of mentoring, we are talking of every relative taking turns to ensure children, wards, or trainees are learning well, in places where each finds love and comfort from those with whom they share deep clan relationships. *We look after our own* is perhaps the unspoken motto here.

> 'one's learning in the Vanua is everyone's responsibility'

Na Veituberi—Touching the heart and soul

Too often, we are taught in school to temper our feelings with some degree of objectivity, while a close look at this epistemology signals a difference—the heart (uto) and soul (yalo) are considered important aspects of the learning trip if a student is to take seriously and not to forget the lessons being taught. Pedagogically, this is what the teacher or nurturer works on—the mind or brain is just as important as winning the heart and soul of the learner if quality education is to take place. When the soul (yalo) is involved, deep learning by the mentee takes place. But to touch the soul, the mentor may need to display values of care, love, and nurturing that enhances the mentee's life. In a small community of a Fijian village, most things like the mentors' behaviour towards mentees and their overall conduct and work will be transparent and critiqued by the other relations and community members. What remains to be seen is how in a big metropolitan city, we can realize or ensure that such a commitment by the mentor is achieved so as to ensure deep heart and soul learning take place.

The word for teacher is dauniveituberi meaning an expert in lifting people, or nurturing students. The teacher lifts, nurtures, and cares for a student's life and learning. This comes with values such as loloma (love-agape). When the student excels, the first question people ask is: Who is your teacher? The evaluation of students' work therefore is an evaluation of the teachers who taught them—in other words, the two are inextricably intertwined. The teacher in this context then ensures standards of quality are met rigorously because teaching and learning is an evaluation of the teacher first and foremost, and the student second.

> 'the evaluation of students' work is an evaluation of the teachers who taught them—the two are inextricably intertwined'

The mentor or teacher is also expected to display certain values or desirable characteristics. Chief among these are dodonu, dina, and savasava meaning to be straight or honest, truthful and clean, and having a record of ethical behavior. In a work on native healing among a group of indigenous Fijians, Katz (1993) talked about similar values and points to these three qualities as necessary attributes of the expert teacher, expert healer, or Fijian doctor.

Perhaps another vital element of mentoring that needs to be mentioned here is leadership. Among the indigenous Fijians studied in Nabobo-Baba's study (2005), the ultimate criteria associated with excellence in leadership (by chiefs or leaders in similar situations as elders or mentors) is judged through their service to the people they serve (qarava) or lead. Authentic leadership safeguards the welfare of people one serves and ensures sautu or well-being of the client or people served or in this case mentored (Nabobo-Baba, 2005).

> 'authentic leadership safeguards the welfare of people one serves and ensures sautu or well-being of the client or people served or in this case mentored'

Many parents, many teachers

The young learn about important Fijian knowledge at home as well as from all other clan members as part of everyday life. All members of a village can instruct, story, advise, or reprimand a young child. Parents are part of the whole teaching fraternity in a Vanua. This means that while the teaching is going on (consciously scheduled or otherwise), the child is additionally learning through established relationships and understandings of respect, commitment, and service as stipulated by custom and through cultural practices. It also suggests a learning context in which teaching and nurturing are shared even though grandparents and parents play a dominant role still. This shared teaching fraternity may mean that in the final analysis the strengths and weaknesses of many teachers are picked up by learners, mostly quietly. The learner is cushioned, however, from the adverse influences of bad teachers because in a small communities teachers of value are well known for their good and exemplary behaviors.

What this may mean is that the mentor is not alone in her duties. The responsibility for child nurturing and care is shared. As change happens in society, such shared responsibility once assumed needs to be redefined and restructured or reexamined to suit changing village or Vanua dynamics.

> 'the responsibility for child nurturing and care is shared'

The potential of online learning may be that teacher education need not exacerbate the dislocation of mentors and teachers from their communities.

Editors

If we accept cultural diversity, perhaps we need to question whether these dimensions may vary between cultures.

Editors

Manner and deportment

In learning and teaching, manner, deportment, and tone are just as important, if not more important, than what is said. A person is judged by their manner of speech. Meyer (2003) has highlighted that in Hawaiian epistemology, the manner of speaking is also important. The way words are strung together determines to a large extent the type of response one gets.

> 'in learning and teaching, manner, deportment, and tone are just as important, if not more important, than what is said'

With regards to important Vanua knowledge, knowing of how to speak is also of the essence. This is not to suggest that all learning is formal and serious. Humour and banter are also used as vehicles of knowledge transmission especially among cross cousins and vitabani. Vitabani is a type of customary relationship between two related groups of peoples or tribes and it involves playing tricks on each other, poking fun and deriving fun and joy—while outdoing each other in a competitive way. A lot is learned through this as well, especially concerning relationships among people. The relationship between mentor and mentee is affected in similar ways as articulated here.

> 'humour and banter are also used as vehicles of knowledge transmission especially among cross cousins and vitabani'

To learn is to keep quiet, listen, and do

In Fijian society, the elderly and chiefs speak, while others remain quiet, listen, and only question to clarify points made. This is because among Fijian, learning is said to be done well by the quietly determined; those that know how to listen and are willing to do work. In ceremonies, for instance, the young sit, look, and learn *hearing verbalized knowledge as well as deciphering silences* (Nabobo-Baba, 2005, pp. 272-273). This process carries on this way until the young are called on by the elders to actually carry out ceremonies. Seeing and listening are therefore important avenues of learning among our people. Mentoring of indigenous students may need to take on board such clan pedagogies with regards to listening and doing as well as close emulation of the mentor or respected elder.

As a result of these cultural experiences, Fijians have developed sustained behaviours and skills in listening. In such situations, story tellers and teachers are expected to give their truths and impart wisdom with eloquence.

> 'language and communicative acts (including silences) that are used, are shared and understood (presumably) between teacher and learner, the mentor and the mentee (dauniveituberi and koya e tuberi/gonevuli)'

Language and communicative acts (including silences) that are used, are shared and understood (presumably) between teacher and learner, the mentor and the mentee (dauniveituberi and koya e tuberi/gonevuli).

Implications for teacher education

One of the major implications is that there is a need for teacher educators to understand the cultural background of student teachers in order that they may bridge the gap

(Thaman, 2003) between teacher education curriculum and indigenous knowledge and epistemology to ensure effective mentoring and learning.

Nabobo-Baba, (2005, p. 302) further adds that there should be understanding and realization that there *are many kinds of knowledge and many ways of knowing the world and* in this case, mentoring or veituberi/veivakatavulici, in the Fijian context is lifelong.

Being taught or to be mentored is a given, an important value that most Fijians growing up learn and experience. It is a part of belonging to a tribe or a Vanua. It is lifelong because all Fijians expect and accept mentoring as an essential part of life. In modern cities and urban life, this situation is changing and continues to change, not always for the better. Working towards change in the understanding one's culture would be what Chin and Benne (1969) describe as normative re-educative. It involves changes in attitudes, values, and skills… not just *changes in knowledge, information, or intellectual rationales for action and practice* (p. 34). Such changes are enhanced through deep reflection to understand one's beliefs, knowledge, and practical reasoning. This requires that teacher educators have space for understanding indigenous students' cultural identities, pedagogies, and epistemologies. In turn, student teachers will feel supported and experience a sense of belonging when this is so.

In conclusion then, this conversation calls attention to cultural understanding of indigenous people in teacher education programs. Teacher educators can use such understandings to promote the development of teachers towards sautu—exemplified as the good, bountiful, and peaceful life. Mentoring and related notions of capacity building that come with it are a part of this good and peaceful life.

'teacher educators can use such understandings to promote the development of teachers towards sautu—exemplified as the good, bountiful and peaceful life'

References

Chin, R., & Benne, K. D. (1969). *General strategies for effecting change in changes in human systems.* New York: Holt, Rinehart & Winston.

Katz, R. (1993). *The straight path: A story of healing and transformation in Fiji.* Massachusetts: Eddison-Wesley.

Meyer, M. (2003). *Ho'oulu: Our time of becoming-Hawaiian epistemology and early writings.* Hawaii: Native Books Inc.

Nabobo-Baba, U. (2004). Silenced pasts and challenges futures. In T. Baba, O. Mahina, N. Williams, & U. Nabobo-Baba, (Eds.), *Researching the Pacific and indigenous peoples: Issues and perspectives* (pp. 17-32). Auckland, New Zealand: Centre for Pacific Studies, The University of Auckland.

Nabobo-Baba, U. (2005). V*ugalei: Voices and silences of what and how we know—Indigenous Fijian epistemology and implications for education.* Unpublished doctoral theses, Auckland, New Zealand: University of Auckland.

Nabobo-Baba, U. (2007). *Knowing and learning: A Fijian approach.* Suva, USP: IPS.

Ravuvu, A. (1976). Fijian religious beliefs. In S. Vatu (Ed.), *Na Veitalanoa Me Baleta na I Tukutuku Maroroi–Talking about oral traditions* (pp. 45-47). Oral Traditions No. 1, Fiji Museum.

Thaman, K. (1997). Towards a Pacific concept of education for cultural development. *Journal of Polynesian Society, 106*(2), 119-124.

Thaman, K. (2003). Decolonizing Pacific studies: Indigenous perspectives, knowledge, and wisdom in higher education. *The Contemporary Pacific, 15*(1), 1-17.

MOLDING THE MOLDERS OF YOUNG CHILDREN IN THE PHILIPPINES: AN INTERVIEW WITH BESSIE RIOS

Bessie Rios
Philippines

 *Bessie is the founding Directress of the Center for Early Childhood Care and Development in the Philippines. She undertakes consultancy services in setting up schools, organization development, curriculum development, personnel administration, working with parents, pupils, and personnel, analyzing school systems, program evaluation, development of sustainable operations, and all other tasks related to efficient and effective school administration. She teaches curriculum development, early childhood education administration, program evaluation, and various topics on appropriate and Biblical parenting practices. She also teaches human resource development including team building and self-development, parenting, and other motivational and inspirational seminars. Bessie also appears as a professional talent on television networks.*

Background profile

Share with us about your own background in early childhood education
I started in early childhood in 1974 as a Public Health Nutritionist supervising more than 50 day care centers in Tondo, the biggest slum colony in the Philippines. After two decades, I decided to take up a Master in Family Life and Child Development from the University of the Philippines. This was a shift in career to concentrate on early childhood education, getting involved with regular preschools, community-based early childhood care and development (ECCD) centers, and some church-based children's ministries, like Sunday School. In 1996, an American missionary entrusted me to evolve his 10-year-old mission agency into a non-governmental organization (NGO) focused on early childhood. Thus, the Center for Early Childhood Care and Development (CECCD) was born. This organization specializes in teaching teachers and other adults engaged in training and teaching of young children. Three years later, CECCD started a Collegiate course. This development required that I pursue a PhD in School Administration, as a requirement from the Commission on Higher Education. My experiences in working with children are not as extensive as my teacher and parent education roles—for example, I presented a radio program for mothers. I also helped owners and Board of Trustees set up, develop curriculum, and manage preschools.

Tell us of your beliefs about early childhood teacher education
Teacher education must achieve a balance between equipping teachers with technical knowledge and paying attention to the transformation of teachers' character and personality. It is important to attend to unsettled hurts.

> 'teacher education must achieve a balance between equipping the teachers with technical knowledge as well as pay attention to the transformation of the teachers' character and personality '

A caring, nurturing touch when educating young children may be hampered when teachers lack commitment or deep focus. They need to view their roles as vocational

> This suggests that teacher education has a responsibility to address the reasons for one's existence.
> **Editors**

rather than as a means for financial security. The heart of the teacher is vital—as John Malwell often emphasizes, *get the heart and the hands will be easier to work on*. The heart is aligned with life purpose. Rick Warren (2002), in his book *The purpose driven life: What on earth am I here for?*, says that meaningful living relates to connecting with reasons for our existence.

Teachers need to be sensitive in educating and caring for children. This must be anchored on sound knowledge about children, authentic assessment, appropriate teaching strategies, efficient classroom management, and favourable relational skills in working with parents. First teachers of children will definitely leave a lasting mark in the hearts and minds of young learners and even their parents. This role, although difficult to quantify, will surely leave an indelible mark in the world we live in.

'first teachers of children will definitely leave a lasting mark in the hearts and minds of young learners and even their parents. This role although difficult to quantify will surely leave an indelible mark in the world we live in'

How have your past experiences formed these beliefs?
My immersion in many preschools and day care centers, coupled with parents' counselling, formed my thoughts about appropriate early childhood teacher education. I often notice that teachers who have internal conflicts relate poorly with children. As I observe in centers, teachers who have low self-esteem are quite confused with their involvement in teaching, and show little of teaching. On the other hand, I have seen teachers who have a mission-focus. They have high motivation and encourage life-transcending experiences with children and their families. They have unwavering spirits and expectant hearts to see that children do not just learn, but that there is some influence in crafting their future. It is not simply education—heart transformation must complement learning.

'they have unwavering spirits and expectant hearts to see that children do not just learn, but that there is some influence in crafting their future'

The Philippine context

You say there are 2.2 million infants and 11.3 million preschool children in the Philippines. How many will receive early childhood education?
There are several laws that govern ECCD in the Philippines—the Republic Act 6972, the Early Childhood Care and Development Act, PD 603, and the Child and Youth Welfare Code. The Republic Act 6972 requires the establishment of a day care center in every barangay (a small district). Despite legal mandates, more than half of the 42,000 barangays in the country remain without any day care or preschool. Only 19% of children aged 4- to 6-years-old go to public and private preschools. If ever enrolled in school, 60% of children ages 7- to 8-years-old drop out when they reach second grade. Many in early childhood are exposed to home-based caring and teaching by any adult left with the child.

Is there any evidence available on the needs and requirements for early childhood education in the future?
A population explosion beset the Philippines. In 1998, there were only 33,184,718 Filipino children, birth through 18-years-old. This number increased steadily over the

One hundred per cent of all our books are from the West. In Thailand I tried to support learning how to run an early childhood centres. I was talking about blocks. I noticed the children were playing with wood and stones, so I had to adapt. In a tribal community in the Philippines, I noticed they had no crayons, so we used bark and banana leaves. So it all depends on how we teacher educators understand the culture of people.

Bessie Rios

years and is projected to peak in 2010 to 36,028,737. The Council for the Welfare of Children came up with Child 21 which reflects the plans and programs for children in the next two decades. It guides national government, local government units, private initiatives, and non-governmental organizations in setting priorities for action and in allocating and utilizing resources to promote the rights of Filipino children. It aims to synchronize family, community, and national efforts towards the full realization of the rights of children by 2025. There is an emphasis on weaving children's rights (survival, development, protection, and participation) with children's life cycles. Finally, it advocates not only for a more focused targeting for children but also for interfacing critical interventions at the various stages of a child's development. A challenge is to advocate for child-friendly budgets as concrete indicators of government commitment and capacity to honor its obligations to children.

CECCD

Share with us about the CECCD.

An average of 250 student teachers, including those in day care centers, attend classes every semester. Each one earns the Certificate of Preschool Education upon completion of projects and proof of acceptable competencies. The program subscribes to the developmentally-appropriate practices of NAEYC. It advocates that adults working with young children support children's rights with a corresponding training on accountability, respect of the rights of others, and sensitivity to National Development issues. CECCD further believes that teachers are facilitators of learning who must cultivate a strong partnership with parents as active stakeholders of child care and education.

> 'teachers are facilitators of learning who must cultivate a strong partnership with parents as active stakeholders of child care and education'

There are 18 units to be completed, divided into three modules:

Knowing the Child
- Child psychology
- Assessing and guiding young children

Teaching the Child
- Foundations of ECE
- Curriculum Development

Managing ECE Centers
- School Plant Design
- Advance Teaching Strategies

The distinctive task of CECCD is molding the molders (teachers) of young children. This is rooted in CECCD's strong adherence to faith and Christian missions. There is a molding and molder relationship referring to the molders as clay which is a favorite play medium of children. The clay is molded and children can create many items out of it. Molders, on the other hand are molded through their learning experiences with CECCD in the context of a Divine Potter or a Master Teacher as the molder.

> 'there is a molding and molder relationship referring to the molders as clay '

Conscience is shaped through spiritual maturity as facilitated through field practice, analysis of relevant theories, and projects unique to the situation of the molders. The significance of conscience is seen as it influences vision, discipline, and passion to change the world for good (Covey, 2004). CECCD adheres to Covey's claim that each person has an immeasurable power and capacity to reinvent his or her life into a supreme power making the reinvention possible instead of purely human pursuit.

Teaching must encourage learners to seek the larger good as opposed to seeking fulfilment in substitutes for that good. Sacramental is defined as eliminating the dichotomy between education and worship, sacredness, and secularity, belief and action, spirituality, and social witness (Moore, 2004). There is an assumption that God is the primary teacher and that all of God's creations are sources of learning. Teaching is an act of walking with sharing with, acting with, remembering with, and constructing meaning with, learners in a learning community. CECCD aspires to offer everything that it does to glorify the Lord. In our own unique ways we want to produce student teachers who are masterpieces and who will be instruments of righteousness.

'CECCD adheres to Covey's claim that each person has an immeasurable power and capacity to reinvent his or her life into a supreme power making the reinvention possible instead of purely human pursuit'

Do you have any research findings on the effects of the programme?
There is no empirical study done yet. We plan to undertake research for more accurate data soon. The impact is seen through observable transformations among student teachers in their values and appreciation of their work with children. Life purpose becomes clearer, too, as they show deeper commitment to staying on with their calling. Feedback from superiors of student teachers validates these observations. Other support is from the growing referrals of previous graduates.

'the impact is seen through observable transformations among student teachers of their values and appreciation of their work with children'

With more than 20 years working in their communities, the teachers and day care workers have considerable experience as teachers and day care workers. Based on their experiences, what skills and dispositions do they bring to their teacher education experiences?
Day care teachers who are under the government have more training compared to those in private preschools or day care centers. The skills shown are evident in teaching strategies, assessment of children and a good understanding of who children are. Those who stay teaching in the day care center for more than ten years show pleasant dispositions and better techniques in handling children's behavior. These experienced student teachers affect their classmates who maybe are not as adept yet. They provide inspiration and share their experiences. Teacher educators make use of exchanges of ideas to reinforce theories or principles relating to teaching young children.

You note that the self-esteem of student teachers is often negatively affected by their working conditions. Can you elaborate on this?
The self-esteem of student teachers in poor communities seems to be affected by their working conditions.

'the self-esteem of student teachers in poor communities seems to be more likely affected by their working conditions'

To invite student teachers to dream of what might be, opens new possibilities in their teaching.

Editors

Having been exposed to deprived families, they have smaller budgets to set up adequate materials in learning environments. Parents who have inadequate finances may manifest many social problems. They may even share concerns and personal burdens that add to teachers' own difficulties, and influence teachers' self-esteem. So, CECCD undertakes specific procedures to mold the molders' self esteem. This starts with mentoring. In addition to technical inputs, relatively informal sessions and multidimensional relationships between CECCD mentors (faculty) and molders (teacher student) take place. The mentor is an individual who serves as an advisor or guide, developer of talent or molder, coach or teacher, role model, interpreter of organizational or professional rules, and carries on all of these functions on a long-term basis. This is like in Greek mythology where Mentor was a trusted friend of Odysseus who helped to advise Telemachus, his son. Mentoring assures students that there is a support from someone who is concerned for their welfare.

'this is like the Greek mythology where Mentor was a trusted friend of Odysseus who helped advise Telemachus, his son'

Another way to raise self-esteem is to expose student teachers to many varied opportunities for personal development. These enable them to become more confident. There is a spiritual touch involved. Sometimes Molders' knowledge may be unenlightened about the truth of God—they may have dark knowledge. Without the Divine Potter there is darkness; without spiritual enlightenment of Christ, all other knowledge, ultimately is irrelevant (Smallbones, 2006).

'without spiritual enlightenment of Christ, all other knowledge, ultimately is irrelevant'

Personal development opportunities are in line with discovering God's purposes for molders. Practicum experiences, as well as other learning experiences, expand the molders' horizons and potential. In our program, the final requirement—the school development plan—challenges molders to go out of their way to organize a plan for their dream school. Seeing how this dream can be packaged in a formal and feasible way assures student teachers of practical steps to make the dream come true.

Have you any examples of how this has impacted on a student teacher's sense of self, and qualities as an early childhood teacher?
Let me share the story of a 35-year-old non-education graduate. This lady, in the initial phase of the program, was not too motivated to learn. Her many years of experience teaching in the Philippines and a short experience with a preschool in the U.S. had raised her confidence. But she just wanted to have the certification and possibly take the Licensure Examination for Teachers. After a semester, she changed in her outlook. Her professional concern turned into a desire for genuine service for others. Leading her less experienced classmates became something that she enjoyed. She graduated second in her class. Today, she has decided to teach in a Philippine school as well as helping in the school of her children. Sharing her learning with CECCD is now part of her vocation. Ultimately, she discovered that living her vocation through her career is far more meaningful and satisfying than merely succeeding in a career.

'she discovered that living her vocation through her career is far more meaningful and satisfying than merely succeeding in a career'

In what ways do you see your program as different to others in your region? And how might you explain this?

Part of being molded is to make student teachers see their roles as part of the plan of the Creator. Molding comes with certain transformations in outlook and character. So, we spend time shaping student teachers' transformations. Mentoring goes beyond regular teaching hours and the imparting of technical knowledge. Some teacher educators go to the extent of even supporting student teachers with their personal concerns.

Student teachers are also given the chance to connect their requirements with job-related tasks. This approach is strengthened by reflective practica where they gain deeper understandings about what they are doing in their classrooms and how this connects with theory. Practical lessons are opportune times for them to resolve their own childhood hurts.

Counseling and personalized guidance are available. Having deep personal relationships with student teachers may sometimes be taxing for teacher educators. The need to support and counsel student teachers can sometimes be demanding, especially for those who have deep personal problems.

CECCD has a Foundation for graduates to inspire them to be partners and encourage them to be a part of achieving CECCD's vision after graduation. They get to set up their dream school through the Foundation's financial and technical assistance. As student teachers take up their courses, CECCD tries to ensure that family responsibilities are not neglected. CECCD allows student teachers to bring children below 5-years-old as well as some family members to help with projects.

Influences on the program

You have travelled extensively and seen programs in the wider Asia Pacific region. How have you adapted your knowledge of other programs and standards to meet the needs of early childhood education in the Philippines?

Professionalizing the practice of early childhood education in the Philippines is a special concern with the passing of the ECCD Law. CECCD integrates the global standards, such as those of NAEYC, into the competencies for student teachers. Other influences are Christian education philosophies such as purpose driven life, faith development principles from Fowler, and moral intelligence theories from varied sources. CECCD uses materials or documents that support the developmentally appropriate practice and the constructivist theory. Additional inspirations are from the works of Charles Malik, Francis Schaeffer, Henry Nouwen, and other writings with similar views.

Roles of teacher educator and student teacher

How do you describe the roles of teacher educator and student teacher?

Teacher educators and student teachers are partners in making lessons enjoyable. Both must be enthusiastic in setting the tone of discussions and discoveries. Teacher educators act as facilitating and inspiring mentors who discover student teachers' potential while at the same time manage interactive learning. Student teachers, on the other hand, perform the role of active learners.

> 'teacher educators and student teachers are partners in making lessons enjoyable and both must be enthusiastic to set the tone of discussions and discoveries'

> Discipline means to guide; to guide means to teach.
> Cheryl McConnell

They fuse their ideas in the development of teaching strategies and apply the things discussed in class in their own ways.

How does your program create the space for this learning relationship?
The program is not too rigid in terms of usual tertiary education classes. Student teachers may come up with their own course requirements that are suited to them. Practicum plans are customized on student teachers' interests. Teaching is not limited to classroom experiences. Camps, group mentoring, focussed discussion, and individual talks are some alternatives.

Molding may imply that student teachers must allow their teachers to shape them in the ways they want them to go. What if these ways are different to the ways student teachers may wish to follow?
Molding is a mutually agreed process where each party respects and gradually adapts to the acceptable transformation that will take place. It is not a one-way process where teacher educators shape student teachers who are passive recipients of any input. There is actually no time limit since molding does not end at graduation. It is heavily dependent on a deep intimacy between mentors and student teachers. Because it is a mutually agreed upon journey, student teachers and teacher educators agree on the directions. This agreement is not something structured. It evolves out of the relationship and trust between mentors and student teachers. In cases of differences, mentors extend understanding while at the same time patiently guide student teachers. The character transformation and alignment to life purpose are more challenging to reckon with.

I am awed to see unseen pictures within their hearts as they dream, feel a deeper sense of fulfilment, and transform their thoughts to craft the school of life for their young learners.

'I am awed to see unseen pictures within their hearts as they dream, feel a deeper sense of fulfilment, and transform their thoughts to craft the school of life for their young learners'

References

Council for the Welfare of Children. (2000). *Child 21: Philippine national strategic framework for plan development for children, 2000-2005: A legacy to the Filipino children of the 21st century*. Retrieved from http://www.cwc.gov.ph/child21.html

Covey, S. R. (2004). *The eighth habit: From effectiveness to greatness*. London: Simon & Schuster.

Early Childhood Care and Development Act, PD 603: The Child and Youth Welfare Code. Retrieved from http://www.cwc.gov.ph/pd603.html

Moore, M. M. M. E. (2004). *Teaching as a sacramental act*. Cleveland, OH: The Pilgrim Press.

Barangay Level Total Development and Protection of Children Act, 6972 . Retrieved from http://www.unescap.org/esid/psis/population/database/poplaws/law_phi/phi_027.htm, (1990).

Smallbones, J. L. (2006). Teaching Bible for transformation. *Journal of Biblical Literature, 124*(3).

Warren, R. (2002). *The purpose driven life: What on earth am I here for?* Grand Rapids, MI: Zondervan Press.

THE LIMITS OF BICULTURALISM: KA HIKITIA AND EARLY CHILDHOOD TEACHER EDUCATION IN AOTEAROA/NEW ZEALAND

Andrew Gibbons
New Zealand

Andrew Gibbons is the Academic Dean at New Zealand Tertiary College, a provider of specialist early childhood teacher education in New Zealand. He graduated from the Auckland College of Education with his diploma of teaching early childhood education in 1992, and has since worked in a wide range of educational settings in both London and Auckland. His research interests connect the philosophy of education with contemporary early childhood education theory and practice, including the recently published book, The Matrix Ate My Baby, *exploring the role of new technologies in early education, and arguing for a philosophy of technology. Andrew is Executive Committee Member and Membership Secretary of the Philosophy of Education Society of Australasia, and co-program chair of the 2009 Reconceptualizing Early Childhood Education Conference.*

Introduction

In 2007 I attended a Ministry of Education seminar introducing the New Zealand Government's draft strategy for Māori in education, known as *Ka Hikitia: Managing for Success*. Māori are the indigenous peoples of Aotearoa/New Zealand having, in 1840, signed te Titiri o Waitangi (the Treaty of Waitangi) with the British. The seminar presenter introduced me, a first generation New Zealander of British decent, to the term *condoned truancy*. This term was used in relation to an instance where a Māori elder is seen to condone a young child's absence from compulsory schooling. This was an important moment for me in understanding the colonisation of Māori education by the British—the significance of separating the child from the most essential link to her education. And it led me to the writing of this paper. A Māori pēpeha, or proverb, suggests:

E tama mā e! Haere atu rā!
Pōpō noa ana te koukou e tāwaia ana e te tāriroriro.
O sons, depart! The owl grieves alone as it is jeered at by the grey warbler.
Mead & Grove, 2003, p. 46

> 'this was an important moment for me in understanding the colonisation of Māori education by the British—the significance of separating the child from the most essential link to her education'

I introduce this pēpeha not simply to highlight a sense of grief that Māori elders may feel in relation to nearly two centuries of colonization of their knowledge of teaching and learning, but to introduce an essential component of that teaching and learning. The pēpeha, Mead and Grove (2003) suggest, is a proverb or saying, also known as a whakatauki, through which ancestral knowledge is conferred to present and future generations. Pēpeha or whakatauki are essential for a culture that regards its language as taonga (a treasure), that connects the people to te whenua (the land), to nga tipuna (ancestors), and to Aitua (God).

The pēpeha above is a lament. As such it speaks of how cultures hold to their values, beliefs, and practices in the face of colonisation. The importance of such resistance is considered in this paper in association with the concept of biculturalism. This paper explores the limitations of biculturalism, as conceived and acted out in Aotearoa/New Zealand, through considering the ongoing colonisation of Māori. It reveals challenges to how we think about, teach, and care for culture in teacher education, and suggests some teacher education practices that might underpin bicultural and multicultural pedagogies. The paper begins with a theoretical framework for thinking about different cultural perspectives of education, before analysing the meaning of *Ka Hikitia* and its implications for teacher education.

First, I must introduce that I was born in the Waikato, a region of Aotearoa/New Zealand, of British descent, with some Indian blood hiding beneath my family's colonial roots. My identity is Pākehā. Being Pākehā in Aotearoa/New Zealand is not an easily distinguished demographic, however it generally is a term that was applied by Māori to the colonial Europeans, predominantly the British partners to the founding Treaty of Waitangi. Pākehā is not a term that applies to, or is welcomed by, all non-Māori in Aotearoa/New Zealand. To orient the international reader further, I would like to point out that Aotearoa is commonly accepted as the Māori name for what the British know as New Zealand. Reflecting the aspirations of this country to be bicultural, I use the term Aotearoa/New Zealand with the exception of reference to the Government, which is known as the New Zealand Government.

> The idea of the commersurable and incommensurable opens conversations about how teacher education might be conceptualised.
> Editors

Theories of differences

Does everyone have the same values about, and purposes for, education? For instance, do we all agree that education should be about ensuring economic prosperity and all that is believed to come with it? If, perhaps, not everyone wants to make it rich, then perhaps here lies a problem of different, perhaps even incommensurable, paradigms and traditions.

> 'does everyone have the same values about, and purposes for, education? For instance, do we all agree that education should be about ensuring economic prosperity and all that is believed to come with it?'

The notion of the commensurable and the incommensurable is a language game which acknowledges the contributions of Wittgenstein and Kuhn to thinking about being and knowing (see for instance Burbules, 2000, who challenges Lyotard's understanding of language games; and Hanks, 2005). Put simply, paradigms that are *commensurate have a common measure* (Dictionary.com, 2008). To be commensurable, then, is to be *measurable by the same standard* (Sykes, 1976, p. 202). To suggest that paradigms are incommensurable, is to claim that they are not measurable by the same standard.

That would seem simple, if it were not for the possibility that there is a problem with the meaning of the word measure. In *...Poetically Man Dwells...* Heidegger (1971) pursues a question of measuring. He suggests *it might be that our unpoetic dwelling, its incapacity to take measure, derives from a curious excess of frantic measuring and calculating* (1971, p. 228).

> 'it might be that our unpoetic dwelling, its incapacity to take measure, derives from a curious excess of frantic measuring and calculating'

A curious excess of frantic measuring occurs where difference is regarded as a problem. Yet for Heidegger, measuring, in a poetic sense gives presence to our differences and these differences reflect different horizons. In understanding a horizon, Young (2002, p. 8) suggests:

My Heideggerian horizon... is non-optional. It is... 'transcendental'... a feature of my existence, something which, as a member of the current epoch of the historical culture to which I belong, I inhabit as a matter of necessity. Embodied in the language I speak... it constitutes for me and my fellows, the limit of what, to us, is intelligible.

The suggestion that different cultures have different horizons, and that it is measuring that gives presence to these horizons, reveals a problem with the idea that we might measure across horizons. More to the point, in a modern Western epoch, a belief that there is only one horizon is revealed by an expectation that all cultural values, beliefs, and practices are measurable by the same standards. In perpetuating this myth, the measurers of the modern West seem to have secured themselves an eternity of frantic measurement.

> 'a belief that there is only one horizon is revealed by an expectation that all cultural values, beliefs, and practices are measurable by the same standards. In perpetuating this myth, the measurers of the modern West seem to have secured themselves an eternity of frantic measurement.'

Lyotard takes this myth as central to the problem of the postmodern. He challenges any tendencies to presume shared understandings between paradigms with reference to Wittgenstein's thinking on language games. Lyotard provides an important perspective on weaving between paradigms and traditions, in suggesting:

Conflicts can arise when people are engaged in discourses that are incommensurable. Because there are no rules that apply across the discourses, the conflicts become differends. To enforce a rule in a differend is to enforce the rule of one discourse over the other, resulting in a wrong suffered by the party whose rule of discourse is ignored. Furthermore the wronged party cannot appeal against the wrong because the rules of its own discourse are not recognized and because to appeal in terms of the rules of the other discourse is already to have given up.
Nuyen, 1988, p. 175, cited in Burbules, 2000.

Here Lyotard is, like Heidegger, challenging a measuring across paradigms, and in particular of the project, in modernity, of attempting to colonise different paradigms through the colonisation of the very measuring of those paradigms. In the context of Aotearoa/New Zealand, Pihama, Smith, Taki, and Lee (2004, p. 33) argue:

Cultural deprivation/disadvantage/difference theories assume there exists a 'norm' in society against which all 'others' can be measured and evaluated. In New Zealand the 'norm' may be generally stated as middle class Pākehā and Māori people are assessed relative to that 'norm'. The emphasis on correcting the cultural background of Māori children is based on the assumption that the environment of the Māori child is a barrier to their achievement within the school system, that Māori children carry with them particular 'cultural baggage' that impedes their development. Underlying such a theory is the notion that the dominant culture and knowledge are "endorsed as 'the culture' of the state schooling system.
(Smith, G.,1986: 3 [sic]).

There is no analysis or challenge to the structural or cultural arrangements of the system itself. *Ka Hikitia* is a central document in understanding the structure and

These six themes open interesting conversations, especially about their implications for early childhood teacher education.

Editors

purpose of the system. Hence it is essential to explore the meaning and implications embedded within its language. It is important to note that this analysis was conducted on the draft strategy, which has recently been replaced by the working strategy. The laudable commitment to consultation that embodies the New Zealand Government's development of education strategies is reflected in some significant changes to the strategy. However some concerns remain.

'the laudable commitment to consultation that embodies the New Zealand Government's development of education strategies is reflected in some significant changes to the strategy'

The draft strategy

In August 2007 the Minister for Māori affairs, Parekura Horomia, and then Minister of Education Steve Maharey introduced a new phase in the restoration of Māori culture. The draft strategy *Ka Hikitia*, meaning 'to step up' was designed to reduce the gaps between students who experience educational success and those who *never really conquer the basics* (Horomia & Maharey, 2007). While *Ka Hikitia* is a strategy specifically for Māori, and hence not specifically a bicultural document, it reflects a commitment to being a bicultural nation, where the two cultures, Pākehā and Māori, are seen to be partners.

Ka Hikitia's (2007) focus on Māori education experiences and outcomes fits within the wider policy of Te Puni Kōkiri, the Ministry of Māori Affairs, of *realising Māori potential* in order to address issues of inequity dating back to the signing of the Treaty of Waitangi by Māori and British in 1840. *Ka Hikitia* acknowledges that educational success for Māori requires self-determination, and that success should not be at the cost of Māori identity. Teacher educators in this nation should then be committed to ensuring Māori have space to determine their educational futures, and importantly their educational histories. However, the nature of *Ka Hikitia* suggests limitations to the possibility of clearing such space.

'teacher educators in this nation should then be committed to ensuring Māori have space to determine their educational futures, and importantly their educational histories'

The strategy has three goals: improving mainstream education, developing Māori immersion primary education known as Kura Kaupapa Māori, and increasing the *involvement* and *authority* of Māori (Ministry of Education, 2007). It is important to accept the intent of all three goals—intent grounded in the Government's obligation to the Treaty of Waitangi, acknowledgement of its own governmental failings and commitments, and belief in a strengths-based approach. However, six interconnected themes are articulated persistently throughout the document as:

Do we sometimes emphasise the differences without celebrating the similarities and connections?

Ros Littledyke

- The expectation that Māori performance in education will be judged by universal outcomes
- The assumption that the purpose of education is economic progress through the exploitation of knowledge
- The requirement that Māori whānau and communities be compelled to enrol their children in a regulated early childhood service and be responsible for participation throughout school years

- The articulation of whānau as consumers of education
- The increasing of demands upon measuring both the intention and ability of schools and centres to meet the needs of Māori
- The intention to personalise learning

These themes reflect a problem with the idea of bicultural education. For instance, a strategy for Māori that focuses on personalising learning in order to ensure *they are active participants in their own learning and are therefore more engaged and purposeful* (Ministry of Education, 2007, p. 4) is a strategy that assumes that the bicultural partners have shared assumptions about personalising learning. Māori have a unique world view that cannot be articulated in generic and rhetorical terms (Pihama et al., 2004), so it is questionable whether terms such as 'personalised learning' and 'knowledge economy' should be employed at all. However, at the very least these terms need to be expressed as open to varying social and cultural interpretations.

'Māori have a unique world view that cannot be articulated in generic and rhetorical terms'

Furthermore, the suggestion by Te Puni Kōkiri that education and knowledge are things to be manipulated for economic purposes suggests that Māori goals and Government goals are enjoined in the rhetoric of what is generally known as new right or neoliberal economic management. It is hard to believe that Māori self-determination so conveniently maps with Chicago school economic government rationality; however, one should be open to this possibility. There is, nevertheless, much disagreement and considerable, if unsuccessful, resistance to this Governmental rhetoric. Ironically, the Government itself suggests that we, the nation, need *to move beyond the rhetoric and actually achieve equity for all in education* (Ministry of Education, 2007, p. 6). Educational purposes and pathways for Māori children are very much predetermined by the rhetoric, and these purposes and pathways limit self-determination. The strategy should be better than this.

'it is hard to believe that Māori self-determination so conveniently maps with Chicago school economic government rationality; however, one should be open to the possibility of this'

Teacher education has an important role in drawing out both the qualities and limitations of *Ka Hikitia*. The strategy itself asserts that teacher education has a fundamental role in ensuring its goals are met, acknowledging a link between the quality of the teaching profession and outcomes for Māori. Teacher education and professional development is expected to support teachers in critical reflection of their own attitudes and beliefs regarding Māori, to ensure that teachers' attitudes and beliefs are challenged, and that teachers are aware of *what works for Māori* (Ministry of Education, 2007, p. 15).

'teacher education has an important role in drawing out both the qualities and limitations of *Ka Hikitia*'

What works for Māori might require non-Māori teacher educators to resist the urge to make decisions for Māori, and instead to work at clearing the spaces that have been cluttered by a Pākehā educational system. Heta-Lensen (2007) suggests that the commitment to bicultural practice in early childhood has done little in securing self-determination for Māori. This may be in part due to the tendency to seek out, in a

> Teachers need also to be careful—they can alienate by asking about culture.
> Melanie Lewandowski

bicultural paradigm, commonalities over differences. It might be appropriate to search for commonalities in cultural values, beliefs, and practices; however, it is dangerous to assume that these commonalities exist. For instance, many aspects of Māori pedagogy (see for instance Ka'ai, 2004; Ritchie, 1994) resonate with early childhood pedagogies around the world; this does not mean they are the same, or that their similarities legitimate action without consultation.

> 'many aspects of Māori pedagogy resonate with early childhood pedagogies around the world; this does not mean they are the same, or that their similarities legitimate action without consultation'

In addition, agreement on the meaning of education, or biculturalism, requires a relationship between cultures that is not grounded in, and subverted by, political or scientific authority (Marshall, 1999). Teacher educators should then consider the political and cultural nature of the knowledge that they are introducing students to. Where a cultural superiority or some form of epistemological supremacy informs teacher educators' practices, they may find it difficult to allow for the possibility that other cultures value alternative and valid ways of knowing.

Epistemological supremacy may be best challenged by drawing out the fragility of any and every knowledge system or science rather than by attempting to show the strengths of any or all. For instance, rather than express the relevance and validity of pēpeha as both scientific and educational, a Pākehā teacher educator might be best enjoined in examining theories as socially constructed narratives. In other words, it is more important to understand that developmentally appropriate practice is no more or less than an important story we tell ourselves in order to make sense of the world and enhance the lives of those who live in it. Teacher educators might also look at the history of such stories about childhood and education, particularly where they have been implicated in colonising practices.

> 'teacher educators might also look at the history of such stories about childhood and education, particularly where they have been implicated in colonising practices'

Another fragile story that has come to take on more authority than it perhaps should is the story about quality early childhood education that so fundamentally underpins teacher education. The unstoppable force that has been the professionalization of early childhood in Aotearoa/New Zealand speaks highly of valuing Māori and Māori communities at the same time as it undermines the right of Māori to determine their own early childhood education through setting up the claim that all Māori children should attend an early childhood service as nationally agreed, and irrefutable.

By contrast Ritchie (1994, p. 3) argues that:
Māori are wary of initiatives that are not Māori-controlled... since experience has taught them that it is only when they are able to exercise their Tino Rangatiratanga (self-determination), that their language will genuinely be supported.

The commitment to bicultural partnership, in itself, seems to be a problem that has historically led to negative outcomes for Māori when dealing with Pākehā. Such negative outcomes have led to the many historical versions of the strategy of getting Māori to achieve for them and for all of us, dating back to, at least, 1840. Heta-Lensen (2007) suggests that biculturalism has led to a slashing of Māori culture into a subordinate relationship. She argues that teacher educators need to move beyond biculturalism to understanding whānaungatanga, an approach which is intended to place more emphasis on Māori values, beliefs, and practices.

While the nation has seen a significant growth in attention to Māori values and beliefs regarding education and teacher education, and to the role of colonisation in subordinating these values and beliefs, there is little emphasis on how to address the tensions between different world views in a systemic sense. The long history of turning to schooling as the solution to problems of Māori education has been, at best, misguided. At worst this is a purposeful disciplining of a culture according to the needs of the dominant group.

What I am asking here is for teacher educators to engage with questioning the very system of which they are an essential component. Teacher educators cannot assume that their programmes have universal application, or that the values and beliefs of cultures can be measured by their own standards and criteria. Furthermore, they should not develop programmes without considering the relationship of the programme to wider social, cultural and political systems (see for instance Pihama et al., 2004). Such an emphasis might start, for the mainstream, with an appreciation of the diversity of beliefs regarding the system itself—in other words, coming to the realisation that there is no Western way to feel superior about. Aotearoa/New Zealand has enjoyed an amazing diversity of *Western* ways to educate children, each having a history of struggle to achieve a status of educational respect in the wider community.

Teacher educators should then be mindful of history, and of the competing interpretations of it. And I believe it is hard as a teacher educator to feel comfortable as Pākehā when exploring the journey of Māori education from pre-colonial and colonial history. Ritchie (1994), Durie (1996), Rokx (1998), and Pihama et al. (2004) express the importance of understanding this history and seeing the strength of Māori culture to resist in any way the violations that have been perpetuated since communities were broken up by European systems of schooling. Rokx (1998) in particular takes adult learners on a positive journey of reflection, one that asks us to think more carefully about the dissonance between a culture's ideals and the very publicly aired educational statistics. In other words, if one accepts that Māori consider learning and education as essential to cultural strength and self-determination, why is it that the education statistics in Aotearoa/New Zealand suggest not only low (relative) achievement but also poor educational behaviour?

> 'teacher educators should then be mindful of history, and of the competing interpretations of it'

As noted above, the intent of *Ka Hikitia* should not be disregarded. The purpose of this paper is not, in other words, to ask teacher educators to dismiss the importance of realising Māori potential, or reject lighting the pathways of self-determination. What is asked here is that early childhood teacher educators, and others, be careful not to measure the educational values of another culture with their own standards. To do so would be contrary to the spirit of being bicultural.

Conclusion

Te Puni Kōkiri (2008) states:
As wellbeing ultimately depends on people having a sense of choice or control over their lives, the framework describes the state of Te Ira Tangata [people's life] as one in which Māori are exercising confident and responsible choices about the quality of their life experiences.

> The Australian context is to raise our children to be independent which cuts across some cultures who respect the role of the grandmother.
> Rhonda Forrest

While the Government's promotion of the well being and self-determination of Māori is to be praised, its guidance of schools, of teachers, and of teacher educators is to be questioned.

The governance of education for Māori, I suggest, remains too embedded in the ways of the Pākehā. Where dissonance in values, beliefs, and practices arise, the Government reverts to a historical position of resisting or subverting Māori self-determination—of labelling those that do attempt to determine their own paths as *truants and condoners*. Moreover, where such government resistance arises, the application of *Ka Hikitia* will continue to symbolise the Government's good intentions while obscuring the maintenance of the status quo.

> 'I accept Heta-Lensen's (2007) acknowledgement that early childhood teacher education has many strengths in its understanding of and respect for the Māori world view, te Ao Māori'

I accept Heta-Lensen's (2007) acknowledgement that early childhood teacher education has many strengths in its understanding of, and respect for, the Māori world view, te Ao Māori. I am concerned however, that the increasing regulation of the early childhood sector, and the rhetoric that demands increasing Māori participation in early childhood education, is undermining these qualities, and engendering early childhood education as a further colonisation of the Māori family. I would like to suggest then that as an early childhood, primary, secondary, or tertiary educator, I would say to the child:

> 'Stay at home with your grandmother. She is far more important to your education than I.'

References

Burbules, N. C. (2000). Lyotard on Wittgenstein: The differend, language games, and education. In P. Standish & P. Dhillon (Eds.) *Lyotard: Just education.* Retrieved from http://faculty.ed.uiuc.edu/burbules/papers/lyotard.html

Dictionary.com. (2008). *Commensurate.* Lexico publishing group. Retrieved from http://dictionary.reference.com/browse/commensuration

Durie, A. (1996, June). *Pathways home: Te hoe nuku roa (The long journey).* Paper presented to the World Indigenous Peoples Conference, Albuquerque, New Mexico.

Hanks, C. (2005). Incommensurability, interpretation, and educational research. *Philosophy of Education Yearbook,* 225-233.

Heta-Lensen, Y. (2007, September). *Kaupapa whānau approaches in educational management.* Paper presented to the Early Childhood Convention, Rotorua, New Zealand.

Horomia, P., & Maharey, S. (2007). *Ka Hikitia: Managing for success.* Retrieved from http://www.beehive.govt.nz/speech/ka+hikitia+--+managing+success+0

Ka'ai, T. M. (2004). Te mana o te reo me ngaa tikanga: Power and politics of the language. In T. M. Ka'ai, J. C. Moorfield, M. P. J. Reilly, & S. Mosley (eds.), *Kit e whaiao: An introduction to Māori culture and society* (pp. 201-213). Auckland: Pearson Longman.

Lather, P. (2006). Paradigm proliferation as a good thing to think with: Teaching research in education as a wild profusion. *International Journal of Qualitative Studies in Education, 19*(1), 35-57.

Lyotard, J-F. (1999). *The postmodern condition: A report on knowledge.* (G. Bennington, & B. Massumi, Trans.). Minneapolis: University of Minnesota Press.

Marshall, J. D. (1999). The language of indigenous Others: The case of Māori in New Zealand. *Philosophy of Education Society Year Book.* Retrieved from http://www.ed.uiuc.edu/EPS/PES-yearbook/1999/Marshall_body.asp

Mead, H. M., & Grove, N. (2003). *Ngā Pēpeha a ngā Tīpuna.* Wellington: Victoria University Press.

Ministry of Education. (2007). *Ka Hikitia–Managing for success: The draft Māori education strategy 2008-2012.* Wellington: Learning Media.

Pihama, L., Smith, L., Taki, M., & Lee, J. (2004). *A literature review on Kaupapa Māori and Māori education pedagogy.* Auckland: The International Research Institute for Māori and Indigenous Education.

Ritchie, J. (1994, December). *Development of a Māori Immersion Early Childhood Education Diploma of Teaching.* Paper presented to the International Language in Education Conference, University of Hong Kong.

Rokx, H. (1998, August). *Atawhaingia te pā Harakekeā—Nurture the family.* Paper presented to the Twelfth International Congress on Child Abuse and Neglect, Auckland, New Zealand.

Smeyers, P. (2006). What philosophy can and cannot do for education. *Studies in Philosophy and Education, 25,* 1-18.

Stewart, G. (2005). Māori in the science curriculum: Developments and possibilities. *Educational Philosophy and Theory, 37*(6), 851-870.

Sykes, J. B. (Ed.) (1976). *The concise Oxford dictionary of current English. London:* Oxford University Press.

Te Puni Kōkiri. (2007). *Strategic outcome and role.* Retrieved from http://www.tpk.govt.nz/en/about/strategic/

Te Puni Kōkiri. (2008). *Māori potential approach.* Retrieved from http://www.tpk.govt.nz/en/about/mpa/

CHAPTER 3

Conversations on teacher education curriculum

In answering the question, 'What is the purpose of education' I relied at that time upon the following observations: Man [sic] lives in a world of objects, which influence him, and which he desires to influence; therefore he ought to know these objects in their nature, in their conditions, and in their relation with each other and with mankind. Froebel, 1886, p. 69

Friedrich Froebel's conception of an early childhood curriculum is a historically significant development for children and adults, firstly in Europe, and then around the world. Froebel did not simply identify how children should play with the things in their world, he identified how adults should know and influence this play. Of course, Froebel was not the first educationalist to develop an early childhood teacher education curriculum—both Martin Luther and Lucius Plutarch (to name just two) guided adults in the nature of early childhood education. However, Friedrich Froebel has perhaps had the most significant role in developing early childhood teacher education with his specific focus on the early years, and his identification of the things and behaviors that might now be regarded as contributing to an early childhood teacher education curriculum.

Conversations on early childhood curriculum, and therefore on what should be essential knowledge for teachers and parents, have continued since Friedrich Froebel's early work in guiding early pedagogical approaches to early childhood education. In this chapter the conversations regarding curriculum cover a broad range of issues, through reference to specific areas of the early childhood curriculum, and to the role of graduate teachers in leading the curricula of the future. The authors in this chapter examine ways to introduce early childhood curriculum to student teachers. In this way, they are giving form to both the early childhood curriculum and to innovations in the teacher education curriculum.

The chapter begins with *The weaving of literacy: An interview with Kathy Ward-Cameron*. In this interview, Kathy discusses an innovative approach to developing teacher awareness of early childhood literacy. Her work with the Illinois Action for Children Early Reading First Program has been developed around a philosophy of introducing literacy strategies to adults in a positive and exciting teacher education environment, emphasizing not only the importance of literacy, but also of happiness as an aim of education (for more on happiness as an aim of education, see Noddings, 2003).

This is followed by a paper by Mary Hynes-Berry and Rebeca Itzkowich entitled *The gift of error*. These writers use mathematics in the early childhood curriculum as a fulcrum for thinking about how student teachers learn about mathematics in early childhood education, and they highlight ways in which student teachers can effectively learn about learning. Particular attention is given to the use of error in making sense of the world, and the ways in which teacher educators can create environments that parallel the child's experiences of error.

The third conversation is entitled *Helping undergraduate student interns meet the challenge of using responsive language*. Kathryn Summers Clark and Ann Noland explore the discourse on responsive language and the challenges that face student teachers in developing communication strategies that enhance the learning of young children. They identify the relational nature of the language that student teachers use, and discuss the meanings of responsive and restrictive language.

Rhonda Forrest concludes the chapter's conversations with her conversations on *The teacher educator's role in students learning to lead*. She places a focus on leadership, arguing that leadership can be taught, and that early childhood teacher education programs have a responsibility for encouraging in teachers the leadership qualities and skills that will be required in the complex and diverse environments that characterize early childhood education. Notably, the many roles of the leader include curriculum leadership. Teacher education is then a key site for encouraging early childhood teachers to lead the development of their centre curricula.

Beginning the conversations

As noted above, curriculum conversations have long occupied teacher educators with complex questions around the purpose of early childhood education, the nature of effective early childhood programs, and the priorities for a student teacher's introduction to theory and practice. In her opening address, Lilian Katz posed that such questions are a key dilemma in teacher education. The following questions provide some scope for engaging with these conversations:

- What roles do teacher educators play in the dissemination of knowledge about what counts as a quality early childhood curriculum?

As noted above, and in both Lilian Katz's and Rhonda Forrest's respective papers, there are many debates about what should be included in an early childhood teacher education program.

- How are decisions about content made in the context of programs that are familiar to you?

Critical literacy is widely regarded as an essential component of being a teacher, yet courses for improving language and literacy skills are rarely regarded as compulsory elements in an early childhood teacher education program.

- What can teacher educators do to support student teachers in their personal and professional literacy development?

THE WEAVING OF LITERACY:
AN INTERVIEW WITH KATHY WARD-CAMERON

Kathy Ward-Cameron
United States

Kathy Ward-Cameron is the founding president of the Early Literacy Institute (ELI), a cadre of early childhood specialists, psychologists, evaluators and consultants who offer consultation, evaluation, and training services to help early childhood programs provide scientifically-based early literacy and learning initiatives for young children. Under her leadership, the ELI team currently provides professional development for Illinois Action for Children's Early Reading First Program in Chicago, Illinois, and oversees early literacy classroom observations and teacher education for a state-wide initiative through the Ohio Department of Education. As a certified instructor on the Early Literacy Classroom Observation (ELLCO) through the Education Development Center (EDC) and Brookes Publishing/Brookes-On-Location, she trains literacy specialists, teachers, and administrators throughout the United States. Through the University of Illinois at Chicago's Center for Literacy and the Chicago Department of Human Services, she served as the evaluator of the Head Start Early Literacy and Youth Development Initiative – Project SOAR, an early literacy program which prepares teens and parents to work side-by-side with teachers to enhance the early literacy skills and development of at-risk children. Kathy also trained facilitators of HeadsUp! Reading early literacy course which is offered through the National Head Start Association and is broadcast via satellite to early childhood programs, libraries, and universities nationwide. Kathy holds a Master of Science in Child Care Administration from Nova Southeastern University and a Bachelor of Science in Early Childhood Education from East Carolina University.

The Early Literacy Institute (ELI)

Tell us about your involvement in the Early Literacy Institute (ELI)
I founded the ELI in 2003 in response to the needs of several large federally funded literacy programs throughout the United States that were having difficulty finding quality professional development in the relatively new field of early literacy. ELI started with a handful of dedicated early literacy specialists based out of Chicago and has grown into an international cadre of researchers, evaluators, trainers, coach-mentors, family literacy coordinators, speech therapists, and even professional dancers and storytellers. We offer program development, professional development coordination, and evaluation and training services to help programs in the U.S. and around the world. This includes schools in South Africa and the Philippines, providing scientifically-based literacy initiatives for young children.

Tell us about the Illinois Action for Children's Early Reading First program. Why it was formed? Who is it targeted at? And, how does the program see the role of the educator?
Illinois Action for Children is an alliance of individuals and groups which supports parents, child care providers, and family service programs. Early Reading First provides federal grants directly to the local level to enhance the reading readiness of at risk preschool-age children, and professional development for teachers in research-based instructional strategies. Illinois Action for Children was awarded an Early Reading First grant in September, 2006. The goal of the three year Early Reading First Project is to increase the language and early literacy skills of over 300 preschool

A feature of early childhood teacher education is its interdisciplinary approach to serving the needs of early literacy. A characteristic of professions is that they relate to, and share their expertise with, others.

Editors

children from very low income families in four child care programs located in the Chicago area, including: vocabulary; phonological awareness; letter knowledge and understanding of the alphabetic principal; and knowledge about print.

The ELI coordinates professional development of the administrators, teachers, assistant teachers, and family child care providers in the project. All staff in the program participate in a series of intensive workshops focused on:

- scientifically-based research on effective strategies for building children's vocabulary, knowledge about print, phonological awareness, and alphabet knowledge
- strategies for creating a literacy- and language-rich classroom environment
- implementation of the Building Language for Literacy and Phonemic Awareness curricula
- working with parents and caregivers to connect classroom learning to home literacy activities.

Coach-mentors (teachers with early childhood experience and master's degrees in reading or early literacy) visit each classroom at least two hours per week to observe, model effective instruction, and confer with teachers to ensure that the curricula are being effectively implemented and that the classroom is providing a sufficiently literacy-rich environment.

A similar, but less intensive, professional development program is provided for the home child care providers who care for the children after school. An initial 5-session workshop focused on dialogic reading is followed by workshops on topics such as promoting phonological awareness through songs and finger plays, developmentally appropriate support for early writing skills, and using public library resources. The classroom teacher (or assistant teacher) introduces learning materials and models their use in bi-weekly home visits. The family literacy coordinators plan and present bimonthly literacy events for families of children in the program. The events are interactive and connected to the themes and literacy concepts being taught in the classrooms.

'the teacher introduces learning materials and models their use in bi-weekly home visits'

What do you understand early literacy to be?
Early literacy encompasses the knowledge, skills, and awareness that serve as the foundation for learning to read and write. It includes oral language development, phonological awareness, letter knowledge, beginning writing, and print awareness.

How do you see early literacy as being taught most effectively?
Children learn best in print-rich, language-rich environments that nurture their natural curiosity about the world; where books are many and varied; where print, including children's writing is attractively displayed; where a variety of fun, interesting reading and writing materials are available; where frequent on-going conversations with adults and other children are encouraged and vocabulary is enhanced; where adults are available and eager to read to an individual or small group, and where children are encouraged to read to each other; where adults enthusiastically co-play, observe, and set the stage for young learners.

The ELI works closely with programs to create and assess literacy-rich environments for young children. Currently, we are partnering with Learning Point Associates and

Literacy education has long been the site of rich debate—from approaches that favor whole language through to those which highlight phonemic and phonological awareness. Whatever position is taken, teachers need to be continually in touch with current research to inform their practice.

Editors

Irrespective of what is provided in the environment— although that is important—it is what is said within that environment that is the key.

Karen Prince

This description of effective teaching, especially of early literacy, affirms the importance of not just the preparation of the learning environment, but also that teachers are wholeheartedly present with their students.

Editors

the state of Ohio on a study using the ELLCO: Early Language and Literacy Observation Tool to help inform early literacy professional development and school improvement efforts throughout the state.

What insights have you gained about the teaching of early literacy?
Several years ago I developed a tool, the ELBO: Early Literacy Behavior Observation, with the University of Illinois at Chicago to measure children's literacy behaviors. In our studies using the ELBO, I discovered that children's literacy behaviors significantly increased the more actively engaged the teacher was in the learning environment. The bottom line is this—children are much more likely to engage in literacy behaviors if teachers are intentional in their practice. It's not enough to have lots of fun 'stuff' for the kids to play with. Teacher involvement and interaction makes all the difference in the world!

'children are much more likely to engage in literacy behaviors if teachers are intentional in their practice'

What are the essential considerations or principles concerning the preparation of teachers to teach early literacy?
The most important consideration or principle is that literacy is integrated throughout the curriculum. Literacy includes all forms of verbal and written communication. It is infused in everything children learn and everything teachers teach.

You have developed some innovative strategies to bring teacher attention to child literacy. Can you explain what motivated you to use an innovative approach to your institute's involvement in the program?
Our philosophy is that teacher education should be effective and enjoyable. If we want teachers to teach with enthusiasm and passion, we need to model that approach in teacher professional development. Learning at all ages and stages should be fun and interactive. So we strive for innovative strategies that are content rich and entertaining.

'if we want teachers to teach with enthusiasm and passion, we need to model that approach in teacher professional development'

What purposes do the retreats serve?
The primary purpose of kick-off retreats is to bring staff together to learn the principles and practices of early literacy, as well as the expectations and goals of the new program and their role in achieving those goals.

'we set out to honor the individual by creating a warm, welcoming environment (comfortable, good food, etc.) to nurture each teacher's spirit and to provide quality learning opportunities by preparing an event that was well-paced, content-rich and presented by the highly qualified, professional trainers'

For the Illinois Action for Children retreat in Chicago we set out to honor the individual by creating a warm, welcoming environment (comfortable, good food, etc.) to nurture each teacher's spirit and to provide quality learning opportunities by preparing an event that was well-paced, content-rich and presented by highly qualified, professional trainers. In keeping with our philosophy, we created an atmosphere of fun. The four day gathering was titled 'Welcome to the Literacy Dance.' The theme of dance emphasized that, for the Early Reading First Program to be successful, each person needed to understand the fundamental steps of supporting early literacy, the specific steps of the dance. Interactive workshops on setting up a literacy-rich environment, integrating literacy into the preschool curriculum, and choosing quality children's books were presented to familiarize teachers with early literacy principles. They were then taken on field trips to classrooms where the principles they learned were being practiced.

Since most teachers and children in the program are African American, another important component of the retreat was to introduce the teachers to the stories, music, and dances of African culture. During the retreat, they discovered strategies for incorporating the arts into literacy instruction while enhancing children's, and their own, awareness of cultural diversity.

How successful were these retreats?
The Literacy Dance retreat was very well received by the participants. At the end of the four days they felt energized and ready to move forward with great enthusiasm. We've been *dancing* together for two years now. There are a few more steps to add before the Early Reading First program ends in September, 2009. Our hope is that the dance will continue and evolve long after we are gone.

Where do you go from here?
The ELI is striving to make the world a better place by sharing what we know and to continue to learn from others about how to help teachers and families create literacy-rich, nurturing environments where young children can reach their highest potential.

Where do we go from here? We'll go where the need is, I guess. At this point, we are researching and designing teacher education and literacy programs for schools in South Africa and the Philippines and retreats for early literacy coach-mentors of other state- and federally-funded literacy programs in the U.S. but we are always open to new opportunities to help spread literacy.

E. D. Nixon said, *Your spark can become a flame and change everything*. The Early Literacy Institute's mission is to be a spark to light the world. We will light the world through literacy.

'we will light the world through literacy'

Cultural diversity opens opportunities for innovative approaches to the teaching of early literacy. But it also opens opportunities to consider that preferences for learning may vary culturally, both in terms of pedagogy and content.

Editors

Journeys of self-discovery can often focus on language… all students can tell their stories

Alison Lutton

THE GIFT OF ERROR

Mary Hynes-Berry
United States

Rebeca Itzkowich
United States

Mary Hynes-Berry has 30 years experience as an oral storyteller in school settings as well as doing professional development with teachers about how to build rich, engaging curriculum out of stories, with a focus on the primary and pre-primary grades. For the last 12 years, she has been exploring the same issues as a faculty member at Erikson Institute for Early Childhood. Her background also includes extensive textbook writing, primarily in language arts; project managing a major primary math program (which included stories) for Encyclopedia Britannica; and work in biblio-poetry therapy, for which she is co-author of what is considered the key text in the field.

Rebeca Itzkowich has worked with young children and their families for over 15 years as a bilingual classroom teacher and program director. For the past 10 years she has been a faculty member at Erikson Institute teaching courses in emergent literacy for new language learners, family and culture, and preschool curriculum. She has been working with preservice teachers in schools helping them develop engaging developmentally-appropriate curricula and culturally-responsive practices.

Introduction

In all the years we have enjoyed working with young children and their teachers, we have noticed that exceptional classrooms are those in which both teachers and students are engaged in the creativity, excitement, and sense of purpose that we believe characterizes lifelong learning. To use Duckworth's eloquent expression, the teachers in these classrooms are 'havers of wonderful ideas' (Duckworth, 1987). Specifically, we are thinking of their wonderful ideas about how to facilitate students' active participation in constructing meaning. These teachers do not look for right answers, but for windows into children's current thinking. The most delightful misconceptions and errors of new learners are received as gifts—as keys that will help unlock the windows and give teachers greater insight into effective ways to deepen children's understandings.

> 'the most delightful misconceptions and errors of new learners are received as gifts—as keys that will help unlock the windows and give teachers greater insight into effective ways to deepen children's understandings'

Our understanding of error as a gift reflects the word's etymology; it comes from the Latin 'errare', meaning 'to wander'. As any good knight errant knows, wandering is not purposeless; it is an attempt to find a path that will lead us to our goal. For the knight, to do one good deed and then another and thus continually prove himself; for the learner, to arrive at deeper understanding about something and then something else again.

In the City College of New York's *Mathematics in the City* project, Fosnot and her colleagues have replaced the traditional linear model of the learning trajectory with one they call the 'landscape of learning' (Fosnot & Dolk, 2001). They describe it in terms that are amenable to both wandering and wondering.

When we are moving across a landscape toward a horizon, the horizon seems clear. Yet we never actually reach it. New objects—new landmarks—come into view. So it is with learning. One question seemingly answered raises others. Children seem to resolve one struggle only to grapple with another. It helps to have horizons in mind when we plan activities, when we interact, question, and facilitate discussion. But horizons are not fixed points in the landscape; they are constantly shifting. Fosnot & Dolk, 2001, p. 18

'unfortunately, in all too many classrooms, we see teachers doing unto children as they were done to in their early schooling'

Unfortunately, in all too many classrooms, we see teachers doing unto children as they were done to in their early schooling; activities are programmed in a highly linear fashion and errors treated as mistakes to be corrected instead of important opportunities for the learning that can result from cognitive dissonance. Consequently, over the years, we have invented for ourselves what Lilian Katz in her opening address to the Working Forum called the principle of congruity, that is, the way we teach teachers should be congruent with the way we want them to teach. This principle harmonizes with workshops and classes with preservice and inservice teachers we have built around activities that will help the participants rediscover themselves as learners.

'the way we teach teachers should be congruent with the way we want them to teach'

With this in mind, we invite you to please play the following quiz, knowing that your responses will be neither collected nor graded. In fact, do not look for an answer key written upside down at the bottom of the page or the end of the article. We did not give one, because the point is not the correct answer but the process. If you can get someone to play with you, all the better. This *Shepherd's Counting System* is displayed at South Wolds' Historical Village Life Museum in West Sussex, England.

How well can you count?

Until the middle of the last century, shepherds in southeastern England used an unusual numbering system. The number names of this system from our 1 to 20 are given in the chart below:

Something to do

1. Write the Arabic numeral next to each number in the left column.

2. Consider the number names:
   • What pattern do you see in how these number names?
   • Do they operate on the same system as the base 10 system we use?

We should have the space to question. As an evolving society we need to encourage and empower our students to question.
Marek Tesar

- Can you see any natural rationale for the shepherd's number system?
- Draw tan-a-figgit sheep. Try to configure them in a pattern to make counting easier.

3. Suggest a name for 25 and then write the names for 26 and 29.

Bonus Challenge
Make up numerals for the first 10 numbers, using the far right column. You can use base 5 notation or make up number signs of your own.

	Yan	
	Tan	
	Tethera	
	Pethera	
	Pimp	
	Yan-a-pimp	
	Tan-a-pimp	
	Tethera pimp	
	Pethera pimp	
	Dik	
	Yan-a-dik	
	Tan-a-dik	
	Tethera-a-dik	
	Pethera-dik	
	Bumpit	
	Yan-a-bumpit	
	Tan-a-bumpit	
	Tethera bumpit	
	Pethera-bumpit	
	Figgit	

Now reflect a bit on the experience of the quiz for you

Did you find this activity:

Intriguing   Fascinating   Fairly pointless   Other

Difficult   Easy   Somewhat challenging but interesting   Other

What might have contributed to how you experienced this quiz:

I enjoy/don't enjoy trivia and puzzles   The questions were confusing

I do/don't feel comfortable with math   Other

We came up with this quiz in the developmental stage of Erikson Institute's Early Mathematics Project—an initiative funded by McCormick Foundation and the Chicago Mercantile Exchange Trust. It grew out of an activity we had developed earlier to re-create for adults the highly complex task a child faces when beginning to develop alphabet knowledge. We could see that an equivalent situation holds in mathematics: adults—or even most 12-year-olds—do not see that rational counting is no simple task; it calls for orchestrating three quite separate systems, each confusing in a different way:

Number names

Once we have learned them, we tend to forget that number names are arbitrary. In English, there are particular problems:

- Some number names have homonyms (*two, too, to*), while others are easily confused because of the very similar pronunciation of very different values (*thirteen/thirty; fifteen/fifty; sixteen/sixty*) (Ginsburg, 2002).
- The number names of the tens in English are irregular. Logically we should say *ten-ty-one, ten-ty-two* (as we say, for instance, *twenty-one, thirty-two*), so that the names reflect the pattern of our number structure, as they do in Asian languages. Research indicates that the English number names are a factor in the difficulty young children can experience in understanding place value (Miura & Okamoto, 1999). In contrast, the *Shepherd's Counting System* is not a base 10 but a base 5 system; in fact interestingly, the number words do not include zero but show place value by changing the number word. *Tethera-figgit* (equal to 23 in base 10) could be represented as 43 in standard base 5 notation.

In many languages, however, reciting the sequence of number names is often a rote memory task. As you may have experienced with our quiz, in order to represent *tan-a-figgit* sheep, you had to translate it, as it were, back to *twenty-two*. So, too, even after they have attained fluency, second language learners tend to conceptualize number values using their first language.

> 'even after they have attained fluency, second language learners tend to conceptualize number values using their first language'

But perhaps the greatest confusion comes from the way children are encouraged to recite the number names in sequence without any reference, that is, without actually using them to count objects. For example, a teacher we know tapped each child on the shoulder to indicate the line order. *You are 1*, she would say, *You are 2; you are 3....* One child in particular would protest angrily, *I am not 3!* and refused to join the line.

The teacher found this behavior inexplicable until our discussion of the Shepherd's counting quiz helped her realize that when the child heard *You are 3* she did not take it to mean she was *third* in line; rather she understood the teacher to be saying that she was 3—which in a young child's world translates to *3-years-old*. As a newly turned 5-year-old, being told she was two years younger was very upsetting. In any case, her confusion about having cardinal numbers used as ordinals is perfectly appropriate developmentally, as is her assumption that the expression *You are 3* had a well established conventional meaning unrelated to number sense. Imagine, for example, the snickers if we counted around a group using the shepherd's system as we got up to *pimp* or *dik*.

As teacher educators, if we model all-knowingness perhaps we may convey to student teachers that their role as teachers is to reside over the learning experience so as to bring conclusiveness and certainty, rather than inconclusiveness and uncertainty to the learning.

Editors

Numerals and number symbols

If you tried to come up with number symbols for the shepherd's system, you may have experienced how young children can find it challenging to tie a number name or value to the written symbol, just as they may find it difficult to differentiate and remember letter shapes. It is instinctive to try to make some connection that will help fix a meaning to the graphic symbol. For some, that leads to an understandable confusion between numerals and alphabet letters. Think, for example, how easy it is to confuse *S* with *5*, lower case *L* with *l* and *0* (zero) with the letter *O*.

This story dictated by two 4-year-olds to describe a game they called *Ants on a Line* is a wonderful example of quite another way of seeing the graphic symbol as a way of representing a meaning that has nothing to do with number value.

And so the whole bunch of ants walked on the ruler but they could only go up to 10 because their moms said 'Only go up to 10 and then you have to come back to O.' And they came back to zero and they felled in the hole because zero is nothing and it has a big hole in the middle. The End. (by Michael and Angel)

For these two, 10 is clearly up from—*more than*—zero, because it is the limit beyond which their mommies say they cannot go. They have some sense that zero is nothing; however, it is the graphic representation—that hole in the middle—that does in the ants. For all the richness of this story, the boys are not really counting. The numbers marked on the ruler are treated as locations rather than as the representation of 'how many'.

Number sense and numerousness

In recent years, brain research has indicated that infants do have a capacity to sense quantity (Holt, 2008; Mix, Huttenlocher & Levine, 2003, 2002). It seems, however, that this early intuitive ability only goes up to about the quantity of three. Somewhere between five and six, children begin to develop true number sense for quantities from 5-100; initially, they link quantity and name/symbol for lower values; however, by age six, many not only grasp higher numbers, they also have begun to naturally explore and develop natural arithmetic procedures such as adding (Ginsburg, 2002).

> 'in recent years, brain research has indicated that infants do have a capacity to sense quantity'

Yet parents and teachers seem so proud of the way young children can perform the rote aspects of number recognition (names and numerals) that they may fail to see that many preschoolers count without counting, that is, they use number names and symbols without understanding that their function is to express how many. It takes multiple experiences and maturation to develop these fundamental understandings:

- The quantity represented by 5 is always the same—it does not matter whether the objects being counted are huge (elephants) or tiny (ants on a ruler), 5 of them means there is one more than 4, one less than 6.
- Our number system operates with a base 10 structure; in two and three digit numbers, the position of a number indicates its value so that in 23, (*tether-a-figgit*), 2 represents twenty (two tens) and the 3 stands for three units. In 10, 200, or 5000, the zeros all have holes in the middle but they are not nothing—they are place holders that indicate values in tens, hundreds, and thousands.

Young children's confusions about how number names, numerals, and quantity are connected can be seen as either a mistake that needs to be promptly corrected or as a gift that needs to be considered seriously. Their imperfect understanding is perfectly appropriate developmentally; furthermore, it is a key opportunity for learning, as we alluded to earlier. We believe then that the more precisely student teachers appreciate the developmental trajectory and the tricky issues that novice learners face, the more effectively they can structure ways to deepen the child's understanding.

> 'children's imperfect understanding is perfectly appropriate developmentally; furthermore, it is a key opportunity for learning'

Let us revisit the experience of the *Shepherd's Counting System* activity. If we were successful we reduced you to feeling like a novice, paralleling the experience young children often face. Instead of handing you a linearly programmed activity, we asked you to accept the gift of error, with its wandering and wondering. At the same time, you may have had some insight into the complex processes involved in learning and into all that must be considered in order to respond accurately and effectively as a teacher.

> 'Katz's principle of congruity requires that we teach teachers in ways that call for the adult to engage in processing material in a way that is parallel to the child's processing'

Engaging in this kind of exercise is an example of what we call 'parallel processing'. Katz's principle of congruity requires that we teach teachers in ways that call for the adult to engage in processing material in a way that is parallel to the child's processing. For us, this term puts emphasis on the processing that is at the heart of all learning. The processing involves two distinct parallels:

- Parallel 1—If I am conscious of what it means to be a novice in a given area, I can recognize and promote how young children move through the landscape of learning, from confusion to misconception to understanding.

If you engaged in the counting activity, you may have felt bewildered as you looked at the unfamiliar names on the chart, just as very young children can be by such number names. At first, you may have even been frustrated by the trial and error process of matching numerals and names and then taking on the more challenging tasks. If you reflect back on the steps you took to arrive at your point of understanding, you can probably see different stages at which you had some partial understanding of the problem. An error that was examined closely became the stepping stone that helped you arrive at a more accurate understanding of the way you needed to proceed. Hopefully, those feelings were replaced by excitement and satisfaction as the penny dropped, and you experienced the benefits of persistence as you broke the code and mastered a new numerical system.

In effect, the process of successfully breaking the code of the *Shepherd's Counting System* results in an experience that meets all the characteristics that define play: that is, it is:

- engaging and personally satisfying. You are absorbed; maybe having fun but taking what you are doing seriously.

Academic learning and skill development can be taught in a short time—intellectual dispositions and attitudes take much longer.

Lily Wong

- intentional. You chose to be doing it.
- creative problem-solving. You are thinking about what you want to do, trying out strategies including negotiating and making meaning.

If you had the opportunity to do this exercise with other people, there is a good chance that you may have broken the code sooner. Research tells us that the greatest cognitive learning occurs in social settings, where more experienced people can scaffold our ideas through guided participation in trying to solve the problem at hand (Schaps, Battistich, & Solomon, 2004; Charney, 2002). Once again, we could be talking about play as well as work. Contrast this authentic exercise to a more traditional professional development training exercise that uses a simulated situation. The adults are given an activity designed for children and asked to respond as would their young students. Because the adults are secure in the knowledge that is required to successfully accomplish the activity, they tend to mimic what they imagine children would do and say.

> 'the greatest cognitive learning occurs in social settings, where more experienced people can scaffold our ideas through guided participation in trying to solve the problem at hand'

The loss is double. First of all, they are not themselves actively engaged in authentic problem-solving. At the same time, they operate on unexamined assumptions about children's thinking. The result may be enjoyable; the group goes home with a make-and-take activity. However, they leave without important insights into what happens when young children persist through misconceptions and partial understanding to construct knowledge.

> 'adults may operate on unexamined assumptions about children's thinking'

As adults, we have beliefs about the way things are that limit our vision like blinkers on a horse; they prevent us from being in a true learner mode—we cannot see beyond what we believe to be the right answer. Errors are seen as mistakes instead of as opportunities to reap the benefits of cognitive dissonance. The power of parallel processing is rooted in the authenticity of the exercise, which gives it the power of play. When adults re-experience themselves as new learners, they bypass their competence as adults and move closer to the consciousness of the young child who experiences learning in a more organic fashion through play. Like the child or the knight errant, they wander through the landscape of learning, with its shifting horizons.

> 'errors are seen as mistakes instead of as opportunities to reap the benefits of cognitive dissonance'

We talked months later to teachers who have participated in exercises like the *Shepherd's Counting System* or the activities we designed around Paul Cox's *Abstract Alphabet: Book of Animals* to help understand the complexities of becoming a reader. They report how profound these experiences have been in terms of helping them rediscover themselves as learners. As a result, their pedagogy has been transformed. Several have felt compelled to bring the activity to parents and colleagues.

- Parallel 2—As teachers, we must be careful listeners and observers of children so that we can learn where they are in their current understandings and what might be an effective way to continue their progress through the landscape of learning.

Think of the two boys playing *Ants on a Line*. Teachers who understand learning as a constructive process can see that their game is not just a cute story but an engaging, intentional attempt to solve the problem of what it means to count up and down from zero to 10, taking into account the graphic representation of number symbols. They know that to address the misconceptions by correcting this story serves no purpose. Rather, they see this story as a wonderful gift, an insight into the children's current thinking. They now have a clue about how to scaffold children's thinking to the next level of understanding. *Ants on a Line* is the kind of problem that teachers who are lifelong learners love to play with. They look at it through three different lenses:

I. Conceptual understanding of the content area
In this case, this refers to number sense. More specifically, teachers should be aware of the four principles of rational counting—fixed number sequence, one-to-one correspondence, order irrelevance, and cardinality—and look for evidence to establish where the child is in terms of mastery. Michael and Angel do know the sequence for counting and are showing one-to-one correspondence as they move their ants from one marker on the ruler to the next. Since the line is established on the ruler, it is not evident that these 4-year-olds have good understanding of the last two principles—and we know that these understandings often do not develop before age 5 or 6.

II. Developmental trajectory in early childhood
Young children—and octogenarians as well—move from understanding the concrete (hands-on), to the pictorial (schematic), and finally to the symbolic level. Furthermore, the younger the child, the more important it is to have repeated concrete experiences. As we indicated above, only as children begin to move through the shift in the ability to reason and abstract that typically occurs between the ages of 5 to 7 can they abstract enough to develop good number sense of two and three digit numbers. The *Ants on a Line* game focuses heavily on the concrete and somewhat on the pictorial. There is little indication that the boys closely link the number symbols with a good sense of the quantity represented by the O in either 10 or the numeral for zero.

III. Unique qualities of the child
One of the rewards in being an early childhood teacher is that children see connections and spin conceptions that reflect their own unique perspective and experiences. These two boys are very aware of how mommies often set boundaries (only go to 10) and of how the world is full of perils such as that hole in zero and finally of how *The End* may precipitously assert itself. The better we know the children, the easier it will be to spot and appreciate this kind of unique insight or processing.

> 'young children—and octogenarians as well—move from understanding the concrete (hands-on), to the pictorial (schematic), and finally to the symbolic level'

Good teachers know that teaching and learning are complex interactive processes. It is essential to keep shifting back and forth between the three lenses to get a good read on each wonderfully unique learner. In other words, both teachers and learners need to play with understanding. Teachers in training bring to the classroom their own experiences as learners and use them as a compass, as guiding principles for their own teaching practice.

If as teacher educators we want to encourage experiencing the consciousness of new learners, we might want to think carefully about the impact of our assessment practices on student teachers' relationships with their learning.

Editors

All teachers have to have knowledge

Liliana Sulikowska

Given that teachers in training bring to teaching their own experiences, the uniqueness of each student teacher underscores the complexity of teacher education, and of the challenge in deciding what it is to be a 'good' teacher.

Editors

Teachers who view learning as a constructive process that occurs within social contexts are likely to provide a curriculum that fosters meaningful learning, and a classroom environment that promotes seeing error as a gift that provides opportunities for new, richer understanding.

References

Charney, R. S. (2002). *Teaching children to care: Classroom management for ethical and academic growth, K-8*. Turners Falls, Massachusets: Northeast Foundation for Children.

Cox, P. (1997). Abstract alphabet: a book of animals. San Francisco: Chronicle Books.

Duckworth, E. (1987). *The having of wonderful ideas & other essays on teaching and learning*. New York: Teachers College Press.

Fosnot, C. T., & Dolk, M. (2001). *Young mathematicians at work: Constructing number sense, addition, and subtraction*. New York: Teachers College Press.

Ginsburg, H. (2002). *Learning to count. In Children's arithmetic: How they learn it and how you teach it* (pp. 3-42). Austin, TX: Pro-ed.

Holt, J. (2008, March 3). Numbers guy: Are our brains wired for math? *The New Yorker*, 42-48.

Mix, K., Huttenlocher, J., & Levine, S. (2002). Multiple cues for quantification in infancy: Is number one of them? *Psychological Bulletin, 128*(2), 278-294.

Mix, K., Huttenlocher, J., & Levine, S. (2003). Quantitative development in infancy and early childhood. *Infant & Child Development, 12*(1), 110-112.

Miura, I. T., & Okamoto, Y. (1999). Counting in Chinese, Japanese, and Korean. Support for number understanding. In C. A. Edwards (Ed.), *Changing the face of mathematics: Perspectives on Asian American and Pacific Islanders* (pp. 29-36). Reston, VA: NCTM.

Schaps, E., Battistich, V., & Solomon, D. (2004). Community in school as key to student growth: Findings from the Child Development Project. In J. Zins, R. Weissberg, M. Wang, & H. Walberg (Eds.), *Building academic success on social and emotional learning: What does the research say?* (pp. 189–205). New York: Teachers College Press

HELPING UNDERGRADUATE STUDENT INTERNS MEET THE CHALLENGE OF USING RESPONSIVE LANGUAGE

Kathryn S. Clark
United States

Ann Noland
United States

Kathryn Summers Clark, PhD, CCLS is the Coordinator for the Child Development Program at Meredith College in Raleigh, North Carolina. She teaches a variety of courses, including infant development, curriculum for young children, and teaming and collaboration. She was one of the developers of the Birth through Kindergarten (B-K) Teacher Licensure Program at Meredith College. Kathryn has traveled to Mongolia and Sweden to present information on best practices in early childhood and to study outdoor learning environments. Recently, she was appointed by Governor Easley to the North Carolina Interagency Coordinating Council. Kathryn is also a member of the B-K Higher Education Consortium and the North Carolina Outdoor Learning Environments Alliance. She has worked in a variety of settings serving young children including early intervention and pediatrics. Most recently, her clinical work has been that of a child life specialist at Duke University Medical Center.

Ann Noland has been a classroom teacher for more than 30 years. Her experience includes teaching in both public and private schools and ages 2 years old to third graders. Presently she is part-time clinical supervisor in the Child Development Program, Meredith College, Raleigh, North Carolina, United States.

Introduction

The relationship between teacher education and the verbal environment created by student interns poses a unique challenge for early childhood teachers. For purposes of this discussion, the term student intern refers to undergraduate students who have been placed in programs serving young children. The quality of the interactions between teachers and young children has been of long-standing interest to teacher educators. How then can teacher educators help student interns develop strategies that will lead to their establishing a verbal environment which, in turn, will contribute to positive teacher-child relationships and improved child outcomes?

> 'the language student interns use when interacting with children not only has an impact on teacher-child relationships and the socio-emotional climate, but it has a significant impact on children's learning and development as well'

There is much agreement that early learning occurs within the context of these interactive experiences (e.g., Kontos & Wilcox-Herzog, 1997). The language that student interns use when interacting with children not only has an impact on teacher-child relationships and the socio-emotional climate of the classroom, but it has a significant impact on children's learning and development as well (e.g., Bowman, Donovan, & Burns, 2001; Eisenberg, 2006; Hendrick & Weissman, 2007; Kostelnik, Whiren, Soderman, & Gregory, 2009).

This paper briefly reviews research that underpins the course content for undergraduate students who are completing their practicum or student teaching experiences, and describes different teaching strategies that attempt to focus the attention of undergraduate students on the language they use with young children.

Verbal environments

The verbal environment of the early childhood classroom is comprised of all verbal interactions that occur within any given setting, including what is said and how it is said, and can be characterized as either positive or negative (Kostelnik et al., 2009). Positive verbal environments are ones in which the teacher is deliberate and strategic in attempting to satisfy the needs of the children and to help them feel valued (Kostelnik et al., 2009). There is concern about the way the information is being conveyed and about the emotional impact of the message (Kostelnik et al., 2009). The adults are nurturing, respectful, and provide positive socio-emotional support. As a result, children tend to develop higher self-esteem, greater sense of belonging, and greater emotional comfort (Eccles, 2007). Furthermore, the use of positive responsive language is more likely to engage children in problem-solving that will facilitate the development of self-control and positive social interactions (Mugno, 2008). It is within a supportive emotional climate that children's social, emotional, and cognitive development may be maximized (Eisenberg, 2006).

Conversely, negative verbal environments are believed to create situations in which children feel unworthy, insignificant, or incompetent as a result of their interactions with adults which are often marked by disrespect, insensitivity, or aloofness (Kostelnik et al., 2009). The teacher dominates these interactions with children and disregards children's ideas or suggestions. As a result, children may not feel accepted or may feel inadequate, confused, or angry (Kostelnik et al., 2009). Research suggests that such environments serve to diminish children's self-esteem and to interfere with their learning of effective ways to deal with emotions (e.g., Hendrick & Weissman, 2007; Kostelnik et al., 2009).

Responsive and restrictive language

The discussion above provides a broader context for considering the quality of the verbal environment of the early childhood classroom, the quality of teacher-child interactions, and subsequent outcomes for children. Several researchers have focused more specifically on the verbal interactions of teachers using the categories of responsive and restrictive language (Cassidy & Buell, 1996; Mugno & Rosenblitt, 2001; Stone, 1993). Among these authors, there is general agreement on how to define responsive language and restrictive language.

Responsive language

Responsive language, generally associated with positive teaching techniques, is defined as language that conveys respect and positive regard for the child. It encourages verbal give-and-take, independence, and reflection on the part of children. Responsive language is elaborative and offers children additional information to support their learning. It implies choice, and offers explanations and reasons to children. Responsive language also presents requests in a respectful way. The

Behind such behaviors is the person who is the teacher. We have a responsibility, therefore, to enable student teachers to explore who they are and why they may act in the ways they do.

Editors

The language we use must be authentic.

Janet Whitten

emotional tone underlying these interactions is one of warmth and nurturance (Cassidy & Buell, 1996; Mugno & Rosenblitt, 2001; Stone, 1993).

Responsive language techniques include using reflections, reasoning, explanations, and elaboration (Cassidy & Buell, 1996; Stone, 1993). The responsive teacher is described as one who is:

an attentive listener who addresses children by name, asks open-ended questions and reflective questions, does not interrupt, and encourages children to elaborate on their own ideas and thoughts. Mugno & Rosenblitt, 2001, p. 69

'The responsive teacher is described as one who is an attentive listener who addresses children by name, asks open-ended questions and reflective questions, does not interrupt, and encourages children to elaborate on their own ideas and thoughts.'

Restrictive language

Restrictive language, generally associated with undesirable teaching practices, is defined as language that conveys teacher authority and control. It discourages children's independence and autonomy. Restrictive language techniques include threatening, shaming, and coercion (Cassidy & Buell, 1996; Mugno & Rosenblitt, 2001; Stone, 1993). It ignores children's feelings and is impersonal (Cassidy & Buell, 1996). The emotional tone underlying these interactions is often one of coldness, detachment, or even hostility. Techniques reflecting restrictive language include lecturing, asserting power and control, and using evaluative statements. Restrictive language may be used appropriately in the early childhood classroom, but it seems reasonable to expect that it would be limited primarily to those times when a child's safety is in question (Cassidy & Buell, 1996; Stone, 1993).

Stone (1993) reported findings from one of the first studies examining teachers' use of responsive and restrictive language. She found that 14 of 30 child care teachers used restrictive language predominantly when interacting with young children. Cassidy and Buell (1996) reported similar results—their data indicated that slightly more than 40% of teacher-child interactions were characterized by the use of restrictive language. As a result of their findings, Cassidy and Buell (1996) recommended that teacher education programs develop specific strategies to focus the attention of undergraduate students on their verbal interactions with young children and require them to reflect on changes they want to make.

'teacher education programs should develop specific strategies to focus the attention of undergraduate students on their verbal interactions with young children and require them to reflect on changes they want to make'

Deborah Mugno (personal communication, March 12, 2008) reported data from her recently completed dissertation that responsive language was an effective strategy to use with young children experiencing emotional or behavioral problems. The teacher first would use statements that interpreted feelings that she thought children were experiencing, connect these feelings to the behavior the teacher was observing, and then offer children choices of what to do next. When teachers used this approach, children demonstrated a positive and significant level of compliance. This led to increased frequencies of positive verbal exchanges between teachers and children. More specifically this process set the stage for further discussions of issues using a give-and-take dialogue. Children had the expectation that they would be treated with respect and given reasonable choices. Teachers' use of responsive language was effective in making positive behavioral change in young children with emotional and behavioral challenges (Mugno, 2008).

Interestingly, her findings also indicated that when teachers used restrictive language such as embarrassing the child, being accusatory or inflicting guilt or shame, the child would respond in a negative way (Mugno, 2008). This provides support for previous research findings that the use of negative, restrictive statements are unsuccessful in changing the undesirable behavior of young children (Mugno, 2008).

Scholars in early childhood education continue to emphasize the importance of verbal communication with young children in the development of teacher-child relationships, and in the choice of the guidance strategies used by teachers. One need only to look at the considerable attention devoted to this topic in early childhood textbooks (e.g., Hendrick & Weissman, 2007; Kostelnik et al., 2009). While these discussions may not use the specific terminology of responsive and restrictive language, the techniques (that is, using reflective statements and stating positive directions) and attitudes (that is, warmth and caring) share many underlying commonalities with this construct. This on-going research and discussion illustrates the continued importance of this topic in teacher education programs as well as its complexities and the interrelatedness of the constructs.

> This raises an essential conversation about using responsive language to build teacher-child relationships when the student or teacher is deaf.
>
> Editors

Strategies

College faculty provides support to undergraduate students in a variety of ways throughout their preservice experiences. Frequent observations are made of student interns as they begin to participate in classrooms serving young children. It should be noted that prior to their practicum and internship placements, student interns have completed coursework that focuses on teacher-child interactions, guidance, and the establishment of a positive verbal and social environment. Despite this, they often continue to use language that reflects their prior personal experiences. For example, student interns often continue to provide vague, nonspecific feedback to children (for example, *Good job*) and to tell children what not to do (such as, *Don't do that*). Indeed, this intuitive knowledge (or common sense knowledge) is knowledge that is based on one's personal observation and experience, and this personal interaction with the environment is a powerful learning experience (Bell, 1991; Lampert, 1984).

'despite this, they often continue to use language that reflects their prior personal experiences'

These practices may not be changed simply as a result of formal knowledge; that is, knowledge that is acquired from reading and taking classes (Bell, 1991; Lampert, 1984). If formal knowledge is to have an impact such that it begins to influence student interns' practice, then they need to have support and experiences that will help them apply the information in a meaningful way and reflect on its application (Bell, 1991; Lampert, 1984). Helping student interns overcome a style of communication that has been so ingrained requires a major shift in their thinking, if there is to be a change in their practice.

'if formal knowledge is to have an impact such that it begins to influence student interns' practice, then they need to have support and experiences that will help them apply the information in a meaningful way and reflect on its application'

In an attempt to address the recommendation that teacher education programs develop strategies that will help student interns think critically about their use of language while interacting with young children in the classroom (Cassidy & Buell, 1996), we have found the discussion of responsive and restrictive language beneficial in focusing the attention of student interns on their interactions with young children and in helping them become more intentional and reflective. The goals underlying the idea of helping students develop responsive language skills to use with young children is threefold:

- to enable the prospective teachers to listen to children and to find out who each child really is as an individual
- to connect and develop an authentic, positive relationship with each unique child
- in this process of listening and developing relationships with children, to discover and find their own voice as a person and as a teacher.

Implementing teacher education

The challenge is to convince student interns to respect and trust children and to focus on what children are doing and feeling. By bringing the discussion back to responsive language, student interns are helped to begin to make this shift to using responsive language.

First, the basic positive guidance techniques are reviewed and discussed. Often this focuses on praise and how to make it meaningful for young children. Specific examples from their classroom observations are discussed. Second, interns discuss why phrases frequently overheard in the classroom for young children are ineffective, and they are encouraged to generate, and then evaluate, alternative phrases. This provides the foundation for subsequent discussions on responsive language. From here the discussion focuses specifically on responsive and restrictive language. Student interns work in small groups to discuss these, and other, restrictive statements and to generate responsive alternatives.

Some examples may serve to illustrate the above discussion. Frequently, a student intern will make a comment such as *Let's put the toys away, okay?* Children believe that the student intern means what is stated and may say *No.* Often, it is her intent to tell children what the expectation is. Therefore, it is important for the student intern to be straightforward and state her expectations clearly, simply, and directly. So instead, she might say something like *It is time for clean-up. Select two toys to put back on the shelf. I will help you if you would like me to.* On the other hand, the student intern might use this same statement (*Let's put the toys away, okay?*) as a way to engage the child in cooperation, but she must be prepared if children reject the proposal.

The phrase *Good job* is an example of how a student intern often provides feedback to young children. This phrase is overused and issued as an automatic response. As a result, it lacks sincerity and meaningfulness. It fails to focus children's attention on the very behavior for which they are being praised. *That's a beautiful picture* is also a

These goals orient teacher education towards relationality built on respect of self as teacher.

Editors

Trust and respect ought to be at the heart of learning and teaching. The development of trust and respect, however, is predicated on building relationship.

Editors

statement that often is overused and is lacking in sincerity and meaningfulness; it is a mechanical response because the student intern does not really know what else to say. On the other hand, when this same statement is a sincere expression of a student intern's appreciation of children's effort, it is transformed into the compliment it is intended to be.

The examples provided above are statements commonly used by student interns and supervising teachers alike. These statements provide a basis of small group discussions and the starting point for individual students to reflect on their own language. In our work in the United States with student interns and cooperating teachers, it seems that these phrases have become too automatic and interfere with developing positive teacher relationships with young children. The phrases may change as trends change, but teacher educators need to help student interns think critically about these and move beyond them.

Thus, it would seem that communication must be sincere and explicit to be credible to young children. Responsive language can be used to interpret and acknowledge the process of children's exploration, the materials they are using, the progress they are making, and the emotions they are experiencing. Using strategies such as acknowledgement and reflection serve to focus children's attention on their effort, the process of their work, or their emotions. The following exemplifies the type of comments student interns find difficult to generate spontaneously:

- *You created a new color with the paint. Tell me what you did.*
- *You spent a long time working on that building.*
- *Clean-up time came too soon for you. It is hard to stop playing,* and
- *Your face is showing me that you are really angry with Sarah.*

Another responsive language strategy that is difficult for student interns to master is asking open-ended questions. Questions such as *What would happen if...* and *How do you think we can solve this problem?* provide children with opportunities to engage in problem-solving and in critical thinking.

Why is it difficult for student interns to learn to generate spontaneous dialogue and use responsive language with young children? Perhaps, as suggested above, it is because student interns fall back on what they have always known and done—their intuitive knowledge. It is easier to do this than to be deliberate in choosing language that is unfamiliar to them. To become skilled in using the responsive language skills they have read about and discussed in class (that is, formal knowledge), they must make the explicit connection between what they are learning in class and their on-going practice. Does this mean there is no place for restrictive language? Certainly not; particularly when children's safety is in question, this may be quite an effective form of communication. This style of verbal interaction should be used as intentionally as responsive language, rather than because of student interns' prior experience with its use.

As part of their observation-based planning, student interns are required to write potential dialogue for their lesson plans. This gives them the opportunity to be more intentional in considering how to incorporate responsive language techniques such as acknowledgement, reflections, and open-ended questions into their language with young children (as well as specifying the steps and sequence of the activity). Writing out potential dialogue does not mean that students have to read or execute the plan exactly as written. It does move them past the idea of *I'll just wing it* and into more intentional teaching. Thus, learning to use responsive language is both a part of the learning process and a result of it.

The language we use to praise children communicates to them what is valued (for instance, effort or ability). The same may be said for the language used in teacher education.
Editors

It would be interesting to find out the extent to which student interns use intuitive knowledge, or whether many ways of responding may have become habitual, even at this early stage, or simply the result of past experiences.
Editors

It's about recognizing and responding to the needs of children.
Kylie Lamont

'learning to use responsive language is both a part of the learning process and a result of it'

After reviewing the basic issues related to responsive and restrictive language and having interns identify changes they want to make in their communications with children, the discussion is expanded and becomes more challenging. Students review sentence starters which include the following examples:

- *Your body (or face) is showing me…*
- *It seems to me that it is hard for you when it is time to…*
- *I know that when you hit someone, something must be bothering you.*

Discussion of how to use sentence or dialogue starters provides an additional opportunity for student interns to think about and to practice using phrases with which they are unfamiliar. Scenarios, such as those described below, are given to the interns who then generate responsive statements either using the sentence or dialogue starters or developing their own unique responses.

These sentence starters are intended to serve as a starting point for student interns who are unfamiliar with responsive language and for those beginning to use responsive language in their practice. This approach does not minimize the value of spontaneity in teacher-child interactions. It is intended to serve as a tool for students as they begin to use language that is unfamiliar and awkward (at least initially) and to be more intentional and deliberate in their language choices. As student interns begin to master this skill, their use of responsive language expands and becomes increasingly evident in their spontaneous interactions with children. Student interns have indicated that these sentence starters provide them with concrete examples from which they can begin to develop their own style of responsive language.

'this approach does not minimize the value of spontaneity in teacher-child interactions. It is intended to serve as a tool for students as they begin to use language that is unfamiliar and awkward (at least initially) and to be more intentional and deliberate in their language choices'

Scenario 1

At a small preschool program each age group has a separately scheduled 45 minute period on the large playground that has a concrete bike trail around its perimeter. The cooperating teacher and her assistant have been supervising the fourteen 4-year-old children on this sunny day from the area beside the bike trail. The class is out on the playground. Evan has been riding a tricycle around and around the bike track (one of his very favorite things to do.). It's time to go inside. The teacher yells, *Time to go inside everybody.* Most of the children begin to head towards the door. Evan keeps riding fast. The assistant begins yelling for Evan to stop. He seems to be in a world of his own and does not stop. The assistant runs over, blocks his path, and physically pulls him off. She says, *Didn't you hear the teacher? She said 'come inside'!* Evan begins to cry and try to get away, kicking and reaching for the tricycle.

Student teachers are sometimes very active in trying out ideas at college, but we are not sure how active they are when they are on field practicum.

Hui Meng Chen

Scenario 2

At a large early childhood center with four classrooms for children 4 years of age, Susan is currently enrolled in one of the classes of 16 children. The licensed teacher has been with this group of children for six months, but has been teaching preschool for three years. The assistant is not licensed but has been teaching for 12 years. Susan's mother is in her early twenties and is a single parent. Susan is her only child. On this day, Susan is carried into her 4-year-old classroom by her mother about 40 minutes after class has started. Susan is holding onto her mother very tightly with her face burrowed in her mother's neck. Her mother tells the teacher that it is her day off but she wants to get their car fixed and wants Susan to stay at school. The teacher peels Susan off her mother and says to Susan, *You know you want to be at school today. We're going to have the paint easel out and new playdough. Be a good girl now.* The teacher puts Susan on the floor, takes her by the hand, and pulls the crying child towards the art table.

A discussion of these scenarios would involve having student interns answer questions such as the following:

- *What is happening in this scenario?*
- *What do the teacher's words and behavior convey to the child?*
- *What might the teacher do or say to be more responsive?*

The discussion of responsive language continues throughout the semester, and student interns are encouraged to set specific goals for themselves related to their use of responsive language. This helps them become more aware of the language they are using and more deliberate in thinking about ways to incorporate responsive language into their repertoire.

> 'providing student interns with numerous opportunities to discuss and to practice using responsive language in the college classroom is a starting point, but learning opportunities must be extended into the arena where they are teaching young children'

Providing student interns with numerous opportunities to discuss and to practice using responsive language in the college classroom is a starting point, but learning opportunities must be extended into the arena where they are teaching young children. In those community-based early childhood settings in which teachers do not use responsive language, it is paramount that college faculty observe the students. It is our practice for faculty to record or tape student interns as they interact with children and implement their lesson plans. This gives student interns opportunities to listen to or view themselves in action. They are often surprised at how often they use restrictive language. Students may also ask their classroom teachers or college supervisors to observe their use of responsive language to record changes over time. Often this marks the beginning of their increasing awareness of their language choices. The following case study illustrates how one author provided this support to a student intern through weekly observations and seminars.

> 'as student interns have opportunities to listen to or view themselves in action. They are often surprised at how often they use restrictive language'

Case study

Chris transferred to the child development program from a local community college as a junior. She had been working for six years at a large commercial child care facility primarily teaching 4-year-old children. For her student teaching placement, Chris was placed in a demonstration classroom with a veteran teacher, Mrs. Smith, which served at-risk children. After Chris's first day of participating in this class, Mrs. Smith called the college supervisor, upset at the way the student intern was talking to the children. Mrs. Smith said that if the inappropriate interactions continued Chris would not be allowed to complete her internship at this site. She described one interaction between Chris and a little boy who was being disruptive; Chris told the child that he was bad and he needed to be good. The college supervisor arranged to be there the next morning to observe. The next morning Mrs. Smith expressed her concern about Chris's interactions with the children, but noted that Chris could really benefit from being in her class. Mrs. Smith had gathered some material on communicating with young children, given them to Chris, and had a long discussion with her about how to talk with children. While the college supervisor was observing, Chris was often sitting down and frequently calling out to individual children in a loud voice to *Stop running*, *Don't do that*, or *Be nice*. Obviously, these negative and restrictive comments were non-specific, vague, and did not tell children what the behavioral expectations were.

The college supervisor acknowledged the challenge Chris was having interacting with children in a specific, positive way and agreed to focus on communicating with children in the student teaching seminar the next day. The college supervisor and the mentor teacher agreed that the college supervisor would observe at least one morning a week during the semester and would focus on teacher-child interactions. Following a meeting with the student intern, it was agreed that if there were not immediate improvements in this, she would not be allowed to continue her placement in this particular classroom.

The next day during the student teaching seminar, students were asked to write a reflection on what they had noticed about communication between teachers and children in their placements. This was the beginning of two sessions that focused on talking with children using techniques that demonstrated respect for the child and incorporated responsive, constructive language. The discussion began with the interns reflecting on their own practice of talking with children. Then specific techniques demonstrated by the mentor teachers were discussed and the interns made a list of these techniques. Mrs. Smith and her assistant were outstanding in establishing relationships with children and using responsive language. Materials that provide an observation checklist to use as a self-evaluation tool and that describe communication guidelines for discussing emotions were reviewed and discussed. Finally, students were asked to write down three personal goals focusing on responsive language techniques that they had for themselves for the following week in the classroom.

Weekly observations and meetings with the mentor teacher, college supervisor, and each intern continued. Concurrently, weekly seminars continued to focus on communication styles, specific wording, and their individual goals. In the classroom, Chris's mentor teacher continued to model and to focus specifically on responsive language. Over an eight week period, significant improvements were noted in Chris's attitude towards the children, her style of communicating, and her enjoyment in the classroom. Her skills in developing curriculum improved as her ability to communicate effectively with the children improved. By the end of the semester Chris said that she thought this had been the most significant learning she had done as a student, and that there was little doubt it would impact her teaching. The mentor teacher, who originally had asked for Chris to be removed from the classroom on her first day, was pleased with the progress of the intern. It was through the process of self-reflection and focusing on responsive language that Chris began to develop a more positive relationship with the children and of herself as a teacher. It was then that she found her own unique voice as a teacher.

> 'it was through the process of self-reflection and focusing on responsive language that Chris began to develop a more positive relationship with the children and a more positive picture of herself as a teacher. It was then that she found her own unique voice as a teacher'

A student intern's voice

Although interns find it difficult to meet the many challenges of using responsive language, they recognize its benefits. One intern said that her mentor teacher was surprised that during her first formal observation, the intern did not say *Good job* a single time, but instead used acknowledgements, specific praise, and reflections of the children's behavior. A first-year teacher reported that her principal described one of her strengths as being skilled in providing specific, positive feedback to children.

The following is from one of our students who is well on her way to becoming a master teacher. She is teaching in an inclusive program that serves at-risk children 3 and 4 years of age with and without disabilities. This is what she had to say about the challenges of using responsive language:

Using responsive language to talk with young children is one of the most challenging and rewarding concepts to learn to use. It often feels like I am stating the obvious, but I have to remember that what is obvious to us is a new discovery for young children. Young children do not often have the language to describe what they are doing, feeling, hearing, or smelling. What better way for them to have a hands-on opportunity to learn new vocabulary than to label it for them! In addition using responsive language is constantly challenging me to find specific praise and feedback for the children and their work. Those descriptions I use with my children to describe their play are often the same observations I remember later in the day to record as part of my anecdotal records. It is the same language I am hearing my children use with one another as their language skills progress. I especially love using responsive language with children who are nonverbal. I wonder how many of them are spoken to at home or by their peers; it seems people often get tired of talking with children when there is no verbal response. However, they may still respond using sign language, picture clues, or whatever communication is set-up for them.

> 'it often feels like I am stating the obvious, but I have to remember that what is obvious to us is a new discovery for young children'

Like anything else we try that is unfamiliar, using responsive language is awkward and I remember feeling very silly. But with support I persevered and developed strategies that were compatible with my style of teaching. After four years of teaching, I cannot imagine my classroom without it. It is worth getting over the initial awkwardness and uncertainty for the betterment of the children. Mewborn 'like anything else we try that is unfamiliar, using responsive language is awkward and I remember feeling very silly. But with support I persevered and developed strategies that were compatible with my style of teaching'

Implications for teacher educators

- Plan to discuss communication early in courses that have placements where students are working in early childhood settings. Focus on its importance and its relevance to developing relationships with children.

  'plan to discuss communication early in courses that have placements where students are working in early childhood settings'

- Spontaneous verbal interactions with young children are a vital step in developing nurturing relationships. Discuss student interns' experiences and understandings of this form of communication. Help them to understand intentional, thoughtful ways of enjoying this kind of age-appropriate interaction with children; for instance, repeating playful sounds and smiling with an infant as one changes a diaper, listening and responding to conversations about favorite foods with 3-year-old children during snacks, and supporting 4-year-old children as they talk about what they did with their families over the weekend.

- Discuss the definitions of responsive and restrictive language. Have student interns come up with examples of both types of language they have heard within their classroom. Have them brainstorm in small groups how to transform the restrictive language into responsive language. Have them discuss other ways they could say the responsive comments that reflect their personal style.

- Give students numerous opportunities to practice using responsive language in small group and large group discussions. Develop scenarios and case studies such as those included in this paper to stimulate their thinking.

  'give students numerous opportunities to practice using responsive language in small group and large group discussions'

- Develop strategies to assist the students in developing their own voice in the classroom such as writing out potential dialogue that incorporates responsive language.

- Develop tools to facilitate discussion of responsive and restrictive language as suggested in the discussion above. Have students generate their own list of sentence starters.

- Guide student observations within their classroom. It can then be used by these same students as a basis for reflecting on their own communication styles and to develop personal goals for continuing improvement. It is certainly helpful if the college supervisor has observed the student intern and communicated with the cooperating teacher by this time.

- Discuss vocabulary choices other than 'sad', 'mad', 'glad' and ways of helping young children with understanding emotional words. This is also a good place to discuss the body language of young children and of adults. Having the student interns develop some role plays themselves in pairs or small groups is an effective strategy to use in conjunction with this tool.
- Observe students in their field placements as soon and as often as possible. Challenging as it may seem, the college faculty members can become a collaborative partner with student interns, helping them set goals and documenting their progress.
- Be aware of one's own language while interacting with undergraduate students. Then use one's own reflections and questions to stimulate critical thinking and problem-solving rather than giving simple answers to students' dilemmas.

Conclusion

As research has indicated, and as described above, it takes deliberate planning and implementation to ensure that a classroom is responsive to children's needs. It also takes intentional planning and practice by student interns to ensure that responsive language becomes a part of their teaching repertoire. Faculty supervisors must observe regularly, record and discuss the students' use of responsive language, and employ strategies that encourage students' reflections on the techniques they use and on the strategies they wish to develop.

> 'it takes deliberate planning and implementation to ensure that a classroom is responsive to children's needs'

Teacher educators must continue to encourage interns to support children through the use of responsive language. Since many mentor teachers do not use responsive language themselves, the strategies teacher educators discuss in class, and demonstrate themselves, help the students translate theory into practice.

Helping student interns develop strategies and techniques, such as responsive language, that will enable them to think critically about their use of language when interacting with young children is a vital process in their becoming intentional and reflective practitioners. Not only does this influence the quality of the language students begin to use explicitly, and deliberately, but more importantly, it impacts the quality of the teacher-child relationship. And as Palmer (1998) stated so eloquently: *good teaching cannot be reduced to technique; good teaching comes from the identity and integrity of the teacher* (p. 10).

> 'good teaching cannot be reduced to technique; good teaching comes from the identity and integrity of the teacher'

Recently, the attention of teachers was refocused on the importance and complexities of teaching:
Teaching is about relationships. The journey of becoming and being a teacher is unique for each teacher and yet depends on others. Gibbs, 2006, p.1

Perhaps we as teacher educators need to reflect more often on the importance of our language and our relationships with our students as we guide them on this challenging journey toward becoming a teacher.

Given that many student teachers will work in multi-cultural settings, teacher education is an important time in which they can reflect on the significance of culture in understanding different beliefs about verbal and body language.

Editors

What this highlights is the value of close relationships between teacher educators and mentor teachers. These relationships provide exemplars to student teachers on what it means to be responsive in our practice.

Editors

References

Bell, N. (1991). *Early childhood teachers' theories in practice: What do teachers believe?* Paper presented at the Fifth Early Childhood Convention, Dunedin, New Zealand. U.S. Department of Education (ERIC Document Reproduction Service No. Ed 341500).

Bowman, B., Donovan, M., & Burns, M. (Eds.). (2001). *Eager to learn: Educating our preschoolers.* Washington, DC: Committee on Early Childhood Pedagogy, National Research Council.

Cassidy, D., & Buell, M. J. (1996). Accentuating the positive? Ananalysis of teacher verbalizations with young children. *Child and Youth Care Forum, 25*(6), 403-414.

Eccles, J. (2007). Families schools and developing achievement-related motivations and engagement. In J. Grusec & P. Hastings (Eds.), *Handbook of socialization: Theory and research* (pp. 665-691). New York: Guilford Press.

Eisenberg, N. (2006). Introduction. In Damon, W., Lerner, R., & Eisenberg, N. (Eds.), *Handbook of child psychology: Vol. 3. Social, emotional, and personality development* (6th ed., pp. 1-23). Hoboken, NJ: Wiley & Sons.

Gibbs, C. (2006). *To be a teacher: Journeys toward authenticity.* Auckland: Pearson Education New Zealand.

Hendrick, J., & Weissman, P. (2007). *Total learning: Developmental curriculum for the young child.* Upper Saddle River, NJ: Pearson Education.

Kontos, S. & Wilcox-Herzog, A. (1997). Teachers' interactions with children: Why are they so important? *Young Children, 52*(2), 4-12.

Kostelnik, M., Whiren, A., Soderman, A., & Gregory, K. (2009). *Guiding children's social development and learning.* Clifton Park, NY: Delmar, Cengage Learning.

Lampert, M. (1984). Teaching about thinking and thinking about teaching. *Journal of Curriculum Studies, 16*(1), 1-18.

Mugno, D. L. (2008). *The relationship between teacher discourse and child response in two therapeutic classrooms for young children with emotional and behavioral problems.* Unpublished doctoral dissertation, Johns Hopkins University, Baltimore, Maryland.

Mugno, D. L. & Rosenblitt, D. (2001). Helping emotionally vulnerable children: Moving toward an empathic orientation in the classroom. In J. Cohen (Ed.), *Caring classrooms/Intelligent schools* (pp. 59-76). New York: Teachers College Press.

Palmer, P. (1998). *The courage to teach.* San Francisco: Jossey-Bass Publishers.

Stone, J. (1993). Caregiver and teacher language: Responsive or restrictive? *Young Children, 48*(4), 12–20.

THE TEACHER EDUCATOR'S ROLE IN STUDENTS LEARNING TO LEAD

Rhonda Forrest
Australia

Dr Rhonda Forrest is a lecturer in early childhood education at the University of New England, in Northern Tablelands of New South Wales, Australia. Rhonda's interests are in leadership, especially self-awareness in beginning leaders. Rhonda has a growing interest in early childhood leadership in developing and post-conflict countries. A second passion is in industrial conditions and rights at work. For the past four years, Rhonda has been president of the UNE branch of the National Tertiary Education Union (NTEU) which is the academic and general staff union. This has provided opportunity to apply her leadership understandings at the highest level of university management. Rhonda has been a teacher, manager and child care advisor as well as being engaged in policy and legislation development in the Queensland Office of Child Care.

> The New Zealand context highlights this issue with many very experienced early childhood practitioners having to enrol in teacher education programs to meet government regulations.
>
> Editors

Introduction

Effective leadership is essential to the well-being of organizations and the individuals within it. Leadership theories can help us understand both our organizations and ourselves, but they must be considered within context. These contexts include early childhood services and the study of these is informed by the discipline of educational leadership. With comparatively few studying the specific area of early childhood leadership, it behoves us to glean evidenced understandings from the rich and fascinating literature within the broader leadership field and then to research its application in our own field.

This paper briefly overviews these areas and proposes that we should enhance the study of leadership in teacher education programs so that our graduates can learn to be wise contributors to the well-being of their early childhood work places. The underpinnings for this commitment are the beliefs that leadership is learned and, therefore, is teachable. Even still, we must consider whether within our crowded teacher education courses, that this discipline deserves space. So we begin by considering the place for leadership in early childhood teacher education programs.

> 'the underpinnings for this commitment are the beliefs that leadership is learned and, therefore, is teachable'

Rationale for teaching leadership

Unlike graduates from most teacher education programs who almost all become classroom teachers, early childhood graduates move to a variety of positions. While many will become room teachers in schools or child care centers, others become directors of centers, Government officers, vocational college teachers, family day care providers, coordinators, and so on. Given the knowledge and skills required for such diverse positions it is incumbent on early childhood teacher educators to teach beyond the limited requirements of classroom teacher training. This suggests a breadth of graduate capabilities that our programs might be designed to build. In the following sections, important components of leadership are briefly identified and justified in terms of their contribution to early childhood teacher education programs. The underpinning theories of leadership are then explored before giving some examples of how early childhood undergraduate and graduate leadership courses have been developed at the University of New England in Australia.

Pedagogical leadership

The general focus of teacher education programs is to support student teachers to be pedagogically sound. Thus, in most preservice teacher education programs, the focus is on curriculum, educational contexts and teaching and learning skills. Furthermore, most practicum experiences align with this focus. That this is essential is not debated, although the degree to which any of the particular discipline areas has preeminence over another is often highly contested in education faculties. Also, given that many graduates from degree courses gain leadership roles early in their professional career, we must acknowledge that they wear the mantle of pedagogical leader often before they develop their own expertise as teachers. This suggests that we ought to educate our student teachers for the pedagogical leadership vocation they may enter.

'given that many graduates from degree courses gain leadership roles early in their professional career, we must acknowledge that they wear the mantle of pedagogical leader often before they develop their own expertise as a teacher'

Organizational mission leadership

It is the responsibility of all early childhood graduates entering the workforce to contribute to the organizational culture of their service in order to support the development and achievement of the service's mission or special characteristic. This involves thoughtful and critical engagement with characteristics of a center articulated by Marshall (2006) as cultural artifacts. Such artifacts are wide ranging, from the physical organization of the environment, to the center rituals, the center philosophy, and the center pedagogy. Artifacts also include symbols such as foyers designed to welcome and value parents, the rituals of daily greeting and farewelling of parents, the inspirational figures such as Montessori, Dewey and Vygotsky, and center ceremonies and celebrations, such as acknowledging the graduation of staff members. The ability to critically examine, question and reshape such artifacts toward vision creation and achievement is both learnable and teachable and, therefore, has a place in early childhood teacher preparation programs.

'the ability to critically examine, question and reshape such artifacts toward vision creation and achievement is both learnable and teachable and, therefore, has a place in early childhood teacher preparation programs'

Administrative leadership

Traditionally called management skills, administrative leadership includes planning, organizing and controlling (Griffin, 1990). These are learnable task-oriented skills needed to survive within complex early childhood settings where there is a growing emphasis on regulations and legal responsibilities to ensure that minimum standards are met and that quality care and education are enhanced (Decker & Decker, 1997).

Leadership is about taking the initiative, building relationships. These keep organisations going. Teams that are not working well together often have relationship issues. Leadership is about creating a safe nurturing culture — a safe environment

Lorelie Paraiso

Some of these responsibilities include such areas as occupational health and safety, children's rights and protection, government regulations, policy development, and record keeping. Student teachers' exposure to, and discussion of, administrative leadership literature helps prepare them to meet these demands.

Personal and interpersonal leadership

The traditional area of human resource management includes the literature on personal and interpersonal relationships. Graduates are fortunate when they leave programs having had exposure to the complexities of conflict resolution, motivation, supervision, communication and teamwork. Such areas are important regardless of whether or not they move directly to leadership positions, for all members of an early childhood service are engaged in the relationship side of the workplace.

Leadership theorists espouse self-awareness as essential to becoming an effective people leader (Drucker, 2000; Covey, 1989; Ginnett, 2001; Palmer & Rittenhouse, 2001; Scharlatt & Weitzel, 2000; Sternbergh & Neary, 2000). Drucker (2000) is typical of these writers arguing that to manage ourselves and be leaders, we must begin by knowing our strengths, articulating our values and being conscious of where we belong. Early childhood programs can actively prepare student teachers to embrace the self awareness journey and thus support them in meaningful human engagement when they reach the workforce.

Advocacy leadership

Rodd (1998) extends the focus of relationship development and maintenance further by building on the importance that others have in relation to the operations of early childhood services. Services for young children and their families do not operate in isolation but impact on, and are impacted by, the wider community. Thus, there is also a need to recognize the broader context in which children's services function in order to engage with leadership approaches that inform the wider community of the benefits of early childhood education. This is where advocacy leadership comes to the fore, at the local community level, and wider national and international level. In terms of influencing public recognition and policy, advocacy efforts in early childhood are an ongoing responsibility of leaders in early childhood education.

Thus, advocacy leadership refers to the strong and positive coordination of advocacy activities. In order to achieve this, graduates need high level personal literacy skills. The ability to read and think critically and then clearly express understandings in convincing spoken and written argument is foundational to harnessing professional passion toward meaningful advocacy. These skills are teachable and learnable and deserve a place in early childhood teacher education programs.

> 'the ability to read and think critically and clearly express understandings in convincing spoken and written argument is foundational to harnessing professional passion toward meaningful advocacy. These skills are teachable and learnable and deserve a place in early childhood teacher education programs'

Having considered our vision of informed graduates from early childhood courses we must determine what we need to teach in order to enhance their leadership potential. Given that leadership knowledge and literature is extensive, and that there are space

> Leadership is recognizing everyone's valuable contributions—that there is no one right way of being a leader
> Angela Russell

constraints on our programs, we must be selective about what we include. This paper proposes some areas of leadership that may form the essentials of such programs.

Teachable leadership concepts

Understanding the context in which leadership theories have developed is essential in student teachers' formulation of attitudes towards early childhood settings they will enter, or are already working in. This is particularly so as many come with preconceived (and often self-limiting) ideas about whether a person is 'born to lead' or whether they can 'learn to lead'. If a graduate believes that they can never be a leader because they do not fit some stereotypical image, then their potential is severely restricted. Furthermore, if they do not understand relational theories of leadership then they may fail to acknowledge their existing leadership role regardless of their level of positional power. The next section considers what leadership theories teach us about whether we are born to lead or learn to lead.

'if a graduate believes that they can never be a leader because they do not fit some stereotypical image, then their potential is severely restricted'

Born to lead or learn to lead

As far back as Plato, theorists formulated the trait theory which codified generalizable skills and traits that were seen as desirable for leaders. These essential leadership traits were seen to emanate only from people of higher class and social status. The theory saw traits as genetically based and passed on through the generations, thus denying the potential for learnable abilities and skills not determined by parentage. Thus, this theory supported the status quo of the social system. It is the basis of the born to lead concept that effectively supported the powerful to claim that they had a right to rule and that the working class could not and should not aspire to be leaders. Under this concept the leaders were identified rather than developed. The identifying factors in 21st century choices of leaders are not as based on social status as they were in medieval England, ancient Japan, or China where birthright was the absolute determinant.

Trait theory leads some to commonly held beliefs about charismatic leaders. Within trait theory in early childhood, leaders may be selected on traits seen as appealing rather than their abilities as leaders. In a recent university assignment, a child care center director explained the dilemma of promoting a worker to room leader based on flawed considerations of important traits held dear by her, staff, and families. She wrote that the employee: *was admired by the parents who often praised her for her devotion. This employee was also very well liked and respected by her fellow colleagues.* The director went on to explain the effects of basing promotion on such traits. She stated: *the cracks began to appear and it became obvious that her lack of experience in the profession, accompanied by the fact that she was unaware of how to properly program affected the routine and the program within the room.* This promotion did not take into account the pedagogical leadership skills required of the position, but rather promoted on personality traits.

While the trait theory still holds carriage for some, leadership theories have progressed and all theories that followed it rejected the seductive born to lead premise and accepted that leadership is learned. These learn to lead theories have developed to encompass a number of perspectives (Marshall, 2006). To illustrate, student teachers applied a number of such perspectives as they planned an early childhood center fête or festival. In brief, these theories include:

- behavior theories that examine the tasks and actions of leaders and sought to teach these to others. For example, skills like planning the fête using an action planning table were taught according to set headings like objectives, strategies, resources, and time allocated.
- contingency theories that acknowledge the importance of context. Under these theories the same action planning would be adjusted to take into account contexts. In our example, the effective leaders might develop wet weather and dry weather plans as well as plan activities suited to their particular ethnic or socio-economic communities.
- power theories that challenge the notion of positional power as essential to leadership and examine new types of power with a focus on the way power is used. These theories would encourage the center leader to consider the application of their power and whether they were using the power of position and control over resources to bring about the action plan success or whether they were using the power of wisdom and respect to support the implementation of plans.
- social change theories with an emphasis on leaders transforming followers to move beyond self-interest and focus on the good of the organization. This important understanding of leadership would encourage the leader to plan the fête so that possibly disempowered families of the center would gain status through recognition of their unique contributions. Thus, the leader would plan in a way that supports the center community to value the diversity of its members.
- meaning-making theories that conceptualize leadership as assisting individuals to make sense of the organizational culture and to transform it to achieve the organization's mission. Leaders who understand this theory would plan collaboratively with the early childhood center community as they recognize that effective planning depends on relationships. Rather than insist on incorporating all sectors of the center, the leader would assist the center community to discover and value its own diversity and the richness of its community. Thus, the center community would grow and change through the planning of the fête.

While all the above theories have different foci as to how to develop leadership capacity, they commonly reject the born to lead theory and recognize that anyone can learn to lead. If we accept this, then we must ask whether teacher educators have a role in teaching student teachers to develop as leaders.

'while all the above theories have different foci as to how to develop leadership capacity, they commonly reject the born to lead theory and recognize that anyone can learn to lead'

In addition, the social change and particularly meaning-making theories move toward a relational view of leadership. In these theories the significance of positional power is questioned. Theorists believe that moving an organization forward is the responsibility of all within it, rather than just with the person at the top. This aspect is called the leader-follower relationship and incorporates the belief that individuals can

This invites an interesting conversation regarding whether social change should be focused on transforming individuals or institutions, and for whose good is the change deemed necessary (the individual, the institution, or both).

Editors

learn to lead and learn to follow. It follows that graduates of early childhood teacher education programs can be prepared to be active participants in the well being of their services, no matter what their position.

'individuals can learn to lead and learn to follow'

Leader-follower relationship

The relationship between leaders and followers is complex (Sergiovanni, 1995). Rather than depending on positional power, a leader's power or influence is derived from aligning their needs and desires with followers (Mitchell, 1990). This relational view does not deny positional authority, but rather, acknowledges that followers have the ability to accept or reject the leader's directions. Furthermore, followers may choose to align themselves to subordinate people and thus make them their leader rather than the one who occupies a position of power. Thus, experiences as a leader may or may not be related to a position, and leaders may have been somewhat down the hierarchical ladder yet have commanded followership. In such cases their power lies in their learned ability to be inspirational leaders (Owen, Hodgson, & Gazzard, 2004).

Graduates can also be helped to understand that constant change in the leaders and the followers results in continual reassessment of this relationship (Foster, 1989). An individual may be a leader for some aspects of life and work and not for others. For instance, educational leaders may be pedagogical leaders and not organizational leaders. Thus, the review and support of classroom programming may be carried out by one while the organization of rosters, and center finances by another. This may also change in time so that one day the followers may align themselves to a leader's directions and not do so the next. For example, at one time you may share the vision of a leader concerning ways of interacting with children and sometime later your values may cause you to reject that same person's direction. Leadership, like all relationships, is subject to review by all that are involved in the relationship. Gronn (1996) describes this dynamic as psychological tugs-of-war in which leaders and followers engage.

'graduates can be helped to understand that constant change in the leaders and the followers results in continual reassessment of this relationship'

Leadership can, therefore, be seen as constantly changing as the leaders and the followers continually reassess their own values and alignments. This leads to a rejection of the appealing cause and effect logic of many leadership theories. For example, a leader may implement all the skills of empowerment (the cause) but that does not mean that followers will automatically be empowered (the effect).

'a leader may implement all the skills of empowerment (the cause), but that does not mean that followers will automatically be empowered (the effect). Being able to dismiss the cause and effect concept helps graduates navigate relationships within their work places '

Being able to dismiss the cause and effect concept helps graduates navigate relationships within their work places. It involves understanding that everyone has

If the leader leaves, the heart can still keep beating

Julie Whittaker

That leadership effectiveness may be judged by the nature of followers' behaviors, provokes conversations about what may be meant by effective leadership, especially in early childhood.

Editors

agency, which is the ability to make decisions about their own behaviors, and that just because a person in positional power acts in a certain way does not determine the way the individual responds. Thus, it is a delusion to believe that effective leadership automatically brings responsible followership. In fact, good and moral leadership can bring out negative responses in followers just as immoral leadership can bring out positive responses.

Understanding that both leaders and followers have multiple sides brings a much richer recognition of the dynamics of the leader-follower relationship and is a key aspect of leadership courses. It is when teaching these particular concepts that students become excited as the concepts have high credibility to them. They will often relate experiences that reinforce the concepts with comments like *now I understand why my good systems don't always work.*

It is one thing to learn about effective leadership skills, but if student teachers are not taught to reject the cause and effect concept then their frustration when their work fails is palpable. Thus, programs need to not only teach valuable skills and processes for effective leadership, but also provide a framework for understanding the practicalities of implementation when people do not act predictably.

Effective and ineffective aspects of leaders

Programs traditionally teach about effective leadership and effective followership and neglect the reality of the negative sides of both. Rather than the study of the latter being dampening on student teachers learning to lead, its reality brings them to a new depth of understanding about the relational aspects of leadership. The value of this learning lies in their recognition of its practical application. Programs should have a balance between understandings of the effective side and ineffective side of both leaders and followers.

> 'programs need to not only teach valuable skills and processes for effective leadership, but also provide a framework for understanding the practicalities of implementation when people do not act predictably or as you might wish'

Understanding the ineffective side of leaders is to acknowledge that they are not always morally driven and benign (Clements & Washbush, 1999). For instance, those that have done some leadership training may know how to support the resolution of interpersonal conflicts, but they may choose not to do so. The agenda of the leader may mean that they want the conflicts between some to continue in order to gain some personal benefit.

Leaders, like everyone, have agency and make choices as to whether to lead effectively for the good of the organization or whether to act in self-interest. Kellerman (2004) describes a possible set of poor leadership styles as incompetent, rigid, intemperate, callous, corrupt, insular, and evil. Interestingly, organizations may value some of these qualities resulting in individuals being rewarded for the negative side of their leadership with increased positional power.

Leaders may also deliberately surround themselves with poor followers. Narcissists may prefer sycophantic follower,s while those with low emotional intelligence may prefer the company of the similarly cold and indifferent. Even those with high emotional intelligence may display manipulative and threatening behaviors and prefer fearful, obedient followers (Hein, 2003).

Understanding the negative sides of leadership may assist early childhood graduates to be more genuinely self-reflective and avoid these leadership behaviors. Furthermore, a wise leader will learn to recognize when followership is lacking and will not assume that superficial obedience means followership.

'understanding the negative sides of leadership may assist early childhood graduates to be more genuinely self-reflective and avoid these leadership behaviors'

Effective and ineffective sides of followers

Followers are not passive recipients and, like leaders, may or may not be morally driven (Clements & Washbush, 1999). For example, they may have a leader who has learnt conflict resolution skills and is implementing them wisely and yet the follower may reject or even sabotage these efforts, as they perceive some personal benefit in doing so. Followers may be controlling, passive-aggressive, dependent, and histrionic, or even masochistic (Clements & Washbush, 1999). At all different levels, related behaviors negatively impact on the leader-follower relationship. Self-reflective followers can be taught and learn principles of followership that may prepare them to identify potentially poor behaviors that neglect their responsibility toward the leader and organization.

'self-reflective followers can be taught and learn principles of followership that may prepare them to identify potentially poor behaviors that neglect their responsibility toward the leader and organization'

Teaching leadership: A model

In accepting the teacher educator role we carry the responsibility to support student teachers' preparation to be teachers, leaders, and followers. The University of New England in regional New South Wales, Australia, has responded by incorporating specific leadership teaching and learning into its early childhood programs. This has been addressed in both undergraduate and postgraduate courses through specific units and practicum.

Undergraduate courses

The Bachelor of Teaching (Early Childhood Education) and the Bachelor of Education (Early Childhood) both have core leadership units. Leadership, and particularly advocacy leadership, requires high level literacy skills. These include exemplary written communication as well as critical reading, thinking, and writing abilities. For this reason a compulsory unit entitled *Professionals in Early Childhood Education* has been developed with a particular focus on students developing the art of professional written and spoken argument.

Further, two compulsory leadership units support the learning of administrative leadership and human resource management. These incorporate self-reflection as an essential component of learning to lead as well as understanding effective and ineffective sides of the leader-follower relationship. Student evaluations indicate high resonance with the significance and practical application of learning to lead and follow within these units.

A designated leadership practicum is another compulsory part of the undergraduate program. In this practicum, student teachers shadow and profile a leader in an early childhood setting. Rather than focusing on teaching and learning of children, this unique practicum is concerned with self-reflection of leadership principles in action. Thus, student teachers experience the implementation of theories of leadership studied in the specific units. Interestingly, many supervising leaders of our students highlight the importance of this practicum and often bemoan not having the benefit of such an experience within their programs.

> 'a designated leadership practicum is another compulsory part of the undergraduate program where student teachers shadow and profile a leader in an early childhood setting'

Postgraduate courses

The Master of Education (Early Childhood) (Honours) program is a research based degree but also incorporates a unit on *Pedagogical Leadership*. Students at this level conceptualize leading young children's learning with respect to multiple contexts such as home, community, culture, media, and education. Further, they critically reflect on establishing personal and professional philosophies of pedagogical leadership.

Furthermore, with leadership as a key element of course work degrees, and with academic expertise in this area, the university attracts doctoral students into higher level investigations of leadership concepts. By creating this community of scholars, students' ideas are presented and contested. Inevitably, the cyclical nature of contributive learning informs and challenges the academics, leading to enriched course work units, and leadership research and practice.

Synthesis

For students in early childhood education programs to emerge as developing professionals they need a complex array of learning experiences. This includes learning to lead. Leadership and followership are multi-faceted concepts that, when examined in an evidence-based course, can support graduates to reach higher levels of professional understanding and behaviors. The challenge lies in acknowledging the essentialness of leadership learning to become a professional and incorporating specific and dedicated leadership units into courses. This broadening from a primarily pedagogical focus is complicated as increasing demands from accrediting bodies reduce educators' independence in designing their teacher education courses.

> 'for students in early childhood education programs to emerge as developing professionals they need a complex array of learning experiences. This includes learning to lead'

Nevertheless, it is worth exploring ways of allocating precious space to these core areas of professional education. The desired and worthwhile outcome would be graduates who are the rounded teachers and leaders required to meet the demands of various early childhood workplaces as well as able to progress in an expanding profession.

References

Clements, C., & Washbush, J. (1999). Two faces of leader-follower dynamics. *Journal of Workplace Learning: Employee Counseling Today, 11*(5), 170-178.

Covey, S. (1989). *The seven habits of highly effective people*. Melbourne: The Business Library.

Decker, C., & Decker, J. (1997). *Planning and administering early childhood programs (6th ed.)*. New Jersey: Prentice Hall.

Drucker, P. (2000). Managing knowledge means managing oneself [Electronic version]. *Leader to Leader, 16*, 8-10.

Foster, W. (1989). Toward a critical practice of leadership. In J. Smyth (Ed.)., *Critical perspectives on educational leadership* (pp. 39-62). London: Falmer Press.

Ginnett, R. (2001). In organizations it takes all kinds. *Leadership in Action, 21*(3), 21-22.

Griffin, R. (1990). *Management (3rd ed.)*. Boston: Houghton Mifflin Company.

Gronn, P. (1996). From transactions to transformations; a new world order in the study of leadership. *Educational Management & Administration, 24*(1), 7–30.

Hein, S. (2003). *The dark side of emotional intelligence*. Retrieved from http://www.eqi.org/history.htm

Kellerman, B. (2004). *Bad leadership; what it is, how it happens, why it matters*. Harvard: Harvard Business School Press.

Marshall, S. (2006). *Issues in the development of leadership for teaching and learning in higher education*. Carrick Institute for Learning and Teaching in Higher Education, Occasional Paper. Retrieved from http://www.carrickinstitute.edu.au/carrick/go/home/grants/cache/offonce/pid/348

Mitchell, J. G. (1990). *Revisioning educational leadership-a phenomenological approach*. New York: Garland Publishing Inc.

Owen, H., Hodgson, V., & N. Gazzard (2004). *The leadership manual*. Harlow, GB: Pearson Education.

Palmer, P., & Rittenhouse, L. (2001). Leadership and the inner journey [electronic version]. *Leader to Leader, 22*, 26-33.

Rodd, J. (1994). *Leadership in early childhood-the pathway to professionalism*. St Leonards: Allen & Unwin.

Scharlatt, H., & Weitzel, S. (2000). Mediocrity at the top: Pulling away from the pack. *Leadership in Action, 20*(5), 1-5.

Sergiovanni, T. (1995). *The principalship. A reflective practice perspective (3rd ed.)*. Boston: Allyn and Bacon.

Sternbergh, W., & Neary, P. (2000). A question of leadership: Should training in ethics be included in leadership development programs? *Leadership in Action, 21*(3), 12.

Continuing the conversations

The above conversations draw upon theory and practice to evidence ways in which teacher educators can enhance the quality of early childhood curriculum through enriching student teachers. More than just providing discussion of the importance and value of leadership, mathematics, language, and literacy in early childhood curriculum, the papers in this chapter have identified important strategies for encouraging student teachers to think about their own relationship to learning, and to learners. Student teachers are, in particular, supported in their making sense of how children engage with the curriculum. Key techniques for supporting student teachers include:

- drawing upon the advice and guidance of associate teachers and mentors in the field

- creating a learning environment that encourages a sense of *sanctuary* for the learner (see for instance Nugent, in Gibbs, forthcoming), and

- at times creating a sense of disruption or imbalance to encourage student teachers to understand and experience different perspectives and practices.

These techniques provide teacher education with more than just effective ways to teach student teachers key content knowledge; they model a range of flexible pedagogical skills that instill in student teachers a sense of possibility and creativity. The argument here is that it is not the content of curriculum that is important, it is how student teachers feel about that content.

When the subject matter is not used in carrying forward impulses and habits to significant results, it is just something to be learned. The pupil's attitude to it is just that of having to learn it. Conditions more unfavorable to an alert and concentrated response would be hard to devise. Frontal attacks are even more wasteful in learning than in war.
Dewey, in Boydston, 1969-1991, p. 176

As a key figure for progressive education, John Dewey emphasized the transformative potential of the curriculum. He argues that teacher educators consider not what ammunition should be used to bombard students in a war upon learning; rather they should consider ways in which students position themselves to the content that constitutes the curriculum. His words suggest an inspirational curriculum might inspire an inspirational teacher. But how do we know in ourselves that we are being inspirational as teacher educators, or that our student teachers are inspired and inspiring? What do inspirational teachers look like? Should we measure and assess inspiration to ensure that the impulses and habits of the teachers of tomorrow are favorable?

In addressing the Working Forum, Lilian Katz reflected upon the importance of nourishing the self. She advised that teachers take the time to enrich their lives in creative and satisfying ways. The teacher that resists such urges in a busy 21st century educational life is perhaps submitting to a 'diploma mill' of education (Peters, 1998). It is not difficult to remember, as a teacher educator, those essential moments when a student teacher has revealed to the class her or his particular passion and skill – a painting, a song, a thought, a relationship. These are intense learning moments. They nourish education, and educators. They underpin a sense of presence and transformation through which the teacher becomes the curriculum. This theme of transformative potential is central to the following chapter, in which the role of the mentor in early childhood teacher education is explored.

References

Boydston, J. A. (Ed.), (1969-1991). *The collected works of John Dewey, 1882-1953: The middle works (Vol. 9)*. Carbondale: Southern Illinois University Press.

Froebel, F. (1886). *Autobiography of Friedrich Froebel*. (E. Michaelis, & H. K. Moore, Trans.). London: Swan, Sonneschein & Co.

Gibbs, C. J. (forthcoming). *A heart to teach: Moments of abundant teacher presence*.

Noddings, N. (2003). *Happiness and education*. New York: Cambridge University Press.

Peters, M. A. (1998). Education and the shift from knowledge to information: Virtual classrooms or automated diploma mills? *Access, 17*(1), 65-78.

CHAPTER 4
Adults as learners in early childhood teacher education

Andy Hargreaves said:

Teachers aren't just well-oiled machines. Computers can never replace them. They are emotional, passionate beings who fill their work and their classes with pleasure, creativity, challenge and joy. Hargreaves, 1998, p. 559

Teaching draws on our capacities to form relationships and to engage in meaningful interactions. In her earlier conversation, Lilian Katz spoke of the need for teachers to nourish themselves. To be nourished means to be willingly connected with others, and willingly connected with the communities of learning in which we work and live. But it also means being connected with ourselves and searching inwards to understand more about the person who is teacher (Palmer, 1998). Such relational connectedness enables the presence of pleasure, creativity, challenge, and joy to be alive in our teaching (Gibbs, 2006). As teachers we are learners; as adults we are learners, too. This chapter opens conversations about adults as learners in teacher education. We share different perspectives on mentoring and also the reflections of a teacher educator's life journey.

Ellen Hall and Alison Maher's paper, *Interns and mentors in learning relationships: An innovative approach to teacher education*, draws upon experiences of mentoring intern teachers at Boulder Journey School in Colorado—a school for children aged from six weeks to six years which is inspired particularly by Reggio Emilia. In explaining their experiences of the teacher education program and mentoring of intern teachers, they share some important challenges. As they write, *the Intern-Mentor learning relationship has challenged us as a community that is committed to social-constructivist learning*. These challenges also affirmed their views that mentoring is relational and therefore requires time so relationships may be nurtured, and of the need for an on-going critical examination of experiences that form the life of the school.

Heather Conroy, along with Wong Lee Leng Jacquelynn, Bey Hwee Kiang, Sylvia Phui, Emelia Prayogo, and Hajarah Rahiman, opens conversations about *Mentoring as a catalyst for change: Empowering teachers through collaborative learning*. Heather is a mentor and critical friend to the other writers who are practitioners in international preschools in Singapore—together they share their journey. This involves setting up a collaborative learning community which depends on forming relationships *based on trust, integrity and a mutual desire to learn about our shared work with, and for, children and families*. When such relational connectedness between mentor and mentee is secure, they found that they had *become excited over small discoveries that find their way into* [their] *teaching* [and that] *this provides the confidence to seek challenges afresh.* As they say, *mentoring, like the act of teaching, cannot be separated from the human being in role of teacher.*

Lindy Austin writes on *Reflective teaching strategies for a reflective educator*. Drawing upon her 40 years of teaching, she weaves and reconstructs her experiences using seven critical reflective strategies and shows how these influenced her pedagogy. Her journey is from a traditional teacher who was *the keeper of knowledge* and one whose job was to transmit subject content, to one who sees teaching as transformative. She makes the point that *it is important for educators to model critical self-reflection especially about contentious and difficult issues,* and that often such transformation is activated by a *disorienting dilemma in the form of a particular life event or experience such as a marriage breakup, job change, or death of a partner.* Lindy's account, therefore, is about relational connectedness and, as such, she makes the point that it requires space and time to reflect, as well as courage to challenge assumptions upon which we live our lives as teachers.

Lily Hok-Neo Wong's paper is *The adult learner in training for early childhood teacher education.* She draws on her Singapore perspective, where a quarter of the population is under the age of 14, and where *increasingly, preschool provision is seen as a common solution to the problem of how to care for, socialize, and educate young children.* This means that more adult learners are entering teacher education programs and, in turn, influences how these are designed and delivered. She suggests that early childhood teacher education programs must respect diversities, especially with regards to age and learning styles. In particular she highlights the need to incorporate different learning strategies and materials, and to vary these by using a range of delivery methods. She also makes the point that we need to ensure that teacher education environments are fair and equitable.

Beginning the conversations

There are several themes apparent in these papers. The first invites us to reconsider how we conceptualize mentoring and being mentored. Traditional models of mentoring often position the mentor as authority and the mentee as novice, or as expert and apprentice. However, the writers in this chapter all suggest that both mentor and mentee are learners as well as teachers.

- How might you describe the nature of mentoring and of being mentored?

- What fundamental principles do you believe ought to underpin such professional development encounters?

A second theme highlights the need for relationship. If we are to develop as teachers, then we need to be relationally connected with others, our communities, and with ourselves (Gibbs, 2006).

- What does being relationally connected mean to you as a teacher?

- How does relational connectedness reveal itself in your teaching?

A further theme relates to the notion of creating space for personal and professional nourishment.

- What spaces do you create in the busyness of teaching for time to reflect and contemplate so that you might be nourished as a person and as a teacher?

INTERNS AND MENTORS IN LEARNING RELATIONSHIPS: AN INNOVATIVE APPROACH TO TEACHER EDUCATION

Ellen Hall
United States

Alison Maher
United States

Ellen Hall is the founder, owner, and executive director of Boulder Journey School, a school for young children in Boulder, Colorado, U.S.A. She is the director of the Teacher Education Program developed at the school through a partnership with the University of Colorado at Denver and Health Sciences Center. Ellen is a partner in Videatives, an educational publishing and professional development company. She is a member of the North American Reggio Emilia Alliance (NAREA) and serves on its board. She is also a founder and member of the board of Hawkins Centers of Learning, inspired by the work and lives of educators David and Frances Hawkins.

Alison Maher is a co-director of Boulder Journey School, Boulder, Colorado, U.S.A. She has been a member of the Boulder Journey School learning community since 1993. Alison supports teachers as researchers, learners, and advocates at Boulder Journey School and in other contexts throughout the United States through the school's study tour and extended study tour program. Alison also serves on the board of Hawkins Centers of Learning and the Friends' School in Boulder.

Introduction

Boulder Journey School is a school for young children in Boulder, Colorado, that welcomes over 200 children ages six weeks to six years and their families. Since 1995, the learning community at Boulder Journey School has been engaged in a study of the educational philosophy and pedagogy of the world-acclaimed infant toddler centers and preschools in Reggio Emilia, Italy. The Reggio philosophy and pedagogy are rooted in classical and contemporary constructivist and social-constructivist theory. Inspiration and ideas emanate from the work of such theorists as John Dewey (1910), Jean Piaget (1966), Lev Vygotsky (1934), David Hawkins (1974), Jerome Bruner (1960), and Howard Gardner (1983).

Constructivist theory proposed by, amongst others, Jean Piaget and Lev Vygotsky, purports that people construct and reconstruct knowledge through ongoing interactions with the environment. While Piaget emphasized children as learners who seek to communicate their understandings of the world through relationships with others, Vygotsky emphasized children learning as a result of relationships formed and maintained within their environment. Thus, social-constructivist learning is a social process that unfolds in a community through relationships created and maintained among all of the protagonists. Loris Malaguzzi, philosopher, founder, and guide of the schools for young children in Reggio Emilia, wrote and spoke extensively of a school based on relationships. In the book, *The Hundred Languages of Children*, Loris Malaguzzi states:

Our goal is to build an amiable school, where children, teachers, and families feel at home. Such a school requires careful thinking and planning concerning procedures, motivations, and interests. It must embody ways of getting along together, of intensifying relationships among the three central protagonists, of assuming complete attention to the problems of education, and of activating participation and research. These are the most effective tools for all those concerned—children, teachers, and parents—to become more united and aware of each other's contributions. Edwards, Gandini, & Forman, 1998, p. 64

'our goal is to build an amiable school, where children, teachers, and families feel at home'

Our interpretation of Malaguzzi's powerful statement has led to a commitment by the Boulder Journey School community to create and maintain a culture of research and participation that includes all of the protagonists in our learning community. In 1998, when we were invited to develop a teacher education program in partnership with the University of Colorado at Denver and the Colorado Department of Education, we were open to the opportunities for research and participation that this program could potentially provide.

A defining characteristic of the Boulder Journey School Teacher Education Program as an innovative approach to teacher education is its existence within a school for young children. We like to say that the program was dropped into the middle of our school. Intern teachers, as participants in the program are called, come from across the country to work at the school for 12-24 months, seeking to earn an early childhood (birth through grade three) teaching license and a Master's degree in either Early Childhood Education or Educational Psychology. As co-teachers with mentor teachers, who are graduates of the teacher education program, intern teachers bridge theory and practice during their time in classrooms as well as during weekly seminars and meetings. When intern teachers graduate, they have, along with their license and degree, one to two years of teaching experience to bring to both public and private sectors as teachers, administrators, professors, and consultants.

Intern teachers become immersed in the culture of the school, establishing long-term relationships with children, families, and faculty. This is in stark contrast to the more common semester-long practicum in which most teacher education candidates participate. Since 1999, over 130 intern teachers have graduated from the Boulder Journey School Teacher Education Program.

The research and participation of intern teachers in the daily life of the school appears to have resulted in a deepening of reflective practice, increased understanding and communication of child development and learning theories, and increased professionalism and commitment. In addition, the program has provided a pool of educated and experienced teachers, some of whom remain at the school as mentor teachers. While the benefits of this program are extensive, the intern-mentor learning relationship has challenged us as a community that is committed to social-constructivist learning. Questions that Boulder Journey School faculty have posed and carefully consider include:

- *How do we define the concept of 'mentor' in our context?*

The common definition of a mentor is a person, usually older and more experienced, who provides advice and support to, and watches over and fosters the progress of a younger, less experienced person (Encarta, 2007). This implies a one-way flow of expertise. Social-constructivist learning, as lived in the schools in Reggio Emilia, lends a different definition of mentor. Carlina Rinaldi (2006), President of Reggio Children, writes:

Those who participate in an educational process, in fact bring their own growth and development into play, and do this on the basis of their own expectations and their own plans. There is a constant relational reciprocity between those who educate and those who are educated, between those who teach and those who learn. There is participation, passion, compassion, emotion. There is aesthetics; there is change.... Learning thus becomes a value because of its force in creating a synthesis of the individual and his or her context, in an affective relationship between those who learn and that which is being learned, a relationship filled with emotion, curiosity, and humor. Rinaldi, 2006, p. 141

'those who participate in an educational process, in fact bring their own growth and development into play, and do this on the basis of their own expectations and their own plans'

The reciprocal, collegial, and collaborative relationship between mentor and intern at Boulder Journey School is evident in their daily interactions. The intern's observations and questions cause the mentor to think about her thinking. The mentor's learning grows as she explains to the intern what she does and the intentions behind her actions. For example, an intern teacher questioned why children at the school were discouraged from bringing toys from home. This provoked an interesting discussion among faculty. Consequently, the intern teacher invited children to set up various scenarios with action figures brought from home, photograph the scenarios, and write stories to accompany the photographs. This intern demonstrated for interns and mentors how toys from home can be resources that enhance, rather than complicate, classroom life.

'this intern demonstrated for interns and mentors how toys from home can be resources that enhance, rather than complicate, classroom life'

Being a mentor has provided me with countless opportunities to further my learning processes as a teacher. Evaluating myself as a teacher, explaining the reasons and thought processes behind my actions, and collaborating with interns to better understand children's learning proves to be invaluable in helping me grow professionally. J. Spruill

- *How can the mentor teacher convey her intentions to the intern teacher within the constraints of a busy classroom day?*

In social-constructivist classrooms, explorations are child-initiated and teacher framed. This means that teachers' actions rely in great part on their observations of the children in classes. Mentor teachers must communicate why they are observing particular groups of children at given moments in time and how reflections on these observations inform the development of further experiences. Documentation (photographs, notes, charts, graphs, videotapes, transcribed conversations, and samples of work) serves as a memory that supports intern-mentor dialogues that occur during less busy times of the day. Lilian Katz writes:

Documentation is an important kind of teacher research, sharpening and focusing teachers' attention on the intentions and understandings of the children as well as their own role in children's experiences. It provides a basis for the modification and adjustment of teaching strategies, a source of ideas, and an impetus of the creation of new ones. Documentation also deepens teachers' awareness of each child's progress. On the basis of the rich data made available through documentation, teachers are able to make informed decisions about appropriate ways to support each child's development and learning.
Edwards, Gandini, & Forman, 1998, p. 39

- *How can mentors support interns in making the important connections between theory and practice?*

As interpreters of classroom experiences, mentor teachers in a social-constructivist learning community share their documented observations of school-related experiences with colleagues, including intern co-teachers in order to make connections between these observations and educational theory. Mentor and intern teachers not only relate classroom moments to established theories, but also challenge and reconstruct these theories based on their observations. For example, intern teachers who documented interactions and relationships among infants began to challenge existing theories about the emergence of empathy in children this age (Piaget, 1965; Kohlberg, 1984).

'intern teachers who documented interactions and relationships among infants began to challenge existing theories about the emergence of empathy in children'

Boulder Journey School Teacher Education Program instructors support ongoing dialogue between mentor and intern teachers surrounding theory as it relates to practice by informing mentor teachers about questions that emerge from interns' readings and discussions during seminars. These questions can be beginning points for conversations among interns and mentors surrounding classroom experiences.

Working as an intern at the school has given me the opportunity to not only learn about the philosophy but to experience it hands on as well. E. Williams

- *What are the enduring effects of the Teacher Education Program on the school as a whole?*

With a social-constructivist focus on the learning community, where individuals build knowledge in collaboration with others and where the knowledge of the group is believed to be greater than the sum of the knowledge of each individual within the group, the participation of each of the protagonists is valued for what they offer to the learning of the others in the community. Thus, we are not solely concerned with what each intern teacher learns during their year or years at the school, but also give value to the traces of the teacher's experiences that become a part of our school's history.

'one intern's research around children's rights which led to a charter of children's rights composed by the children, has become a long-term research project that has touched all of us—children, families, and educators around the world'

Strong connections between center communities and teacher education lend a sense of fluidity to programs that may give student teachers abilities to not only adapt to, but welcome, change.

Editors

We ask children to bring in things from their homes reflecting their cultures—what they are comfortable with. It has changed us as teachers—we listen to the children rather than them listening to us.

Nanisi Mabbs

For example, one intern's research around children's rights led to a charter of children's rights composed by the children and has become a long-term research project that has touched all of us—children, families, and educators around the world.

Additionally, in a social-constructivist learning community, each of the protagonists contributes their unique background and experiences to the culture of the school. The culture of the school is thus created and recreated through the contributions of all of the protagonists. For example, two intern teachers began the school year with prior expertise in, and love of, painting. As members of our learning community, they initiated and organized experiences with paint among both children and adults. These experiences unfolded in a way that they may not have, had these two teachers not been participants in the Teacher Education Program. Even when they leave the school, the contributions of these two intern teachers will remain.

- *In what ways do we acknowledge the experiential uniqueness of each intern, each mentor, and each intern-mentor relationship?*

While intern teachers, as graduate students, typically enter Boulder Journey School's Teacher Education Program with an openness and a willingness to learn, some interns bring a knowledge of social constructivist learning, while others are new to this way of thinking about teaching and learning and some are entirely new to the field of early education. Mentor teachers are also in different phases of their learning journeys, with varying years of experience in a variety of contexts. Such differences are considered when placing intern teachers in practicum classrooms with mentors.

- *How does the process of enculturation affect new interns?*

Intern teachers resonate with the chapter 'Conversation with a Group of Teachers' in the book, *Making Learning Visible*, especially the passage in which a new teacher says:

Thinking about myself and my first days, I felt I was a researcher, but more in the sense of someone who was searching for solutions, even immediate ones. I was looking for something, and especially for someone who would say to me straightaway, 'Do this, do that' or 'Look, this is how we do things here.' Gambetti, 2001, p. 118

Very quickly intern teachers realize that they are not going to be taught 'correct' and 'incorrect' methods of teaching, neither in the classroom nor in seminars. So they use the more common strategy of imitation, doing everything that their mentor teacher does without questioning why; the whys soon follow as their comfort as members of the school community, as well as their comfort with social-constructivism, grows. As the year unfolds, intern teachers begin to share the common language and fundamental values that define the school's culture, and at the same time, they begin to compose their own understandings surrounding the education of young children. The process of journaling and sharing reflections on classroom experiences supports interns' development of personal philosophies of education.

'journaling and sharing reflections on classroom experiences supports interns' development of personal philosophies of education'

- *How and for what purpose do we engage in ongoing critiques of one another?*

We think that the culture of the school must embrace open and honest dialogue as one of the most significant tools for professional development. Mentors model this form of communication by questioning their own practice as well as that of their colleagues, which supports the social-constructivist learning of children and adults in the school. The ever-present question, Why? permeates this way of being and doing. Gradually, intern teachers, as a result of their immersion in the school's culture, feel comfortable participating in debate.

Our colleagues in other countries endorse the significance of this culture of reflective practice as well:

We can say that Reggio has helped us to create a crisis in our own thinking, and so helped us to transgress dominant discourses and practices. Through critical inquiry and reflective practice we have been able to understand how our own thinking and practices are inscribed in dominant discourses, which has opened up a new space and helped us to understand that there are other possibilities—alternative discourses or counter-discourses. Working in relation to Reggio has helped us find critical and productive questions: How has the child, knowledge, and learning been constructed in the Swedish context? Are there other ways of constructing the child and ourselves as pedagogues which can open up for an emancipatory practice in early childhood institutions? What tools and practices can help this deconstruction and reconstruction of dominant and counter discourses and different pedagogical practices.
Dahlberg, Moss, & Pence, 1999, p. 134

- *How can mentors and interns seek support from others in areas that are personally challenging?*

Open and honest dialogue within a social-constructivist learning community leads to an understanding of the individual strengths and challenges of all the protagonists. Participants in such a community come to understand that they can turn to one another for support and encouragement, and that the quality of work increases considerably when collaboration is an inherent part of the school's culture. The creation of a faculty resource guide at Boulder Journey School was the result of many conversations about our own unique strengths as well as the strengths of colleagues within the school community. Intern teachers use the resource guide, as well as experience substitute teaching in classrooms throughout the school, to learn about the varying contributions of mentors. Thus, what begins as a reciprocal learning relationship between one mentor teacher and one intern teacher eventually becomes a reciprocal learning relationship among all of the educators in the school. For example, an intern-mentor team with little gardening experience may utilize the resource guide to locate a teacher in another classroom with knowledge of plants, soil, and landscaping.

> 'open and honest dialogue within a social-constructivist learning community leads to an understanding of the individual strengths and challenges of all the protagonists'

The environment and philosophy at Boulder Journey School supports a cooperative process. Teachers as well as children are heard, respected, and encouraged to grow. D. Spahn

As a school community, our ongoing challenges include:

- *Maintaining a strong sense of community, recognizing that at the conclusion of each school year almost two thirds of our faculty leave the school and thus, at the beginning of each school year, the same number of faculty are new*

We want our students to be reflective so we need to be as well… a reflective journey… if you aren't growing, you aren't modeling.
Mary Hynes-Berry

The importance of space for contemplative reflection cannot be underestimated. Such space includes the physical, social, emotional, and temporal. When such conditions are not present, contemplation may more likely be superficial. This raises questions about spaces we create for reflective contemplation in teacher education programs.
Editors

Having almost two-thirds of the school's faculty leave each year is incredibly challenging. On the other hand, if mentors can remain committed to maintaining the school's vision, it can be refreshing to bring new voices into the community. Clearly, strong leadership is critical here. Teachers hold knowledge of the history and values of the school community, which can be combined with the new perspectives and new expertise that each year's interns bring to the school.

During their internship, intern teachers develop individual philosophies of teaching and learning that can be shared with colleagues in new contexts when they leave the school and begin teaching elsewhere. Through the creation of an alumni network at Boulder Journey School, we have had the opportunity to maintain long-term relationships with graduates of the Teacher Education Program.

By being a mentor teacher, I have the opportunity to help improve the education system in Colorado and in the United States. C. Hunt

> 'by being a mentor teacher, I have the opportunity to help improve the education system in Colorado and in the United States'

- *Maintaining strong professional development opportunities for mentor teachers who are no longer participating in formal seminars and recitations through the Teacher Education Program*

We have challenged ourselves to create opportunities for mentors to continue their studies through book talks, through visits and consultations with scientists, artists, anthropologists, and leaders in the field of education, and through conversations sparked by the sharing of documentation during inservice and meetings. Mentors also continue their own learning through their ongoing research with materials. Our work with materials, as adult participants in the learning process, informs our study of, and work with, children who make meaning of the world through their interactions with the materials in their environment.

- *Maintaining a balance between time with children and time for children, acknowledging that a reciprocal learning relationship requires time for discussion, deliberation, disagreement and debate in order to contribute significantly to the professional development of both mentor and intern*

Each year brings new structures and strategies for offering adults the time they require for professional development. These structures and strategies are developed to support current school goals; as our goals evolve, new structures and strategies are required. For example, a year ago one of our school goals was to better support children in their explorations and representations with materials, such as clay, paint, paper, and wire. One strategy was to offer intern and mentor teachers time to work with these materials, acknowledging that adults' experiences with materials could potentially increase their comfort with, and knowledge of, materials' properties, affordances, and constraints.

- *Maintaining the visibility of children's research in a school that educates not only children but also adults*

The teachers' reflections about children's learning and their own learning cannot overshadow the visibility of the children's research: their questions, their hypotheses,

Teachers, as well as teacher educators, draw from the person they are including in their interests and passions. This prompts us to consider how we nourish these in teachers and teacher educators.

Editors

and their ideas, which they represent and express through many languages. Adults and children engage in a parallel learning process that is complimentary, equally relevant and equally important to the learning of the entire school community.

Concluding implications

While the Boulder Journey School Teacher Education Program is unique in many ways, this project has implications for early childhood contexts as well as for teacher education. These include:

- recognizing the importance of teaching teams that can include formal and informal mentoring

- considering how new teachers are immersed in the culture of schools

- creating and maintaining a school culture in which teachers are learners, and

- extending a school community to develop a network of learners that extends beyond the walls of the school.

References

Bruner, J. (1960). *The process of education*. Cambridge, MA: Harvard University Press.

Dahlberg, G., Moss, P., & Pence, A. (1999). *Beyond quality in early childhood education and care: Postmodern perspectives*. London: Falmer Press.

Dewey, J. (2004). *How we think*. Boston, MA: D.C. Heath & Company. (Original work published 1910.)

Edwards, C., Gandini, L., & Forman, G. (1998). *The hundred languages of children: The Reggio Emilia Approach — Advanced reflections*. Westport, CT: Ablex.

Encarta World English dictionary: North American edition. (2007). London: Bloomsbury Publishing.

Gambetti, A. (2001). Conversation with a group of teachers. In C. Guidici, C. Rinaldi, & M. Krechevsky (Eds). *Making learning visible: Children as individual and group learners* (pp. 116-135). Reggio Emilia, Italy: Reggio Children.

Gardner, H. (1983). *Frames of mind: The theory of multiple intelligences*. New York: Basic.

Hawkins, D. (1974). *The informed vision*. New York: Agathon Press.

Kohlberg, L. (1984). *Essays on moral development. Volume 2: The psychology of moral development*. San Francisco: Harper & Row.

Rinaldi, C. (2006). *In dialogue with Reggio Emilia: listening, researching and learning*. London: Routledge.

Piaget, J. (1965). *The moral judgment of the child*. New York: The Free Press. (Original work published 1932.)

Piaget, J. (1966). *The origins of intelligence in children* (Margaret Cook, Trans.). New York: International Universities Press. (Original work published 1936.)

Vygotsky, L. (1962). *Thought and language*. Cambridge, MA: MIT Press. (Original work published 1934.)

MENTORING AS A CATALYST FOR CHANGE: EMPOWERING TEACHERS THROUGH COLLABORATIVE LEARNING

Heather Conroy
Singapore

with Wong Lee Leng Jacquelynn, Bey Hwee Kiang, Sylvia Phui, Emelia Prayogo, and Hajarah Rahiman, Singapore

Heather Conroy is an Australian early childhood educator with 20 years experience working as an early childhood teacher, director, and administrator in both public and community based sectors, as well as working as a university lecturer in Australia. Since 2003, Heather has worked as a teacher educator in Singapore. She is currently Senior Director of Pedagogy with EtonHouse Preschools, a Singaporean-based education provider of both preschool and primary education. EtonHouse also operates several schools in China. As well as lecturing in curriculum and pedagogy at the EtonHouse Education Centre, she provides direct classroom support for teachers in several of the EtonHouse preschools, to assist educators to further strengthen their understandings of observation, integrated learning, and documentation as a tool for reflection. Heather provides professional development for teachers in centres. She is responsible for the development of policies which aim to enhance aspects of quality across the EH settings.

Sylvia Phui is an Assistant Teacher in an EtonHouse Preschool in Singapore. She says, 'working and being with children, has brought me much joy. Children constantly amaze me with their competence. They have indeed opened my eyes, my ears, and my heart. I feel that they have taught me much more about myself and life, than I have taught them. I look forward to going to work everyday, giving meaning to my life as well as theirs'.

Bey Hwee Kiang is a beginning early childhood educator who enjoys learning with and from children. Designing spaces for children is an interest which she hopes to pursue and realize, if possible, in the near future, in Singapore.

Emelia Prayogo is pursuing a Specialist Diploma in Preschool Education (Leadership), having recently completed a Diploma in Preschool Education (Teaching). She works with a group of Nursery 2 children (3 and 4 year olds) where she is using observation and documentation as tools in valuing children's learning and in reflecting on her teaching.

Jacquelynn Wong is a student pursuing a Specialist Diploma in Preschool Education (Leadership) with EtonHouse Education Centre. She has a Master of Business Administration (International Business) and Bachelor of Science (Management). She says, 'I started without a clue about early childhood education. I've learnt a lot and I am hoping to learn more towards contributing to research in early childhood education'.

Hajarah Rahiman teaches a Nursery 1 class of 12 children. She says, 'I have always had a passion for being a part of a child's journey of learning and discovering the ways of the world. As Robert M. Hutchins said, 'the object of education is to prepare the young to educate themselves throughout their lives.' I hold strong to this in my personal philosophy of early childhood education and am glad to have achieved my teaching goals alongside support from my mentor and colleagues.'

Introduction

Each day, educators make many complex decisions related to curriculum design and delivery within their classrooms, as well as their interactions with children, peers, and parents. The ability to critically reflect on practice and to evaluate one's performance in the classroom is not only an indicator of professionalism, but also holds the solution to many of the problematic situations which hold the educator's attention on a day-to-day basis.

This conversation explores the role of the mentor working as critical friend within a context of a small group of practitioners and student teachers in Singapore, in order to support the practitioners' reflections on practice as they explore challenges within their teaching. The relationship between mentor and practitioner is one which has been founded on trust, respect and a mutual desire to learn more about our shared work with, and for, young children and their families. Through reflective practice, the mentor aims to support the practitioners' exploration of issues which arise as they interact with a complex set of beliefs and values. Through the establishment of peer support networks, opportunities are created for practitioners to collaboratively construct new meanings about classroom practice. Practitioners are thus empowered to take increasing responsibility for enhancing their teaching, creating stronger linkages between theory and practice in the classroom. As such, mentoring enables a valuable form of teacher education and personal-professional development.

> 'mentoring enables a valuable form of teacher education and personal-professional development'

Contexts for learning

This story traces the learning journey of a group of practitioners and student teachers who work across four international preschools in Singapore. As the storyteller, the mentor has used the metaphor of a journey to create an image of a group of collegial travellers with a reasonably open travel plan in that we had no fixed itinerary. However, we shared a common vision, or end point—that of accepting responsibility for creating an optimised educational experience for the young children and families with whom we worked. In working towards this goal, we saw possibilities for our own growth and regeneration as practitioners and classroom-based researchers.

The Singaporean context

Singapore, as an early childhood educational context, has experienced a period of extensive change particularly within the last decade. In 1999, a steering committee was formed to oversee the development of a range of new initiatives including the development of a kindergarten curriculum framework. This framework was launched by the Ministry of Education (MOE) in 2003 and incorporated the MOE desired outcomes of preschool education in Singapore. In his foreword, Minister of Education Shanmugaratnam highlighted, as key principles underpinning the curriculum, the significance of the child's holistic development and integrated learning through play (MOE, 2003).

Intensive government supported training agendas to increase the number of qualified early childhood teachers have been introduced, and include most recently a requirement to enhance the professional rigour of courses by increasing the number of required training hours from the current 700 hours for diploma students to 1200 hours in 2009 (Preschool Qualification Accreditation Committee [PQAC], 2008). Consequently, there was a heightened level of debate amongst the Singaporean early childhood community as to what constituted quality provision of early childhood care and education, both in relation to program delivery for adult learners and the effective provision of preschool education.

> 'there was a heightened level of debate amongst the Singaporean early childhood community as to what constituted quality provision of early childhood care and education, both in relation to program delivery for adult learners and the effective provision of preschool education'

In response to demands for qualified early childhood teachers, EtonHouse International (EH), a Singaporean-based early education provider, opened its own teacher training institution at the end of 2005—the EtonHouse Education Centre (EEC). It was intended that EEC graduates would proceed to employment in the international preschools owned and operated by EH. As qualified educators whose teaching was newly informed by current research, it was anticipated that these graduates would play a role in implementing changed practice within centres.

The mentor, who serves as the group's narrator, is an Australian early childhood educator who has worked as a teacher educator in Singapore for approximately six years. Initially employed as a lecturer in curriculum and pedagogy at the EEC, the role of mentor was proposed as one who would work across the training centre and preschools, to further support the graduates as they moved into roles of classroom practitioner. Specifically, the mentor was identified as a curriculum support person who would facilitate curriculum change towards a more integrated, play-based teaching approach. The mentor was to model (and, at times, to challenge) practice; to prompt critical reflection on practice; and to support ongoing professional development for both new and experienced practitioners.

Our story is a work in progress, constantly evolving as we have discovered new challenges and inspirations. In sharing, we have acknowledged the power of storytelling as a meaning-making tool which, in turn, can be shared with others. Several of the educators whose stories are shared by the mentor, are beginning practitioners who had recently completed their early childhood diploma. As student teachers adopted roles of classroom educators, the mentor–beginning practitioner relationship re-defined itself as the mentor worked beside the new teacher and shared in a process of critical reflection. We saw our journeys as being characterised by a process of collaborative learning with, and from, each other.

> 'we saw our journeys as being characterised by a process of collaborative learning with, and from, each other'

EtonHouse international preschools

EtonHouse international preschools provide educational programs for both local Singaporean children and children of expatriate families living and working in Singapore. Across the individual preschools, there may be up to 12 different nationalities represented in any one classroom. This cultural diversity is further reflected in the cultural and educational training backgrounds of its many local and expatriate teachers.

Curriculum

Previously EH preschools had been working with an adapted version of the National Curriculum Foundation Stage Early Learning Goals (England) (2003). Favoured by some, this curriculum document was seen by others working in the preschools to be overly prescriptive and somewhat de-contextualised given the Singaporean setting. Management endorsed a move towards integrated (inquiry based) learning, which relied on ongoing observation and research of children's interests and ideas as the basis of curriculum design. The identification of a dedicated curriculum support person to serve as a catalyst for change served as evidence of management's commitment to changing curriculum design and delivery.

Philosophy

The move towards integrated learning within the centres was based on a philosophy strongly influenced by socio-cultural and social constructivist theories (e.g., Vygotsky, 1962; Rogoff in Elliot, 1994); drawing inspiration from Reggio Emilia in Northern Italy. As such, the EEC student teachers were actively engaged in a process of constructing new understandings about children and their learning and redefining what constituted the adult role in early childhood classrooms. It was hoped these understandings would enable the students, in their own classroom as beginning teachers, to be active participants in the curriculum change process.

The change process

Management decided in 2006 to initiate the change process initially in one preschool only. Whilst they chose the setting, individual teachers elected to be part of the change process. They also decided that practitioners in other settings could elect to participate, having observed the change process in the first setting. In many ways, this was sensible in that should tensions have arisen between conflicting beliefs and practices, the conflict could be contained within one setting, as opposed to spreading across all preschools. The mentor-centre relationship was then constructed as one of visiting colleague and critical friend who worked as lecturer with student teachers at the EEC, then moving with beginning practitioners into their own classroom. It was anticipated that beginning practitioners may need support to translate theory into practice as well as articulate their beliefs about teaching and learning to colleagues and parents.

> 'it was anticipated that beginning practitioners may need support to translate theory into practice as well as articulate their beliefs about teaching and learning to colleagues and parents'

Whilst management articulated a desire for the EH preschools to move towards a more integrated approach to curriculum delivery, the mentor felt it essential that practitioners be empowered to shape their own teaching as part of this change process. It was the mentor's aim to support practitioners to critically reflect on their existing practice and to seek out, rather than to have imposed upon them, challenges within their teaching. When teachers engage in a process of reflection on their practice in collaboration with another, possibilities are created to construct new meanings about teaching and the practitioner's role as a co-constructor of children's learning. The desired outcome from the mentor's perspective was to create, as Pelo (2006) proposed, a *culture of inquiry* (p. 50), amongst the practitioners—a context within which practitioners would come to value the uncertainty of their teaching as a source of inspiration and a means of further exploring the learning-teaching relationship.

Curriculum is not neutral—culturally, politically, economically, pedagogically. This highlights for us the situationally-specific nature of curriculum.

Editors

Lilian Katz spoke earlier of alliances against teacher educators. However, in this instance there is a synergy between the roles of lecturer and mentor which challenges perceptions of the theory-practice divide.

Editors

> Sometimes our mentees are more resourceful than we think.
>
> Karin DuPlessis

'the desired outcome from the mentor's perspective was to create a *culture of inquiry* amongst the practitioners—a context within which practitioners would come to value the uncertainty of their teaching as a source of inspiration and a means of further exploring the learning-teaching relationship'

Initial expectations of the mentor and practitioners

As narrator of the story, the mentor acknowledges that her perspective is only one of many. Comments were invited from several of the beginning practitioners about their perspectives on the mentor-beginning teacher relationship. Initial dialogue indicated that the beginning practitioners sought *efficacy* (Cheyney, 2008, p. 14) in their teaching, rather than quick fix solutions. As such, the mentoring process was defined by beginning practitioners as:

Providing appropriate guidance which caters to my individual learning progression and current knowledge… two-way active communication. Kiang

Beginning practitioners wanted mentoring to provide:
Constructive and non-biased feedback, sharing experiences and information that will enable me to develop further… it may even at times be emotional support, because starting out as a teacher is not as easy as it seems. Hajarah

They also saw the potential to influence the learning of the mentor, that is, that learning would be reciprocal:

The mentor learns about alternate perspectives… the interactions with the mentee also help the mentor in reflecting on his/her own thinking, beliefs and practice. There is always something new to learn from another person. Jacquelynn

The mentor acknowledged the rich potential for perspective taking within these conversations as well as the possibilities for consolidation and clarification of her personal beliefs and values as quality outcomes of mentoring interactions.

Relationships at the heart of learning

The relationship between mentor and practitioner developed out of interactions within which reciprocal trust and integrity were essential components. There was also a mutual desire to learn about our shared work with, and for, children and families. The mentor believes that teaching is about forming relationships—forging connections with individuals (adults and children) which are based on open communication and respect for the learner and the learning process. Similarly the mentoring relationship was seen by the practitioners as one based on trust.

I do not want to be second guessing the sincerity, accuracy, and appropriateness of the mentor's advice. Sylvia

Initially, our relationship began as one of lecturer and student in classrooms where textbook theory dominated most of our discussions. Indeed, student teachers had to wait until their field practicum experiences before they began to see how research-based theory related to hands-on practice. As they moved into classrooms in their practicum, so began a new relationship—not simply one of lecturing to, but one of facilitating and supporting the development of professional early childhood educators. This involved processes of modelling and *guiding the participation* of these new teachers (Rogoff, cited in Elliot, 1994, p. 9).

Together, we began a collaborative relationship of building bridges between the research and theory which supported our professional work as educators, applying theory in real life situations. We explored the values which informed our teaching. We attempted to build bridges between what we knew and what we wanted to learn, between reality and the ideal. We believed we had much to gain as we began a partnership of learning with, and from, each other. We committed to the process of learning about our learning. One cannot talk about the serious matter of understanding teaching without a sense that this meant something to both parties. The shared responsibility for the problem at hand both defined, and influenced, the practitioner-mentor relationship.

> 'we committed to the process of learning about our learning. One cannot talk about the serious matter of understanding teaching without a sense that this meant something to both parties'

Both parties need to come together with an open mind… believing that they will learn and gain something from the relationship. Both parties must first be receptive to perceptions and approaches that differ to their own. The spirit to explore together and look on the relationship as a journey that they are taking together. There may be situations that are new to both parties or opportunities to implement something new or different together, and even if it is something routine, there are different ways of looking at it in that particular instance… The willingness to share, the willingness to allow the other party to share without the intention to criticise but to discuss and provoke each other to think positively and more in depth on the issue(s).
Jacquelynn

Social-constructivism as a framework for learning

According to Millikan (2003), *the construction of knowledge is a subjective process that proceeds in a spiralling rather than a linear way* (p. 87). Within a social-constructivist framework, individuals construct highly personalised understandings based on their own experience and understandings of events, or interactions. The practitioner interprets or filters these interactions through a complex series of values and beliefs to make meaning of their day-to-day classroom experiences. At times the meanings are subjective, emotive, or perhaps too complex for the individual practitioner to map a way forward. Working in isolation, they may in fact not see the wood for the trees. Collaborative dialogue encourages practitioners, through a process of supported reflection, to discover new aspects of their teaching. As Jones said:

knowledge is constructed by the learner through action on the environment and interaction with peers… knowing is embedded in collectively shared meanings and depends on validation in significant relationships. cited in Carter & Curtis, 1994, p. 3

Mentoring supported a process of collaborative reflection, of meaning making based on the support of others who shared knowledge about learners' interests and aspirations, as well as the complexities of the learning context in which both mentor and practitioner found themselves. The process of collaborative dialogue supported reflection which assisted practitioners to identify their problems—that which captured their attention in a teaching day, and which caused them to think again. Malaguzzi suggested that teachers:

need to understand that professional growth comes partly through individual effort, but in a much richer way through discussion with colleagues, parents, and experts in a variety of disciplines. cited in Millikan, 2003, p. 85

As such, Malaguzzi proposed the notion of *shared meaning making and modification of personal theories,* (cited in Millikan, 2003, p. 86). Therefore, the relationship between mentor and practitioner was one that enabled the practitioner to reveal their own insights:

The mentor does not have to provide all the answers. I do not need my mentor to 'spoon feed me'. I would like someone to explore (with me) and experience the process of investigation and learning that would be most meaningful. Sylvia

Cheyney (2008) proposed the notion of building internal capacity whereby teachers undertake collaborative action to both define and investigate their own learning. Within a social-constructivist paradigm, scaffolding, or temporary support (Elliot, 1994) occurs after an assessment of the individual learner's current competency and aims to guide and share responsibility for, but not to take control of the learning process.

With reference to Vygotsky's theory... I see the mentor assuming the role of the necessary scaffold or support system that allows me to move forward and continue to build new competencies. Sylvia

Lilian Katz (1972) proposed a hierarchy of developmental stages which outline anticipated stages of preschool teachers' professional competence as a result of building personal and professional confidence. As confidence builds, the learner is thus empowered to move to the next level, demonstrating greater autonomy and overall awareness of the potential of their role as a professional educator. Each developmental stage, for example the initial developmental stage of survival, (Katz, 1972) holds implications for the ongoing professional development needs of practitioners. Mentoring, as a form of teacher education, articulates positively with Katz's first stage, providing guided (context specific) support around the specifics of the beginning practitioner's day-to-day teaching encounters.

Critical reflection: Learning to listen

Embedded within the notion of shared or collaborative meaning making is the practice of learning to listen for the meanings shared by others. In Reggio Emilia, educators acknowledge the significance of the pedagogy of listening which they interpret as a reciprocal process involving sensitivity and openness to the meanings which are being constructed as part of the listening encounter (Rinaldi, 2006). As practitioners dialogue about their decision-making processes, the mentor is offered the possibility of gaining access to other perspectives—to connect with the personal reality of their teaching. Similarly, as we engage in conversations about our shared experience in the classroom, we have the potential to support each other in uncovering issues that require further thoughtful consideration. Therefore, *it is critical within the mentoring relationship that there is one who listens and sees my doubts and offers suggestions on how I could adopt and work towards my goals... a sounding board.* Sylvia

Lilian Katz's (1972) description of developmental stages has been influential. Given our changing societies, we are curious as to whether these stages continue to be reflected in today's teachers and mentors.

Editors

'embedded within the notion of shared or collaborative meaning making is the practice of learning to listen for the meanings shared by others'

Critical reflection: Influencing practice

The forging of strong relationships requires sensitive acknowledgment of the practitioner's reality both within and outside of the preschool context, and consideration, as has been stated, of the practitioner's stage of professional development (Katz, 1972). The mentor must recognise the practitioner's personal and potentially culturally influenced expectations as to what constitutes each individual's philosophy of teaching and learning, or ways of knowing (Carter & Curtis, 1994). This practice of getting to know the person inside of the teacher created for us the potential of building quality relationships.

Rather than impose herself on a classroom (which in the beginning could well have been seen as a threat), the mentor responded to invitations to work with teachers. Working regularly side by side with teachers and children supports the perspective of the mentor as a colleague and critical friend, rather than a distant visitor. The mentor role is free of any supervisory or appraisal component, freeing the practitioner and mentor to talk without an evaluative component—the relationship is one of listening and sharing, not passing judgement. This allows conversations to take flight in terms of the depth and breadth of content. Over time, the invitations have become open as in: *come whenever you can; when can you come back?*

'working regularly side by side with teachers and children supports the perspective of the mentor as a colleague and critical friend, rather than a distant visitor'

As critical friend, the mentor brings her own knowledge base and culturally defined set of values into play, and she builds relationships with children and practitioners. The mentor needs to be highly sensitive in this regard, constantly reflecting on the significance of her own background in terms of context and *western* perspectives and practices. The beginning practitioners, however, work in international education settings, exposed to many diverse cultures on which they reflect their value systems.

'I think it is so much more interesting for two people of different cultural backgrounds to share and explore unfamiliar ground than for two people who are so like-minded that it leaves no room for further exploration'

I think culture is a valuable input to the exchange in the relationship. Whilst there could be potential for conflict, there exists also the potential for more learning… both parties (have the opportunity to) review and share cultural differences to find the common ground on which both can proceed to achieve a common objective (in our case supporting children's development). It is not a matter as to whose cultural approach is better, but what works for the situation at hand. I think it is so much more interesting for two people of different cultural backgrounds to share and explore unfamiliar ground than for two people who are so like minded that it leaves no room for further exploration. Jacquelynn

> The evaluation of a teacher's practice ought to be guided by this commitment to understand 'the person inside of the teacher'.
>
> Editors

Reflection facilitates transformation.
Bambi McLean

Hajarah: A case study

Hajarah began the 2008 teaching year (having graduated the previous November) with a group of 12 children aged between 2 and 3 years. I reflected on one of my visits to her classroom, where she and I were offered the opportunity to analyse her practice against the backdrop of her personal philosophy statement.

Mentor:
Monday morning began as busy as ever and progressed through a flurry of tasks including transitions between indoor and outdoor environments, snack, and diaper change. Both staff were focused and extremely efficient in their management of routines—however, interactions with children whilst warm, seemed rushed and repetitive. Hajarah sat down at a painting experience and proceeded to invite various individuals to the table. I sat at another table and waited for children to come. The initial two children who joined me chose to draw, as did the friends who joined them. We drew together for the whole of indoor time, beginning a relationship with each other just as much with the materials with which we worked. After the children had departed, Hajarah and I had the opportunity to talk:

Hajarah:
What you did today, having a conversation with children… that is what I want to do… but we don't do that here. That's one of my goals. Why don't we do that here?

This experience was offered to us as a point to pause, to reflect upon what really mattered to us in our teaching. As we worked collaboratively, we had the opportunity to jointly construct (new) meanings (Rogoff, in Elliot, 1994) which responded to our shared understandings about teaching and learning.

The significance of time

It takes time to build reflection into busy teaching days. Timetables are packed, contact hours are long and at times we find it difficult to find regular times to talk. E-mail conversations are a useful but less preferred option. The beginning teachers and I prefer to engage face-to-face, often within the actual context of the classroom, so that we can embed our conversations into the reality of our teaching. However, we have learned to see time as a friend in supporting our thinking processes. Reflection is about thinking again, about analysing and synthesising our thoughts to better inform our understanding of the matter at hand—not necessarily about 'right' answers. At times we all need to pause in our thinking and survey the scene—to review progress and consider what might be (next). A question posed one day can be significantly enriched if left to be mulled over:

Do you remember when we talked about how the environment defines children's behaviour…? I have been reflecting (on) how I see that in my classroom. Emelia

> 'at times we all need to pause in our thinking and survey the scene—to review progress and consider what might be next'

These questions may come weeks after initial encounters and, at times, surprise us in terms of the richness of discussion that ensues. As beginning practitioners, individuals are consumed with working out the practicalities of their day-to-day interactions with children (Katz, 1972). However, we acknowledge the wisdom offered to us through reflective practice, placing our teaching under a magnifying glass to better understand our interactions. In the relationships we have built, we have learned to feel comfortable with change and challenge. Together we have learned to ask more questions than to simply seek the answers. We acknowledge the beginning nature of our research journey into making sense of our experience and have learned to understand that sometimes we do not know—however, in time we may come to know.

Teachers as researchers: Empowering self and others

Jones proposed, under optimal conditions of safety and challenge, human beings are inherently curious, intrinsically motivated, self directed learners.
cited in Carter & Curtis, 1994, p. 3

The educators with whom I work bring amazing strengths to their teaching. Their willingness to take risks in teaching, attempting something they had never undertaken before, is a significant quality to bring to a change process. We reminded ourselves to keep track of our small steps as well as keeping the goal in our focus. We have become excited over small discoveries that find their way into our teaching. This has provided the confidence to seek challenge afresh. We have come to understand, as Fillipini proposed, that:

reflection on practice allows the educators the opportunity to construct new meaning and understandings, and the possibility of moving towards new theories.
cited in Millikan, 2003, p. 80

> 'their willingness to take risks in teaching, attempting something they had never undertaken before, is a significant quality to bring to a change process'

Together, we have begun to see ourselves as researchers in our own classroom contexts.

Implications

A basic tenet of early childhood practice is to access learners' deep, personal satisfaction of self-motivated learning. Through reflective practice the mentor aimed to support practitioners in identifying their own personal and professional goals, developing confidence in their decision making and their ability to translate beliefs into practice. The mentor has served as a companion or guide to this process, conscious of the need for practitioners to steer, and to set the pace of their own development, but keen always to suggest new possibilities.

Creating strong teachers requires a major investment of time, finance, and expertise. To ensure sustainability in our teacher education programs, we must be prepared to extend that investment of time and support ensuring that student teachers continue their ongoing professional learning as strong classroom practitioners. The mentor relationship, forged out of an existing student-lecturer relationship, builds upon existing understandings of trust and knowledge about each other's belief systems (cultural, contextual, and philosophical). In this way the mentoring relationship acknowledges the individual learner within a context.

Cheyney (2008, p. 16) proposed that collaborative learning communities support:

teachers to make their voices heard, initiate their own discussions, pursue answers to their own questions, take initiative for their own change, and ultimately grow as professionals.

Being a companion supports the relational role of critical friend who is then more able to both affirm and challenge teaching practices and beliefs.

Editors

Teacher education must also encompass the notion that the act of teaching cannot be separated from the human being in the role of teacher. Dispositions which support teaching behaviours of self-directed learning, reflexive practice, and innovation can be developed through collaborative relationships that sensitively aim to build onto the strengths of all parties involved. Individuals who have been engaged in a mentoring experience can, in turn, become mentors in their own right, thus creating a full circle of learning as the beginning practitioner brings their own experience and learning to support a new relationship of teaching and learning.

> 'teacher education must also encompass the notion that the act of teaching cannot be separated from the human being in the role of teacher'

Classroom-based research, which aligns closely with the mentoring relationship, can expand our understandings about what happens in early childhood classrooms, as well as how teachers interpret and enact curriculum. It supports stronger understandings of what constitutes teaching, which may inform and enrich teacher education courses, as well as induction and intern programs.

Conclusion

Teaching is about building relationships of trust which demonstrate genuine interest in the personal and professional growth of the learner. Mentoring, as a form of teacher education, may not suit all practitioners. However, for those who believe in the social constructivist principle that we learn with and from others, rather than in isolation, mentoring provides a valid and valuable framework which both affirms and challenges learning.

> 'teaching is about building relationships of trust which demonstrate genuine interest in the personal and professional growth of the learner'

A final last word from one of the beginning practitioners:

The basis for an effective mentor-mentee relationship is a belief, between both parties in the relationship, that you can learn something from it; that your honesty will be reciprocated… it requires humility from both parties to look beyond their experience and knowledge and to believe that there could possibly be another perspective or approach that is more appropriate to the context. I like the idea of a full circle of learning. It makes it so much more meaningful from this point of view… we need to think how we can get others to believe in the value of such learning to perpetuate the cycle. Jacquelynn

References

Carter, M., & Curtis, D. (1994). *Training teachers: A harvest of theory in practice.* St. Paul, MN: Redleaf Press.

Cheyney, K. (2008). Collaborative learning communities. *Exchange, 180,* 10-16.

Elliot, A. (1994). Scaffolding learning. *Every Child, 1*(2), 8-9.

Katz, L. (1972). *Developmental stages of preschool teachers.* ERIC Clearinghouse on Early Childhood Education (ERIC Document Reproduction Service No. ED057922).

Millikan, J. (2003). *Reflections: Reggio Emilia principles within Australian contexts.* NSW, Australia: Pademelon Press.

Ministry of Education. (2003). *Nurturing early learners: A framework for a kindergarten curriculum in Singapore.* Singapore: Preschool Education Unit Ministry of Education.

National Curriculum Foundation Stage Early Learning Goals (England) (2003). Retrieved from http://www.opsi.gov.uk/si/si2003/20030391.htm

Preschool Qualification Accreditation Committee (PQAC) Revised standards for 2009 (2008, April). Briefing session for Singapore training institutions.

Pelo, A. (2006). Growing a culture of inquiry: Observation as professional development. *Exchange, 172,* 50-53.

Rinaldi, C. (2006). *In dialogue with Reggio Emilia.* London: Routledge.

Vygotsky, L. (1962). *Thought and language.* Cambridge, MA: MIT Press. (Original work published 1934.)

REFLECTIVE TEACHING STRATEGIES FOR A REFLECTIVE EDUCATOR

Lindy Austin
New Zealand

Lindy Austin has played an active role in education for over 40 years now and has worked in the early childhood, primary, secondary, special education, tertiary, and vocational sectors. Initially she held educational positions such as teacher, advisor, principal, and manager in the Aotearoa/New Zealand education system. She was an ANZAC fellow in 1985. This enabled her to study fulltime and complete a postgraduate special education qualification in Brisbane, Australia. From here she worked as a full-time lecturer within the vocational and university sectors in Queensland, Australia. Recently she returned to Aotearoa/New Zealand where she was appointed as Deputy Program Head (Early Childhood) at Manukau Institute of Technology. She has worked extensively in the Asia-Pacific Basin, and completed her Doctor of Teaching through Charles Darwin University, Northern Territory, Australia. Her special interests are reflective practices, communities of learners, and transformative learning.

Introduction

The aim of this paper is to make public a means to illustrate how the use of seven critical reflective strategies influenced my pedagogy. Even though their influence on my pedagogy occurred over a duration of 40 years, I have only been able to cognitively document these critical reflective strategies in the last decade. My doctoral thesis provided an avenue for this to occur. Consequently, I could better understand how these critical reflective strategies influenced my pedagogy. This was, and is, for the betterment of my practices and student teachers. Of interest, more often than not, the use of these critical reflective strategies was intuitive and not consciously incorporated into my teaching. The influence of these will be discussed, and are identifiable in an already growing list of recommendations for reflective strategies for educators. To enhance critical reflection in adults, specific and sequenced steps can be developed to support and enhance the reflective process.

Requesting students to reflect upon their lived experiences, beliefs, assumptions and values is the first step. This initial practice of asking students (and others) to reflect has long been a recommendation by those concerned about bias and prejudice. Studies conducted by Ziegahn (2001) established that reflection of personal experience is empowering for learners because they confront the contradictions of everyday life. Therefore, the first critical reflective strategy is:

critical reflection is included within all discussions and training programs for student teachers.

> 'reflection of personal experience is empowering for learners because they confront the contradictions of everyday life'

Along with exemplars, the next six critical reflective strategies will be integrated within my journey of reflective pedagogy.

My pedagogical journey begins

Around the mid-1950s the first developmental phase of my early childhood journey commenced. At the age of 14 years I believed I had achieved my childhood dream to teach. I was a Sunday school teacher of 34 preschool children. The bible story and the choruses sung were my choices. Planning the lessons was my responsibility alone. The control was mine. My teacher identity was being formed due to personal, spiritual, social and cultural, and historical aspects of the late 1950s (Zembylas, 2003). Enroling in teachers college a few years later, to train as a junior class teacher, was a continuation of this first phase of my journey.

Initially my pedagogy was very traditional—similar to those of my childhood experiences. My pedagogy, which was subject-oriented, was of questionable value for students (Sutton, 2005). My primary goal for the students was the acquisition of knowledge. In other words, I was the holder of all the knowledge and power. The school curriculum was my bible and new content taught was built on previous knowledge. For a short period of time I was satisfied with my pedagogy. However, I was beginning to have doubts about traditional methods of teaching. I started to consider issues such as providing a program that catered for the learning needs of all students regardless of ability, class, race and gender. Humphries and Martin (2000) assert that assumptions regarding learner homogeneity and the existence of a *level playing field*, are not addressed in subject-oriented pedagogy. This was definitely the case in my classroom.

> 'assumptions regarding leaner homogeneity and the existence of *a level playing field*, are not addressed in subject-oriented pedagogy'

As Lindy the teacher, I began to critically self-reflect upon my pedagogy. This necessitated my taking on the role of external observer to critically examine my own teaching practice and the multiple meanings and identities which influenced my pedagogy. I examined why my non-inclusive practices did not cater for individual students' learning needs. Why was I not providing for the learning needs of the students when I was conscious of the underpinning inclusive pedagogical theories? What was influencing my theory in practice? Was I, as stated by Imel (1992, p. 2), *espousing to one theory but using another in practice*. Why did these contradictions and doubts exist? Why did I allow limited interaction between the children? Why were most areas of the curriculum delivered in whole-class methodology?

At the commencement of any new course, teacher educators should encourage, by modeling this themselves, the use of reflection with student teachers. Teacher educators should actively encourage student teachers to understand the interconnectedness between their personal lived experiences, their new understandings of these lived experiences, and the course content. The second reflective teaching strategy is evident in my pedagogy today which is that:

I endeavor to model and encourage reflection initially and the attachment of multiple meanings and identities to lived experiences in all classes.

> 'teacher educators should actively encourage student teachers to understand the interconnectedness between their personal lived experiences, their new understandings of these lived experiences, and the course content'

We share our culture with other professional colleagues around the world. Storytelling is really important. Listening around the fire and listening to grandparents, parents. It's all about sharing.

Marek Tesar

During this early period of my teaching career, I forced myself to reflect critically upon my pedagogy while constructing knowledge from the socio-historical context in which it occurred (Baumgartner, 2001; Sutton, 2005). I was attempting to bring about change in my pedagogy and believed I had the ability to alter the classroom environment for the betterment of the students (Gershon & Straub, as cited in Henderson, 2001). To change my style of pedagogy it was necessary for me to examine my negative childhood school experiences, maybe re-examine them, acknowledge how they were controlling my pedagogy, and then reject those which I considered detrimental (Austin, 2008).

For instance my primary schooling took place during the 1950s when pedagogy was very traditional and formal. The most vivid of my flashbacks are located in the middle schooling years. As a 9-year-old pupil I was placed in a mixed class of children, most of whom were similar to me and came from working class backgrounds. My memories present the teacher as an elderly European bachelor. All pupils feared 'him'. His 'maleness' was not the issue, but his desire for all power was. I observe myself as a tall, skinny girl who was constantly trying to be invisible so 'he' could not see me. My desire to be a teacher was not kindled by these childhood schooling experiences. Schooling experiences for me as a tall skinny girl were associated with the emotion of fear. In this era of formal and fearful pedagogy, most pupils sat in double wooden desks that had seats and desks jointly constructed. Both the seats and desk lids lifted up. In many ways these desks resembled conjoint twins: firmly agglutinated yet struggling to be separate. The teacher's desk was situated on a platform at the front of the room, which allowed the teacher to survey pupils in his kingdom. The pupils' desks were arranged in straight single rows down the classroom. 'He' surveyed 'his' class from 'his' platform. Everyone was petrified of 'him'. 'His' concept of good teaching was to use negative emotional teaching techniques which gave 'him' power and enhanced 'his' status as teacher. Instead of using emotions with his pupils as tools of freedom, this teacher used emotions as tools of oppression.

I was able to utilize these childhood emotional experiences when I reflected upon my pedagogy. These experiences provided me with the confidence in my ability to change my pedagogy (Henderson, 2001; Willis, 2007). I had discovered a process which empowered me to conceptualize my pedagogy within a broader educational content. Consequently, I was able to make the crucial connections between my conceptual understandings, children's learning, and curriculum documents. My reflective journey was well underway.

The reflective journey continues: Systematic reflective practices

The emergence of my reflective process documented here occurred over many years. Similar to the time and space I required to develop reflective practices, another reflective strategy emerged, namely:

it is essential that educators ensure they allow time and space within their classes for critical reflection.

'it is essential that educators ensure they allow time and space within their classes for critical reflection'

Time and space is crucial in developing critical reflective skills. Students require time to rethink, reconstruct, reexamine, and then reframe an issue. This is regardless of the mode of discussion.

That our emotional experiences as a child influence how we come to understand our pedagogy, opens conversations about the significance of early personal experiences on shaping who we are as teachers.

Editors

Many years later I was able to identify my reflective process with a method of reflection described by O'Connor and Diggins (2002). These writers describe their method of reflection as 'ways of knowing'. Huitt (1998) describes ways of knowing as having the ability to think critically and logically about a personal experience to gain a unique, personal, and deeper understanding of that experience.

My journey to become a critical self-reflective practitioner more or less followed a series of four identifiable phases:

- I gave little thought to my real life experiences—it was represented by silence. Additionally, I gave little acknowledgement to the emotions in my professional life. I relied on others to justify my pedagogy. I accepted blindly that a subject-oriented or mechanistic approach to teaching was acceptable for my students. Teaching was a technical enterprise.
- My social relationships and values systems were constructed by my families, culture, and school situations (Zembylas, 2003), all of which were ordained by various authoritative educational, religious, societal, and cultural sources. This received knowing from authorities was not challenged personally at this stage of my life.
- In fact, this situation suited my needs at the time. This subjective knowledge provided an acceptable reason to continue my traditional method of teaching. Why would I want to consider perspectives other than my own? Why would I want to challenge my fundamental pedagogical beliefs and values and assumptions?
- Over time I realized that there were other perspectives to knowledge and commenced the procedure of critically analyzing my traditional method of teaching. In other words, I began to challenge the validity of my fundamental pedagogical beliefs and values and assumptions. This process is known as 'procedural knowledge'.

Consequently, I constructed knowledge, which *integrated the best of all four of the above ways of knowing* (O'Connor & Diggins, p. 47). I examined my pedagogy and integrated my findings with other perspectives and analyzed how they contributed to a holistic pedagogical picture. Because I invested so much of self into my teaching, there was a merging of my personal and professional identity.

> 'because I invested so much of self into my teaching, there was a merging of my personal and professional identity'

At the same time, my identity changed from a teacher who used a subject-oriented or mechanistic approach to one who practised and modeled transformative or critical self-reflection. I was beginning to hear and listen to my own voice and then act upon this knowledge to bring about change. My identity as teacher—the keeper of the information—was shifting to that of facilitator where the students were encouraged to become active learners and take control of their learning (Austin, 2008).

> 'within a sensitive and supportive environment I challenge student teachers to reflect on the origin of their own beliefs, assumptions and, values'

Now within a sensitive and supportive environment there is another reflective teaching strategy:

As teacher educators, does our guidance of student teachers reinforce the view that in order to teach one must appeal to authority (whether that be knowledge or people).

Editors

All teachers have beliefs—some are held strongly, others less so. In reflecting the diversity of beliefs in our societies, teacher education programs ought to create spaces where all are able to communicate freely about beliefs whether those be based on religious, emancipatory, scientific, or other ideologies.

Editors

We have a huge responsibility to get the feel of the group. So that we can work with that group… multiculturalism, for instance, is such an emotive topic… there tends to be a bit of *there's a right way* and *there's a wrong way to do it.*

Cheryl Payne

I challenge student teachers to reflect on the origin of their own beliefs, assumptions, and values.

By working through the cognitive or experiential processes, students are able to ascertain why they hold specific beliefs, values, and assumptions. Challenging students with perplexing questions requires them to make sense of the inconsistencies between their values, assumptions and beliefs, and lived experiences. To examine the origin of their beliefs is very pertinent to some students who have very strong religious beliefs, for instance. In some instances, they may be inclined to blindly accept the dogma of a variety of organizations, cultures, and contexts.

Critical self-reflection has the potential to lead to transformation. The process of transformation is often set in motion by a 'disorienting dilemma' in the form of a particular life event or experience such as a marriage breakup, job change, or the death of a partner. Therefore, another reflective teaching strategy is:

it is essential for educators to ensure that extra support people are in place for students, when required.

According to Mezirow (as cited in Merriam & Caffarella, 1999) these crises are often the catalyst for transformation and create emotional turmoil while working through the transformative process. With all of the adult students I teach, I ensure that a variety of extra counseling services are available to meet the diversity of their needs. These could take the form of individual mentors, psychologists, counselors, and religious people. Being responsible for contentious topics within some early childhood courses has meant responsibility for ensuring that support staff were constantly in place if traumatic situations arose for student teachers, as they experience each others' trauma.

Theoretical links to practice

Linking reflective practices with theory was the next developmental phase of my journey. My teaching was changing due to several factors, including understanding the assumptions which underpinned my awareness of my teaching, developing critical practices and participating in pedagogical and theoretical discussions with my colleagues. Consequently, another reflective teaching strategy within all of my classes is:

I encourage students to contribute in the exchange of ideas and to offer critical contributions.

Teacher educators should manage these by creating opportunities for all students to make meaningful contributions—especially the how and when aspects of reflection.

Of immense importance for me, were the introduction to transformative learning and then the theoretical discussions of Mezirow's six essential practices for transformative pedagogy. Mezirow (1998, p. 5) posits that transformative learning *offers a theory of learning that is uniquely adult, abstract, idealized, and grounded in the nature of human communication.* Mezirow would argue that this theory is both a developmental process and a process in which learning is understood by using a prior interpretation of one's lived experiences and constructing a new or revised interpretation of that lived experience in order to determine future behaviors. Empirical research conducted by Grimmett (1989) and Preece (2003) concurs with Mezirow's theory and states that within the framework of transformative learning, learners' assumptions, values, and beliefs are challenged. Consequently, our cultural assumptions and presuppositions have a direct bearing on the meanings derived from these personal lived experiences.

Additionally, Mezirow asserts that transformative pedagogy enhances opportunities for critical self-reflection. Developing a sound understanding of the theory enabled me to underpin my teaching with these six essential practices to foster transformative learning.

> 'transformative learning *offers a theory of learning that is uniquely adult, abstract, idealized, and grounded in the nature of human communication*'

From the late 1990s to the present day, most of my pedagogy has occurred within a group setting in which all students are encouraged to be active learners—experiential learning (Sutton, 2005). However, to enable students to critically reflect upon and challenge their beliefs, assumptions, values, and perhaps prejudices, the learning environment has to be supportive and trusting. For a disposition to change, teacher educators should give deliberate acknowledgement of all players' emotions and feelings—affective learning (Sutton, 2005). Additionally, I am cognizant that transformative learning has the possibility of being time consuming. To become transformative learners, some students require more time to work through this change process of the reconstruction or rejection of reconstruction of lived experiences (Sutton, 2005; Taylor, 2000). Instead of:

merely adapting to changing circumstances by more diligently applying old ways of knowing... students could discover a need to acquire new perspectives in order to gain a more complete understanding of changing events and a higher degree of control over lives. Mezirow, 1995, p.3

> 'for a disposition to change, teacher educators should give deliberate acknowledgement of all players' emotions and feelings—affective learning'

Due to my use of Mezirow's six essential practices and weekly reflective journals with one group of adult students I teach, one of them modeled his practice on my pedagogy. Bob stated:

Your practice of Mezirow's six essential practices was so effective, and I found the template for our weekly reflective journals so effective that I used both these myself in my educative role with intern volunteers following my completion of study at the Ministry Training Centre.

My doctoral findings noted most students use critical self-reflection as a method to examine the broader issues of general practices, rather than as a tool to question or examine their own underlying beliefs or assumptions of their personal practices.

> 'most students use critical self-reflection as a method to examine the broader issues of general practices, rather than as a tool to question or examine their own underlying beliefs or assumptions of their personal practices'

It is not sufficient to examine only the broader issues of practices. Students need to be encouraged to critically reflect about their own orientation to key issues and examine their own underpinning values, beliefs, and assumptions. Therefore, another reflective teaching strategy is that:

it is important for educators to model critical self-reflection especially about contentious and difficult issues, but ensure that the focus of the reflection is on the students.

The following comment demonstrated how I challenged the belief system of a group of adult students.

I remember a specific class discussion where Lindy intentionally challenged the Christian beliefs of the interns. She proposed a question about whether we thought someone living in a remote tribe who'd never heard about God or his provision of salvation in Jesus before they died would go to heaven. I remember the question and ensuing discussion made me feel agitated because some shared beliefs were opposing to what I held at the time. Lindy shared her belief near the end, and although it was contrary to mine at the time I never felt dishonored. In fact, the whole exercise made me realize that I had assumed my belief on this issue from others' convictions and not my own.

Conclusion

Over a period of 40 years I changed from a traditional teacher to a transformative teacher. However, until commencing my Doctor of Teaching, I was not able to cognitively describe the processes which I had progressed through. The critical reflective strategies which changed my pedagogy and are now long established, were purely intuitive. At the time they seemed to be the correct pedagogical changes to implement. This on-going reflective journey has been challenging, frustrating and sometimes, sheer hard work. However, this journey has been worthwhile—especially with the creation of a positive, supportive yet challenging, learning environment for students.

References

Austin, L. (2008). *Developing critical self-reflection with intern volunteers working in a faith-based organisation.* Unpublished doctoral thesis, Charles Darwin University, Darwin, Australia.

Baumgartner, L. (2001). Four adult theories and their implications for practice. *Focus on Basics, 5*(B).

Grimmett, P. (1989). A commentary on Schön's view of reflection. *Journal of Curriculum and Supervision, 5*(1), 19-28.

Henderson, J. (2001). *Reflective teaching professional artistry through inquiry* (3rd ed.). NJ: Prentice-Hall.

Huitt, W. (1998). *Measurement, evaluation, and research: Ways of knowing.* Educational Psychology Interactive. Retrieved from http://chiron.valdosta.edu/whuitt/col/intro/wayknow.html

Humphries, B., & Martin, M. (2000). Unsettling the learning community: from 'dialogue' to difference? *Community, Work & Family, 3*(3), 279-295.

Imel, S. (1992). *Reflective practice in adult education.* Retrieved from http://www.ericfacility.net/ericdigests/ed346319.html

Merriam, S., & Caffarella, R. (1999). *Learning in adulthood: a comprehensive guide* (2nd ed.). San Francisco: Jossey-Bass.

Mezirow, J. (1995). Understanding transformation theory. *Adult Education Quarterly, 44*(4), 222-223.

Mezirow, J. (1998). *The theory and practice of transformative learning: A critical review.* The Ohio State University. Retrieved from http://ericacve.org/mp_taylor_01.asp

O'Connor, A., & Diggins, C. (2002). *On reflection: Reflective practice for early childhood educators.* Aotearoa New Zealand: Open Mind Publishing.

Preece, J. (2003). Education for transformative leadership in Southern Africa. *Journal of Transformative Leadership in Southern Africa, 1*(3), 245-263.

Sutton, I. (2005, November). *Transforming pedagogy in our secondary classroom: Preservice teachers and community-based action learning.* Paper presented at the Global Perspectives in an Integrated Curriculum Conference, Charles Darwin University, Darwin, Australia.

Taylor, E. (2000, October). *Fostering transformative learning in the adult classroom: A review of the empirical studies.* Paper presented at the annual meeting of the International Conference on Transformative Learning, NY.

Willis, P. (2007). Transformative pedagogy for social capital. *Australian Journal of Adult Learning, 47*(3).

Zembylas, M. (2003). Emotions and teacher identity: A post-structural perspective. *Teachers and Teaching: Theory and Practice, 9*(3), 213-238.

Ziegahn, L. (2001). *Reflection and transformation in the intercultural context.* Retrieved from http://www.edst.educ.ubc.ca/aerc/2001/2001ziegahn.htm

It's challenging to build trusting relationships between students and college teachers.
Katherine Rugg

THE ADULT LEARNER IN TRAINING FOR EARLY CHILDHOOD TEACHER EDUCATION

Lily Hok-Neo Wong
Singapore

Dr Lily Wong is the Executive Director of Advent Links-SAUC, an education center for children and family studies. She is an educational psychologist and a professor of psychology and education. She holds a doctorate in Educational Psychology and Counseling from Andrews University in Michigan U.S., and a Bachelor's and Master's in Education from Adventist University of Philippines. Her post-doctorate study and research in complex instruction was from Stanford University, and Quality Infant and Toddler Caregiving from Syracuse University, U.S. As a research assistant at the Hewitt Research Center, Michigan, she screened and summarized research on early childhood education funded by a U.S. Office of Education grant. She has a teacher's credential from the State of California. In Singapore she is accredited as a supervisor and a trainer for preschool education courses. She is a member on a number of policy, ethics and program committees, including MCYS, NCC, SAGE, World Forum International Representative, Scholastic Book Council, Educational Research Association Singapore, AECES, OMEP, NAEYC, APA, and AERA. She has researched and published on various issues concerning family, children, and education. She was awarded the Woman of the Year (Family Life) US, and Long Service Award from the Ministry of Community Development and Sport, Singapore.

> Government regulation on teacher qualification status, in Singapore, as well as in other countries, has changed student teacher demographics.
> Editors

Introduction

Preschools have emerged as core educational institutions in Singapore. They are widely regarded as a much needed and ever increasing phenomenon. Singapore, referred to by her neighbors as a 'little red dot', is a country with a young population—a quarter of its population fall within the range of birth through 14 years of age. Increasingly, preschool provision is seen as a common solution to the problem of how to care for, socialize, and educate young children.

> 'increasingly, preschool provision is seen as a common solution to the problem of how to care for, socialize, and educate young children'

This solution contributes to two further, and related, problems: that of ensuring quality preschool experiences for all children, and of developing a professional workforce able to work within guidelines of quality preschool education. The response in Singapore has been a fast tracking of adults through teacher education programs, necessitating a massive retraining of early childhood education workers. As a result, in the last decade the total percentage of trained and graduated early childhood teachers has moved from 33% to 95%. Further analysis of enrolment statistics for the 1016 graduates from one of the 20 training institutes found that between 2002 and 2007, 72% of those working in the early childhood education industry met Singapore's newly introduced credentialing requirements through attending evening classes. What is more interesting is that the average age of this group was 41.4 years.

> 'what is more interesting is that the average age of this group was 41.4 years'

The reflections in this paper are based on my role and experiences at Advent Links–SAUC, a business arm of the Southeast Asia Union College. Advent Links–SAUC offers certificates, diplomas, advanced diplomas, and graduate diplomas in early childhood education that are accredited by the Ministry of Education, Ministry of Community Development Youth and Sports, and the Preschool Quality Accreditation Committee in Singapore.

A Bachelor of Arts in Childhood and Family Education is offered in collaboration with Edith Cowan University, in Western Australia, while a Master of Arts in Early Childhood Studies is offered in collaboration with the University of East London, in Great Britain. Advent Links-SAUC attracts both student teachers and qualified teachers from a wide variety of cultures and religious backgrounds.

Feedback from quarterly evaluation exercises shows that what motivated student teachers to choose the training program at Advent Links-SAUC was its effectiveness in teaching and learning and its focus on the needs of adult learners. This paper explores the trend towards older adult learners becoming the most likely teachers of very young children and argues that early childhood teacher educators, both in Singapore and elsewhere, ought to carefully consider the specific needs of adult learners in the development of effective teacher education programs. It outlines a range of instructional design strategies aimed to account for these specific needs.

Customizing instructional strategies for adult learners

In my conversations with student teachers, it appears that while both mature and teenage student teachers have similar views on the role of preschool, they have different views on what it means to be a teacher in early childhood. For instance, more mature adult learners perceive that teaching and caring for young children is not a *sexy* job. Teacher educators, therefore, need to consider their andragogical approach (see for instance Knowles, 1984), in order to ensure that greater successes may be achieved.

> 'more mature adult learners perceive that teaching and caring for young children is not a *sexy* job'

The adult student comes to the learning experience with a unique set of background experiences, needs, desires, and anxieties. Hence, while the main components of curriculum design may remain consistent in terms of objectives, subject matter, teaching strategies, methodology, logistics, communications, and evaluation, training the adult learner calls for a different approach—one that is more sensitive to the different needs of adult learners. In Singapore, two key elements that engender this uniqueness are age and existing (often extensive) experience in working with children. These characteristics may differ from those of younger student teachers (mostly in their late teens) who, though they finished their training from a local polytechnic, did not immediately enter the workforce in the child care or preschool setting.

The mandatory curriculum framework provided by the Singapore Government through the Preschool Qualification Accreditation Committee remains undifferentiated for all adults. In other words, the particular needs of adult learners are not considered in the development of the teacher education curriculum framework. This attempts to ensure uniform standards and expected outcomes for the profession. However, when the details of each curricular component are closely examined, the specific needs, preferences, and desires of adult students demand not only an understanding of their learning styles, but a healthy respect for their individuality as adult students. Likewise, while the academic requirements remain similar, there is often a vast difference in the mindset and psychological makeup in adult learners taking early childhood education classes. Perhaps then, the academic requirements should be different.

The key to effective teacher education lies in customizing the instructional strategies according to the composition of each class. To be successful, the teacher educator has to:

- understand each unique adult learner intimately
- recognize the common threads or characteristics that bind the entire group, and
- adjust instruction and learning encounters for their greatest benefit.

'the key to effective teacher education lies in customizing the instructional strategies according to the composition of each class'

This knowledge enables close interaction between adult learners and teacher educators and encourages students to grow intellectually, socially-emotionally, and spiritually as they form friendships and make life choices.

Respecting the diversity of adult learners

Teacher educators should understand the needs of all learners, regardless of age, and their preferred learning styles—visual, verbal, participatory, or simple instruction—thus making it necessary for them to facilitate a variety of learning activities, or teaching styles. However, adult learners may vary in the extent to which they are:

- intrinsically motivated, therefore making teacher-selected rewards rather ineffective
- creative, independent, and self-directed, thus making teacher-oriented lectures rather boring or unchallenging
- cognitively complex, thus making learning easier or more difficult in relation to the tasks and assignments
- practical and real-life oriented, and having less patience with, or interest in, theory or details
- interested in short-term solutions rather than questions, puzzles, or issues—that is, the extent to which they are willing to invest time
- operating within personal philosophical frameworks, intellectual biases, or religious prejudices, that make learning more difficult to break through.

'teacher educators should understand the needs of all learners, regardless of age, and their preferred learning styles—visual, verbal, participatory, or simple instruction'

The list can go on endlessly. One key theme that develops out of these characteristics is that of the teacher educator acting as a facilitator of learning rather than a transmitter of facts, knowledge and skills. With this in mind, during the planning process the teacher educator needs to analyze the backgrounds of the adult learners, to develop the most appropriate learning strategies, and instructional methodologies. Thus, the teacher educator provides for a variety of learning strategies and options that meet and appeal to adult learners.

This opens conversations as to whether teacher education programs should be streamed according to criteria such as age, gender, life experience.

Editors

I like the word 'genuine' when we are talking about mentors.

Rachel Tong

These characteristics illustrate the complexity evident in all learners, as well as the variance that may be apparent in different cultural contexts.

Editors

Recognizing that adult learners vary greatly in their pace of learning, learning experiences must allow for different levels and rates of comprehension, application, analysis, synthesis, and evaluation. Flexible schedules and multiple levels of expected competencies and achievements make for more effective andragogy.

Success depends on what the adult learner takes rather than what the teacher educator gives. Based on an understanding of adult learners' profiles, self-concepts, readiness, motivations, and learning orientations, the teacher educator shapes different experiences that help the adult learner to overcome personal barriers. In this regard, the notion of 'Kiasu' is relevant for describing the partnership of learning and teaching of adult learners and teacher educators. The common Chinese dialect has three 'Ks' that serve as the underpinning knowledge of the adult learning behavior:

- Kiasu (afraid to lose out)
- Kiabo (fear of getting nothing), and
- Kiasee (afraid of dying for something).

'success depends on what the adult learner takes rather than what the teacher educator gives'

> 'Kiasu' illustrates that for andragogical approaches to be meaningful and effective, there is a need to account for cultural 'underpinnings'.
>
> Editors

These three factors sum up the teaching and learning partnership for adult learners in a society where meritocracy is the underlying ideology of education. They reflect the cultural and linguistic diversity of adult learners in Singapore. One implication of Kiasu for teacher educators relates to the adult learner's self-assessment. It is important, for instance, to guide adult learners to compare their learning results with their own self-imposed goals and criteria, rather than peer-to-peer comparisons.

A word perhaps should be said about allowing for differences in retention as well as the application of concepts. Adult learners tend to make better sense of materials and ideas that are clearly relevant to their lives. They tend to develop the practical applications in what they learn through reflective learning—taking into consideration the interactions between content, process, and premise. They prefer to learn well rather than fast (depth versus speed), and retain the knowledge longer as a result of their personal involvement rather than what they are told (others' perspectives).

Finally, it is important to consider the maintenance of a safe emotional environment for adult learners. For instance, adults require space to answer questions and practice skills without fear of failure, ridicule, or violation of confidentiality. While it is vital that teacher educators open up ethical dilemmas and seek best practices to resolve them, it is equally important to make provision for avoidance or handling of topics that cause emotional or moral distress.

'while it is vital that teacher educators open up ethical dilemmas and seek best practices to resolve them, it is equally important to make provision for avoidance or handling of topics that cause emotional or moral distress'

Promoting a fair and equitable environment for honest self-assessment is more than simply a pedagogical imperative, it helps to bring out the true impact and meaning of professionalism. However, it is easy to drift into debates that can very quickly get out of hand and result in embarrassing situations For this reason, planners of teacher education programs need to approach the subjects without prejudice, remain honest, fair, ethical, and transparent, while also maintaining a high moral-ethical professional position at all times. Interventions should be planned to avert or pre-empt the different unexpected consequences of dealing with sensitive issues and questions.

Conclusion

Andragogical approaches remain theoretical or conceptual until they are put to test in the classroom. Teacher educators, equipped with lesson plans that cater to different learning styles, can vary learning activities to meet the different needs of specific learners more effectively. This is especially the case when adjustments are based on knowledge of the preferences and needs of the adult learners. Here are four recommendations that I would like conclude with:

- respect diversities, especially with regards to age and learning styles

- adapt different learning strategies and materials to meet the needs and goals of the adult learners

- vary learning activities and delivery methods to engage each individual learner

- provide care for the learner's emotional and physical safety, and have a fair and equitable learning environment.

References

Knowles, M.S. (Ed). (1984). *Andragogy in action: Applying modern principles of adult education.* New York: Jossey Bass.

Continuing the conversations

Teachers, as adults, are also learners. This chapter positions relationships and reflection as critical aspects of being adult learners. If we are to be those passionate, emotional beings that Andy Hargreaves speaks of, who fill our teaching with *pleasure, creativity, challenge, and joy* (1998, p. 559), then we need to be relationally connected to others, our communities, and ourselves.

As Nel Noddings (2003) points out, happy schools and early childhood centres are places in which there are adults who recognise the aim of education and life itself is happiness. Allowing ourselves to be mentored, offering ourselves to mentor, and opening ourselves to critical self-reflection, all contribute to this. Such excursions into the life of the self and the lives of others need not be tortuous, but indeed can be enriched by celebrating the pleasures from both personal and professional experiences. Erica McWilliam puts it nicely when she says:

I simply think we can learn something about the lived conditions in which teaching and learning takes place by thinking about the pleasures that are available to us as teachers—how we explain them and how we feel them. McWilliam, 1999, p. ix

The lived conditions in which teaching and learning occur encompass the whole person, including their thinking, feeling, and beliefs, as well as the life experiences that contribute to shaping these. This chapter, then, highlights that it is not theories and concepts of adult learning, in themselves, that are essential to early childhood teacher education. Rather, it is the nurturing of relationships through which we show our openness and responsiveness to each learner.

The next chapter continues this conversation by drawing upon the contexts of early childhood teacher education when this is presented online. In a simple sense, this both amplifies as well as reconfigures aspects of this relationality in teaching and learning, and helps us further appreciate what relationship means in early childhood teacher education.

References

Gibbs, C. J. (2006). *To be a teacher: Journeys towards authenticity.* Auckland, New Zealand: Pearson Education.

Hargreaves, A. (1998). Emotions of teaching and emotional change. In A. Hargreaves, M. Fullan, & D. Hopkins, *International handbook of educational change* (pp. 558-575). Dordrecht, Netherlands: Kluwer Academic Publishers.

McWilliam, E. (1999). *Pedagogical pleasures.* New York: Peter Lang.

Noddings, N. (2003). *Happiness and education.* New York: Cambridge University Press.

Palmer, P. J. (1998). *The courage to teach: Exploring the inner landscapes of a teacher's life.* San Francisco: Jossey Bass.

CHAPTER 5
Conversations on learning online

Yet the very challenges associated with developing, implementing, and evaluating online and distance learning are perhaps the very factors which contribute to the potential of distance learning for engendering meaningful educational experiences for learners. The 'tyranny of distance' is a challenge to the educator to think about not only how to get things right, but what are the right things to get. Gibbons, 2006, p. 2

Online early childhood teacher education is widely regarded as a positive contribution to early childhood teacher education, and the development of the early childhood profession. In the United States, online programs have been highlighted for their significant contribution to a national need for early childhood teachers (Education Commission of the States, 2002). More than simply fulfilling a perceived need for more qualified early childhood educators, online early childhood teacher education provides the very possibility for some student teachers to study and earn a qualification whilst remaining in their communities and most importantly in their early childhood centres.

The conversations in this chapter narrate challenging and successful journeys in the development of online learning for early childhood teacher education. The chapter begins with reflections upon the immense difference online learning can make for the lives of early childhood teachers.

Rose Davies begins these conversations. Her paper is entitled *Learning online: Experiences and challenges of including the excluded in higher education in the Caribbean*. In this paper, Rose draws upon the voices of students in a Master of Education in Leadership in Early Childhood Development program in evidencing the value of online learning for students in remote communities.

The chapter then considers a flexible delivery program that was developed in Australia through the prompting of student teachers. This paper by Louise Hard, Wyverne Smith, Melanie Angel, and Genna Smith is entitled *Developing leadership self-belief in early childhood preservice teachers: Flexible learning approaches*. They discuss the development of an online component of an early childhood leadership course, identifying both challenges faced and benefits realized. Their focus on both leadership and flexible delivery of course content emphasizes the widening scope of online learning literature, and the potential to provide different ways of thinking about, and implementing, essential elements of early childhood teacher education.

Judy Goth-Owens' paper is entitled *The power of relationships online in early childhood teacher education*. She provides a deeper look at the value of online communities in contributing to student teachers' development. Her conversation emphasizes the role of the program, and the teacher educator, in creating a vibrant online discussion forum that enables the student teacher community to develop important reflective and communicative skills.

Finally, Julie Whittaker and Katrina Ludeman recount the first steps of developing a specialized early childhood education web-enhanced mode of early childhood teacher education. Their paper is entitled *Moving forward by looking back: Piloting a web-enhanced teacher education program*. The immense value of piloting a program with a student teacher cohort, and listening carefully to the voices of student teachers, is highlighted in the development of discussion forum capacity for New Zealand Tertiary College's eLearning platform.

Together these papers provide multiple perspectives on online learning in early childhood teacher education. Following are some prompts to invite conversations around this significant area of development in teacher education.

Beginning the conversations

The papers in this chapter identify and discuss many of the positive contributions of online learning to early childhood teacher education. In addition, they invite critical reflection on our assumptions regarding optimal learning environments, both face-to-face and online. Conversations on online learning as technology for educating teachers are not all glowing in their commendations and aspirations. Many concerns are raised given assumptions about the nature of best education (generally) and teacher education (specifically) practices. Just one concern is the absence of the face-to-face contact between teacher and learner.

However, many of the criticisms of online learning are far too certain of the benefits of a face-to-face reality (see for instance Gibbons, 2006). In other words, they idealise more traditional modes of learning. It might be more appropriate to draw upon the development of online learning to reflect upon many assumptions regarding what counts as good teacher education.

The following questions may help in reflecting upon the potential of online learning to effect positive transformations to early childhood teacher education.

- In what ways is relationality evident in online learning?

- How can relationality be both accounted for and enhanced in early childhood teacher education programs?

- In what ways do our values and beliefs about modes of communication and interaction impact upon our design and delivery of teacher education programs?

- How do our views on technology influence the ways in which we engage in teaching and learning?

LEARNING ONLINE: EXPERIENCES AND CHALLENGES OF INCLUDING THE EXCLUDED IN HIGHER EDUCATION IN THE CARIBBEAN

Rose Davies
Jamaica

 *Rose Davies is passionate about early childhood education generally, but even more excited about the developments and prospects for the sector in Jamaica presently. She has a Bachelor's degree from University of the West Indies (UWI); Master degree from Erikson Institute, Chicago, and a PhD in Education from the UWI, Jamaica. Rose has been working in the field of early childhood for over 35 years and has experience as teacher, centre director, training coordinator in this field, both in the United States and Jamaica. She is presently employed as senior lecturer with tenure at the Institute of Education, UWI, Jamaica, is Chief External Examiner for early childhood education in teachers' colleges, and also responsible for overseeing the development and monitoring of standards and quality of the Early Childhood Diploma program offered in teachers' colleges. She has been influential in the development of Bachelor and Master level courses in ECE at the UWI; teaches in Master's degree programs at UWI, as well as for the University of South Florida's degree program offered through a local college. Her research interests are in teacher preparation, development, and performance, especially at the early childhood level. Rose has published in local and international peer-reviewed journals. She has served on the Early Childhood Commission of Jamaica and other boards concerned with child welfare and development, and has co-directed internationally funded projects in ECE in Jamaica.*

Introduction

Within the English-speaking Caribbean, access to tertiary level education has always been significantly less than for other levels of the education system. In 1997, only 7% of school graduates were enrolled in tertiary level education (Leo-Rhynie, 2007). The Heads of Government of the Caribbean Community (CARICOM) at that time indicated that by year 2005, this percentage should be increased to at least 15%.

Tertiary institutions responded by increasing the diversity of programs offered and the pathways for entry into and exit from them, as well as by expanding the range of modalities through which programs could be delivered. These initiatives were expected to increase access and attract a broader base of clients seeking to enrol in tertiary education.

The University of the West Indies in the Caribbean

The University of the West Indies (UWI) is the largest tertiary level institution serving the English-speaking Caribbean with three university campuses located in Jamaica, Trinidad and Tobago, and Barbados, and several university centers in the non-campus territories. In its Strategic Plan for 2002-2007, the UWI signaled its intent to expand tertiary enrolment by broadening its client base through more flexible matriculation arrangements and diversified program delivery modalities. The first effort to offer courses online at the UWI was initiated in 1998 by the Institute of Education (IOE) at the School of Education. These courses were trialed and by the year 2001 were considered to be sufficiently successful for the UWI to give full permission for the School of Education to offer the Master of Education in Teacher Education solely online. Other programs were gradually added including the Master of Education in Leadership in Early Childhood Development which commenced in 2004 (Miller, 2005).

Including the excluded in tertiary education

Until the first experiment with online teaching, most courses at the UWI were taught in the face-to-face mode with the exception of a very small number offered via print-based learning materials. The face-to-face delivery mode excluded a large group of individuals interested in pursuing tertiary level studies, but whose personal circumstances were not accommodated by the face-to-face approach. This group included:

- individuals who were unable to enrol in a fulltime program because of the economic need to remain gainfully employed while pursuing studies
- individuals whose family and work responsibilities limited their ability to participate in out-of-home activities, and
- individuals whose geographical location restricted their access to tertiary institutions. Geography is a particularly relevant factor for many no-campus countries in the Caribbean where there is no access to graduate university programs other than online, or a limited offering through University Centers (Evans, 2007).

> 'geography is a particularly relevant factor for many no-campus countries in the Caribbean where there is no access to graduate university programs other than online'

The most significant role of introducing online technology at the UWI, therefore, was the opening up of doors of opportunity for thousands of eligible students who would otherwise not have been able to realize their dream of tertiary education. The introduction of online programs has brought about a dramatic increase in student enrolments at the UWI. The convenience and flexibility of being able to participate in higher education from home base has been enthusiastically embraced by the formerly excluded group.

> 'the most significant role of introducing online technology was the opening up of doors of opportunity for thousands of eligible students who would otherwise not have been able to realize their dream of tertiary education'

The Master of Education in Leadership in Early Childhood Development

The Master of Education in Leadership in Early Childhood Development (MELECD) program offered at UWI was developed in response to the dearth of trained leadership in Early Childhood Development (ECD) in the Caribbean. With donor support from the Inter-American Development Bank (IADB) in 2001, the UWI embarked on the task of developing a Master level program to address the need for qualified leaders for the ECD sectors of countries within the region.

The MELECD program aims to provide existing and potential leaders in ECD with a base of relevant knowledge and skills necessary to advance the development of local ECD sectors (including, for example, advocacy, administration, human resource management, curriculum and training, research, project development, and current issues and trends in ECD). Issues and Trends in ECD in the Caribbean—one of the required courses—is the subject of this paper's reflections. The first cohort of 25 very eager and enthusiastic student teachers started this course with me in January 2005.

The desire of students to be included in a tertiary education program, however, brought its own challenges as they encountered the realities of adjusting to an unaccustomed mode of learning, balancing the unanticipated demands and events of home, work, and community, and managing their time effectively to meet the semester requirements of the various courses. This paper, then, focuses on the challenges and positive experiences of being a first time online teacher educator working with a group of first time online students; and examines the role of technology in the delivery of this particular course as well as the broader implications for future development of the UWI's online product. In doing this I draw on current literature on online education and make reference to other information sources including e-mail correspondence between the student teachers and myself, online conference discussions and completed course evaluation questionnaires.

> As we meet the needs of students previously excluded from accessing teacher education, there may still be a remaining group, or indeed a new group, of potential candidates who remain excluded for a variety of reasons—e.g., connectivity, access to computers. However, while we may wish to give computers to the unconnected, this does not mean that we necessarily should.
>
> Editors

Facing the realities of online learning— Some challenges

Before discussing the course and its challenges in some detail, it is important to highlight the positivity with which both the students and I welcomed this new learning experience. As the course teacher educator, this was my first experience of teaching online. The *Virtual-U*, developed at Simon Fraser University in Canada, was the system chosen by the School of Education as the platform for offering online programs. In the introductory online conference where student teachers introduced themselves and shared their expectations of the course, I was very encouraged by the level of motivation and enthusiasm they expressed.

'I was very encouraged by the level of motivation and enthusiasm they expressed'

What more could a teacher desire? The following e-mail sent to me by one of the students aptly captures the spirit of the group toward their academic venture:

> My colleagues told me to e-mail to you my dreams and aspirations concerning this present course. First of all I give God thanks for you and your vision, because now you have turned my dream into a reality. For the past six years I have wanted to study early childhood education and my excitement about this course is overwhelming. I intend to finish this course by the grace of God within two years.

The distance learning delivery model

In the literature on distance education, Taylor (cited in Reddy & Srivastava, 2002), identifies five models associated with delivery techniques:

- printed materials only
- multimedia, which includes printed study guides, selected readings, videotapes, and audio tapes and computer based conferences
- telelearning, which is based on the use of information technologies, such as audio conferencing, audiographic communication systems, video conferencing, and broadcast television and radio
- flexible learning which combines high quality interactive multimedia with access to an extensive range of teaching-learning resources and enhanced interactivity through computer-mediated communications offered through the internet, and
- intelligent flexible learning model which involves the use of automated response systems to reduce the variable costs of computer-mediated communication.

The *Virtual U* system falls somewhere between the first two models, as a high level of print materials is involved and little or no audiographic or videographic materials are accommodated. This was one of the first challenges the student teachers noted in their regular e-mails. They complained that although relevant and interesting, the readings were *too much, a tall order, and overwhelming*.

Technological malfunctioning

Student teachers and course teacher educators alike were given orientation in the use of the *Virtual U* system and were also provided with guidelines for necessary upgrading of their own personal computers to make them adequate for what would be required for online interaction during courses. However, despite this, the *Virtual U* technology had problems during the semester that the course was offered. The conferences were occasionally inaccessible to some students (mostly the non-Jamaicans); the U-Chat feature functioned only sporadically and some student teachers frequently had difficulty accessing files or downloading and printing them from the computer. In many cases, student teachers discovered and acknowledged that these problems were due to their own failure to bring their computers up to the standard required by the course, for example, by installing Acrobat Reader™. They were forced to take remedial action in order to keep up with the pace of the course units. The e-mails came to me at a frantic pace relaying their frustrations:

My computer just went crazy and it took me 45 minutes to get it working again.

Virus took up my computer so bad I have been unable to use it, I have lost files and some of the information I saved are not available to me and has caused me much stress.

The materials from the pdf files cannot be copied.

This is so frustrating; remind me never to sign up for another online course again!

The student teachers' frustrations were understandable. Difficulties at home with logging into sessions or using e-mail at times made them feel isolated from the group and when they were finally able to log in, they felt overwhelmed by all the work that had piled up for them to complete. These student teachers were seldom able to submit

---

Student teachers' responses that readings were 'too much', 'a tall order', and 'overwhelming' raise interesting curriculum and pedagogical challenges for online teacher educators.

Editors

assignments on the given deadline dates and were constantly writing to apologize and request additional time. They expressed a strong sense of guilt for not being able to keep up with their assignments.

In addition to the technology challenges, some student teachers faced a range of personal problems that would have been a justifiable reason for them to abandon their studies. Some of these situations are shared below.

> 'some students faced a range of personal problems that would have been justifiable reason for them to abandon their studies'

Personal challenges

Student teachers' discussions posted on asynchronous conferences were very revealing and supportive of each other. Personal events such as a student teacher giving birth, the marriage of someone's child, or the death of a parent, were all openly shared and received responses of congratulations or condolences. Some student teachers sent e-mails to me explaining the severity of their personal crises being experienced. One student teacher, who later dropped out, had marital problems which ended in divorce. The poignant story of one student living in a violent community, the effects on her family, and her struggle to remain in the program is captured in this brief excerpt from one of her e-mails:

I am sorry about posting my assignment a little late. Last night I was afraid to have the lights on in my house so late due to the extreme violence which has taken over my community. For the last few weeks it is the last thing I hear at night and the first in the morning. Gang violence has taken over so much so that half of the residents have abandoned their homes. I cannot move right away because of my financial commitment to this program. I will try my best to keep up with the work, but when I get home from work I do not have enough daylight time to get the readings done and to work online. Many times I have to abandon my work to comfort my children. I am really in a tight spot.

Two student teachers from the same country had to cope with a natural disaster involving severe flooding of entire communities. One of these students had additional difficulties on the job in which she as head of the Municipal Day Care Services, was fighting with her government to prevent the closing of three day care centers that were well needed in their respective communities. Simultaneously she had to cope with the hospitalization of her husband and children on account of illnesses resulting from the flood conditions. Her challenges were enormous, but she still tried to keep connected to the course. She used a local Internet café to keep up with the course activities as her own home had been flooded out. In spite of it all she wrote this to me in an e-mail:

Please whisper a prayer for me wherever you are as I am in need of strength and prayers to cope with the challenging situations I am faced with at this time. I do not intend to give up. I'm really determined to continue the program regardless of the challenges, because I believe the knowledge acquired will help me to bring about change in the situation.

> 'please whisper a prayer for me wherever you are as I am in need of strength and prayers to cope with the challenging situations I am faced with at this time'

Teacher education needs to open spaces for our lived experiences, including hardships, whether face-to-face or online.

Editors

I have found the knowledge gained to be very useful in helping me deal with various situations in my work environment.

Other students were challenged by their own lack of organization and lack of self-discipline which interfered with their approach to learning tasks. They shared all these sentiments with me in their e-mails. During their moments of frustration, their e-mails expressed a yearning for the face-to-face approach, which they felt would allow them to be more spontaneous in discussions, allow them to get immediate clarification or feedback on a matter, and so on.

Helping students to 'hang in'—the facilitator's role

As facilitator, I constantly responded to student teachers' letters to reassure them that they had the ability to complete the course and to encourage them to be courageous and persistent. I suggested ways that they could organize and manage their time to allow periods for doing their readings and assignments. I invited them to send me e-mails about their problems and concerns as often as they needed to. At times I sent out a brief general letter of encouragement and reassurance to all student teachers. Their appreciation of these timely notes was evident in expressions such as:

Your letter was just what I needed at this time or, Thanks for your very warm and supportive response to my problems. You have encouraged me to go on.

What was most surprising to me was the determination expressed by student teachers to complete the program in spite of the personal and other challenges they faced. They seemed, for the most part, to be intrinsically motivated to make use of the opportunity to access tertiary level studies which had for so long eluded them.

But I had reason to believe that the long desired dream to study at the tertiary level was only part of the explanation for the students' tenacity. I sought to identify the positive experiences that could have accounted for the other part of the story. These came more clearly to light as I read and analyzed the information contained in the e-mails, conferences, and course evaluations. As I engaged with more of the literature on online learning, I found that many of the positive outcomes I had discovered were supported in the research of online experiences of others.

Some positives of learning online

Coping with stress

Using the online mode played a role in helping the student teachers to cope with their personal fears and stresses. They seemed to derive a high level of comfort from being able to express their personal fears and concerns by writing about them and sharing them with the group in e-mails or conference postings.

> 'students seemed to derive a high level of comfort from being able to express their personal fears and concerns by writing about them and sharing them with the group in e-mails or conference postings'

Lindh and Soames (2004) concluded from research conducted on an online university course that online students benefit from closer interactions with their facilitator and peer group members than students in face-to-face classrooms. They explain that:

unlike the traditional classroom setting, where a student would be considered as dominating the class discussion to the possible annoyance of other students, or feel inhibited in disclosing uncertainties, misunderstandings, etc. the student engaged in e-mailing has privacy to air one's thoughts and can share concern with the tutor in confidence.
Lindh & Soames, 2004, p. 132

I found this to be true, as every student teacher (as long as there were no technological difficulties) shared their views, feelings about many things in personal e-mail correspondence with me.

Building a learning community

Some of the activities in the course were built around work in small groups. Student teachers fashioned their own ways of interacting and working together online to complete group projects. As they grappled with their various personal and program challenges, they learned to rely on each other more and more for support, both in the small and larger groups. Using the online technology led them to forge their own support structures to help each other cope with emerging challenges during the course. Their interactions exemplified those of cooperative learning. An example of student teachers pulling together to overcome a difficulty they were experiencing with another course, is seen in the following e-mail exchange:

Student 1
Hi colleagues, I am using this medium to contact you all about the accounting course module. I don't know about you but I am having difficulties with the course. I am requesting (just a suggestion) that we begin to share our strengths and weaknesses in conferences so that we will be better prepared for the exam.

Student 2
I too am having difficulty with that component of the course and have made up my mind for the worse. But I am convinced that if we can do as you suggest, we can stand a chance of succeeding. Thank you for taking the initiative.

Student 3
I share the same sentiments with you both. I am having grave problems with this module. This course should be taught face-to-face… I am willing to share whenever we are ready to study.

'student teachers fashioned their own ways of interacting and working together online to complete group projects'

In the research conducted by Lindh and Soames (2004), students found working in groups to be the biggest problem. Student teachers enrolled in my course found group work to be very helpful to them. They had formed a learning community among themselves and relied on it for support when needed. One stated in response to the course evaluation question, 'What strategy or method of the course did you find most helpful and why?':

I found the group work experiences and the conferences very useful. I was able to learn about individuals in a way that I would not normally learn about them. I was also able to interact with them more than usual and learn from each other. I learned to compromise with others through group work.

In spite of the negative response to group work expressed by their research subjects, Lindh and Soames (2004) recommended small group work as a critical component of

How do you know a student's soul if you've not seen them? The handwriting, voice, facial expressions are all telling of a person's character.
Iwonna Florczyk

Requiring student teachers to take the time to write responses demands that they create space and time for reflection as well as the production of the response.
Editors

both online and campus-based programs, as interactive activities within groups allow deep learning to take place.

Quality of learning resources and assignments

Fox and Donohue (2006), in a very insightful paper on trends and practices in early childhood teacher education online, raise the issues of quality and efficacy of such programs. They make the point that work must be done to improve the standards and effective practices *to ensure online teacher education leads to increased knowledge, enhanced teacher performance, and improved outcomes for young children* (p. 30). They emphasize the importance of relevance of content to online student teachers' learning experiences, and its practicability.

> 'work must be done to improve the standards and effective practices to ensure online teacher education leads to increased knowledge, enhanced teacher performance, and improved outcomes for young children'

In student teachers' evaluations, the quality and relevance of the course materials and assignments received the highest ratings by the majority of course evaluation questionnaire participants (12 out of 19 questionnaires returned). Follow-up comments indicated that the course materials offered student teachers practical and helpful support in the various tasks they had to do for the course as well as in their own job situations. Most of the student teachers were not practicing as classroom teachers as they were now in leadership positions. Some of their comments are noted below:

The course materials provided a wealth of information which assisted me in responding to conference discussions, doing assignments, and providing information for further research.

The materials provided were very relevant and served to stimulate my interest to further research and widen my knowledge base in the subject area.

I was able to apply what was learned to what I am engaged in at present.

The materials were very useful and relevant to the Caribbean situation.

Two of the three course assignments could be very easily applied to the practical work situation of student teachers. One assignment required them to prepare an advocacy package containing information and strategies they would use in advocating to achieve a particular goal. They had great fun doing this assignment as they had so many situations requiring strong advocacy to effect change. They were able to select a real case from their own program or community as the basis for their advocacy work and prepared materials that they could put to effective use immediately.

In recognition of the role they would have to play as leaders in their community, the student teachers learned how to develop project proposals. Their final assignment involved developing a project proposal for funding to improve an identified area of need in their ECD program or community. Again, this task was most welcomed by them. In at least two instances, student teachers refined and submitted their final proposals to funding agencies and in at least one of these instances funding was approved to improve a program for children with special needs.

People are often unaware of the fact that they are self-reflecting.

Leigh Reddish

Personal development

In spite of the difficulties student teachers encountered in using the online technology, they derived some benefits in their own personal development, beyond increasing knowledge in the content area. Some of these benefits included:

Improved skills in computer technology

Many of the student teachers rated themselves poor with regard to their readiness to use technology at the beginning of the course. However, in order to keep up with the course activities, they were forced to improve their computer skills, which showed significant improvement by the end of the course.

> 'many of the student teachers rated themselves poor with regard to their readiness to use technology at the beginning of the course'

Increased self-discipline and self-regulation

During the early sections of the course, some of the student teachers continually sent me e-mails deriding themselves for lacking self-discipline and focus. However, with continued encouragement from the facilitator and peers, they showed significant improvement in achieving better control and management of their time and had improved in the areas of self-discipline and self-regulation by the end of the course.

> 'with continued encouragement from facilitator and peers, they showed significant improvement in achieving better control and management of their time and had improved in the areas of self-discipline and self-regulation'

Less inhibited participation

Online contributions of course participants to asynchronous conference discussions were very rich as each student teacher freely expressed views for or against the topic. In a regular face-to-face session the contributions might not have been as balanced as there are always student teachers who dominate the discussion and student teachers who are more reserved.

Implications for future development of UWI's online programs

Overall, the Issues and Trends course received a very positive evaluation by student teachers. Some of the factors that contributed to this have been presented in this paper. The lessons learned in terms of what online student teachers appreciate and find helpful within our local university context are also clear.

> 'one or two successful courses do not an effective online program make'

However, one or two successful courses do not an effective online program make. There are several other courses with several other teacher educators for the MELECD and other programs.

The UWI must move quickly to establish and standardize best practices in all its e-learning offerings because in an increasingly competitive environment; students are free to choose or refuse program offerings based on their perceived quality or lack thereof. The implications for improving the UWI online product must revolve around the following urgently needed activities:

- setting standards for all online delivered courses at UWI
- selecting and training teacher educators who are willing to provide consistency of quality in online teaching
- investing in more up-to-date and versatile online delivery platforms
- investing in the development of interactive materials and teaching aids, grounded in local cultural and practical experiences for all courses, and
- increasing support systems for online students.

Conclusion

This paper has examined the experiences of a highly motivated cohort of student teachers who for the first time were able to access tertiary education through online technology at the UWI. Although they faced challenges with using the technology and also in their personal lives, most of them pursued the course to the end. Learning by way of online technology played an important role in learner enhancement that went far beyond expanding their knowledge base. Learning online fostered the development of positive attributes that included improvements in:

- computer competencies
- self-discipline and self-regulation
- appreciation for co-operative learning, and
- greater willingness to share views and make contributions to group discussion.

The role of teacher educator, and quality of course materials and assignments were also seen to be important factors in motivating and retaining students in an online course. In order to enhance its own online product, the UWI will need to invest resources in improving the human, material, and technological infrastructure on which quality online programs can be built.

References

Fox, S., & Donohue, C. (2006). Trends and promising practices in early childhood teacher education online. The view from New Zealand. *He Kupu, 11*(1), 29-34.

Evans, H. (2007). Information and communications technology in professional development of teacher educators and teachers. In M. Hamilton & A. Perry (Eds.), *The UWI Quality Education Forum, 13,* Jan; Jamaica: University of the West Indies.

Leo-Rhynie, E. (2007). Prospects and challenges of the tertiary education sector in Jamaica. In K. Hall & R. Cameron (Eds.), *Higher education: Caribbean perspectives*. Jamaica: Ian Randle Publishers.

Lindh, J., & Soames, C. (2004) A dual perspective on an online university course. *Electronic Journal on e-learning, 2*(1), 129-134. Retrieved from http://www.ejel.org.

Miller, E., (2005). Teacher education and information and communication technology. In E. Miller, J. Tucker, & H. Morris (Eds.), *EduVision: Enhancing teaching and learning through partnership and technology innovation: Institute of Education, University of the West Indies*. Jamaica.

Reddy, V. V., & Srivastava, M. (2002). From face to face to virtual tutoring: Exploring the potential of E-learning. In *Motivating & Retaining Adult Learners Online* (pp. 11-22); Virtual University Gazette. Retrieved from http://www.geteducated.com

DEVELOPING LEADERSHIP SELF-BELIEF IN EARLY CHILDHOOD PRESERVICE TEACHERS: FLEXIBLE LEARNING APPROACHES

Louise Hard
Australia

Wyverne Smith
Australia

Melanie Angel
Australia

Genna Smith
Australia

Wyverne Smith is an Early Childhood Education lecturer in the Murray School of Education, Charles Sturt University (CSU), Albury, New South Wales, Australia. She teaches a variety of subjects including 'Leadership and Management in Early Childhood' and 'Wellness and Well-Being'. Before coming to CSU, Wyverne worked at the University of Southern Queensland and in leadership positions at a wide variety of early childhood educational settings.

Louise Hard is currently the Head of the Murray School of Education at Charles Sturt University. This role involves managing and leading a school of 17 academic staff and five administrative staff serving over 400 on-campus and 13,000 distance students. She teaches in both internal and distance education subjects in the Bachelor of Education (Early Childhood and Primary) and the Bachelor of Teaching (Birth to Five Years). She co-teaches with Wyverne Smith the course Leadership and Management in Early Childhood. Her doctorate focused on leadership in the field of early childhood education and care and was titled, 'How is leadership understood and enacted in the field of early childhood education and care?' Her research interests include leadership, wellness and wellbeing, and administration.

Melanie Angel decided to attend university four years ago, with a life-long dream to obtain a degree. Her love for and interest in children and their development led her to complete a Bachelor of Education (Early Childhood) at Charles Sturt University. Her engagement and effort in her studies resulted in commending marks and acceptance into a Graduate Program for the Australian Public Service. Whilst she will be taking a break from teaching children in a classroom situation, she hopes that her position with the Federal Government will lead her into working for the Department of Education in the future.

Genna Smith was a student of Charles Sturt University. She has recently completed a double degree of Bachelor of Early Childhood Teaching (0-5years) and Bachelor of Speech and Hearing Science. She completed her studies with distinction and gained employment at a local child care centre. Within this position she is further developing her understanding of early childhood education and the issues that surround working in this field. She is preparing to undertake the Junior Preschool Team Leader position in January 2009.

To be an on-line teacher you need to be an on-line learner.

Rachel Talapati

Introduction

The field of Early Childhood Education and Care (ECEC) is such that often teachers are required to move into formal leadership roles early in their careers. It is understandable, therefore, that preparation for leadership has received increasing attention in recent years (Ebbeck & Waniganayake, 2003; Rodd, 2006). One challenge is to engage student teachers in theory related to leadership while also developing skills in management. In particular, student teachers need to build the capacity to engage in leadership activity, mindful of the professional contexts they enter.

'one challenge is to engage student teachers in theory related to leadership while also developing skills in management'

In this paper we acknowledge that management and leadership skills are both important for early childhood professionals. Such an interpretation is pertinent to the ECEC field as many positional leadership roles, for example, directors of long day and preschool services, have both management and leadership responsibilities (Ebbeck & Waniganayake, 2003). This, however, is not to suggest that leadership opportunities are absent from non-managerial positions.

Leadership research indicates some specific challenges for aspiring leaders in the ECEC field including professional identity, workplace culture, and notions of team-based leadership (Hard, 2006). Student teachers need to build their own professional identity and develop an appreciation of this complex leadership environment to work effectively as leaders. Our work with preservice teachers requires us to address leadership and particularly the notion of leadership as it plays out in the ECEC field. This challenges student teachers to think about leadership in ways that are incongruent with dominant social constructions of leadership. For example, early childhood practitioners refer to leadership as a non-positional activity describing it more as team based leadership.

'student teachers need to build their own professional identity and develop an appreciation of this complex leadership environment to work effectively as leaders'

As academics working with third year early childhood students in a Bachelor of Education course, the challenge was to have student teachers access the leadership literature and make connections to their own lived experiences. In 2007 we were challenged by our student teachers to provide subject content and design learning opportunities which afforded them increased flexibility in their studies. Basically they wanted to be and learn off-campus more often, partly because they had two days per week allocated to a professional experience placement.

Initially, as teachers we struggled with this notion pondering on how best to provide such opportunities while maintaining credible and authentic learning experiences. Challenges included working with a structured and constrained timetable, elearning availability, and team teaching. In addition we had developed the opportunity for our student teachers to engage in a real life conference with our neighbouring municipal early childhood group. This posed a logistical and professional challenge for us, and the student teachers were required to work together quickly and effectively to achieve a positive outcome.

As learners we also faced the challenge of engaging with the elearning environment and using it as an educational tool. For us, this involved a pilot project where we were able to use an online environment to engage with our student teachers, provide resources, chat sessions and forums, as well as online learning modules.

We decided that a blended learning approach would suit our context and address student life needs while meeting subject objectives involving leadership theory and practice. Blended learning enhanced the leadership theory and practice because it required students to study independently and be self-motivated. Students were no longer simply the recipients of information, but were now required to initiate learning, engage with content, and articulate their learning to others. These skills are required in both management and leadership.

> 'blended learning enhanced the leadership theory and practice because it required students to study independently and be self-motivated'

Leadership and identity

Social understandings of leadership traditionally are heavily imbued with images of the sole political or religious leader, often male, stoic and heroic. When one examines the highly feminised field of ECEC, this traditional image of leadership is absent. In this context, how is leadership understood and enacted? In a 2005 study, Hard examined how ECEC practitioners understood leadership and saw it enacted in the field (Hard, 2005). Findings indicate a complex field dominated by a discourse of niceness but underpinned by challenges such as horizontal violence (Farrell, 2001) and an expectation of working as a team. Horizontal violence, in this sense, refers to:

psychological harassment, which creates hostility, as opposed to physical aggression. The harassment involves verbal abuse, threats, intimidation, humiliation, excessive criticism, innuendo, exclusion, denial of access to opportunity, disinterest, discouragement, and the withholding of information McKenna, Smith, Poole, & Coverdale, 2003, p. 92

> 'social understandings of leadership traditionally are heavily imbued with images of the sole political or religious leader, often male, stoic and heroic'

Hard (2005) attributes these apparently competing discourses (niceness and horizontal violence) to the field being undervalued and poorly remunerated, which contributes to a low level of professional esteem and a limited professional identity. It may be that individuals with such a professional identity are vulnerable to behaving in ways that diminish others to assert themselves through behaviours such as horizontal violence. Randle (2003) suggests that self-esteem is a major predictor of behaviour and perhaps in the ECEC field the interpretation of low social kudos and remuneration may contribute to poor self-esteem. Hard (2005) proposes that this culture has the effect of deterring aspiring leaders since they are often expected to behave as part of the group rather than undertaking positional leadership roles.

It is apparent that there are multiple understandings and a complex array of issues related to leadership in the ECEC field. This presents a challenge for academics to explore these issues and prepare student teachers to work in such contexts. Our intention as teacher educators was to develop in student teachers a robust identity which would enable them to understand and deal with the systemic leadership issues

There are shifting sands of leadership— students need to learn how to be leaders and followers... leadership and followership are both learnable.

Rhonda Forrest

they will face in the field. This professional identity would inoculate student teachers to some degree and enable them to work as leaders not constrained by the negative behaviours (such as horizontal violence) which often result from feelings of low self-esteem.

As the semester progressed, we were increasingly aware of the relationship between blended learning and the development of leadership and management skills in the student teachers. Evidence of their ability to work in teams and their independent engagement with the leadership online modules was indicative of emerging leadership maturity.

> 'evidence of their ability to work in teams and their independent engagement with the leadership online modules was indicative of emerging leadership maturity'

More meaningful leadership models

Traditional leadership models provide little to the ECEC field as they have often espoused male images in positional roles. In contrast, emerging work by Sinclair (2007) and Wheatley (2005) provide alternative ideas of leadership which may be more appealing to those in the field of ECEC. These authors present views of leadership which are much more holistic and humanistic. Wheatley (2005) links leadership with interconnectedness, creativity and thinking beyond the individual. She challenges readers to embrace the spiritual dimension of their lives and work and acknowledge the emotional aspects.

> 'Wheatley links leadership with interconnectedness, creativity, and thinking beyond the individual and challenges readers to embrace the spiritual dimension of their lives and work and acknowledge the emotional aspects'

It is one of the great ironies of our age that we created organisations to constrain our problematic human natures, and now the only thing that can save these organisation, is a full appreciation of the expansive capacities of us humans. Wheatley, 2005, p. 21

She proposes organisations where the leaders create opportunities for people to work together developing a shared sense of purpose, exchanging and creating information, learning constantly, paying attention to the results of our efforts, coadapting, coevolving, developing wisdoms we learn (Wheatley, 2005, p. 27). She sees leaders as people who nurture people and connect them to each other.

They trust that we can create wisely and well, that we seek the best interests of our organisation and our community, that we want to bring more good into the world. Wheatley, 2005, p. 30

These images of leadership are in sharp contrast to those defined in traditional, heroic leadership models (Sinclair, 2007). They present a view of leadership enactment that embraces the human spirit and understands the connectedness between people as central to effective work. Perhaps for ECEC personnel, Wheatley's ideas provide possibilities to harness the egalitarian rationale of the field (Hard, 2005) and tap into the desires people have to improve circumstances for children, families, and staff through a collaborative and fulfilling endeavour.

Sinclair provides further scope to new ways of viewing leadership in her book *Leadership for the Disillusioned: Moving Beyond Myths and Heroes to Leading that Liberates* (Sinclair, 2007). This text is part of her evolving thinking and research around leadership. She highlights the role of the body in leadership in contrast to previous constructions focused on it as solely a brain activity. Body can involve a physical presence, changes to physical activities and expectations and *an appetite to experiment with bodily conventions* (Sinclair, 2007, p. 109). She challenges leaders to embrace well-being and teaches yoga to others to promote time for oneself, and doing things that are not about knowledge, careers, or material values. Sinclair discusses the notion of less-ego in leadership and embraces Eastern thinking to suggest alternatives.

Stepping back from the ego therefore requires both knowing yourself and letting go of yourself. Letting go of these personal scripts has powerful liberating effects. When we cease trying to control others, we find freedom for ourselves as well as for them. By allowing others priority, less-ego leadership becomes possible. Sinclair, 2007, p. 170

'Sinclair highlights the role of the body in leadership in contrast to previous constructions focused on it as solely a brain activity'

As teacher educators, we too were exploring new ways of teaching leadership by challenging traditional conceptualisations in our current university context. We were somewhat unconsciously taking a leadership role in our teaching of this subject. Like Wheatley we were co-adapting and co-evolving as we redesigned our subject and, as Sinclair suggests, we were exploring less-ego as we put our traditional methods of teaching on hold. We needed to release our control over teaching and learning methods to afford student teachers the opportunity to more meaningfully explore team work, engage in self-directed learning, and finally share this learning with their peers.

Blended learning

In 2007, we faced the challenge of engaging our student teachers in the leadership literature to build their leadership capabilities. We needed to provide flexibility in learning and depth in their engagement. There is much talk in academic circles about the changing nature of teaching and moves to increase study options for student teachers by the provision of various forms of learning. Part of these discussions includes the notion of blended learning which is defined as:

the thoughtful fusion of face-to-face and online-learning where the strengths of each are blended into a unique learning experience congruent with the context and intended purpose.
Garrison & Vaughan, 2008, p. 5

It was our intention to include elements of face-to-face teaching alongside online learning to afford our student teachers a sound but challenging engagement with leadership theory and management practice. The elearning component offers flexibility and opportunities for learners to make choices that suit their learning style. The face-to-face component provides the human support and scaffolding (Graham, 2006) as well as opportunities for student interaction and collaboration. Kvavik and Caruso's survey of higher education student teachers found that students value interaction and are concerned about *reduced communication with their instructors* (Garrison & Vaughan, 2008, p. 87).

The importance of body and the physical presence of teachers is often underemphasized. This challenges us to consider how online programs address the physicality of teachers and their presence.

Editors

Offerman and Tassava (2005) state that face-to-face contact helps students to see themselves differently as learners as a result of discussing, questioning, and engaging in an energetic and enthusiastic environment. According to Garrison and Vaughan, it seems important that subjects are in fact designed to optimize student engagement (2008) and Holmes and Gardner discuss the need to promote self-assessment and reflection (2006).

> 'face-to-face contact helps student teachers to see themselves differently as learners as a result of discussing, questioning, and engaging in an energetic and enthusiastic environment'

With these criteria in mind, some important requirements of a blended learning course are:

- students need to see themselves as *producers of information* rather than *just consumers*
- there needs to be a process of communal construction of knowledge
- students need training in use of technologies
- authentic tasks, group work, projects, and peer presentations need to be *built in*
- assessments need to benefit students
- classroom time needs to include *communal discussion and group work*
- students need to be given the chance to lead discussions and experienced students need to take on the role of mentor.

(sourced from Holmes & Gardner, 2006, p. 111)

> 'students need to see themselves as producers of information rather than just consumers'

In addition to these pedagogical guidelines, on a very practical level authors such as Vaughan (2007) suggest that blended learning can also address the cost of commuting which is a real issue for our student teachers. The flexibility of having classes off-campus provides increased options for family and work obligations and can mean that students are more likely to choose or remain in a course (Dziuban, Hartmann, Judge, Moskal, & Sorg, 2005).

> 'the flexibility of having classes off-campus provides increased options for family and work obligations and can mean that students are more likely to choose or remain in a course'

Challenges in the new environment

Despite these positive elements, there are some challenges in using blended learning. Vaughan (2007) states that among students in two studies, some had an expectation that fewer classes meant less work. Some had *inadequate time management skills*, some had *problems with accepting responsibility for personal learning*, and others had *difficulty with more sophisticated technologies* (Vaughan, 2007, p. 85). For us in our work in this leadership subject, these were real issues which we shall explore in the coming sections. What was apparent was incongruence between our student teachers wanting to have flexibility and accepting the associated responsibilities. Elearning *can provide significant opportunities for students to create and acquire knowledge for themselves* (Holmes & Gardner, 2006). In addition to the issue of student expectations, teachers faced issues of time commitment, lack of support for course redesign, difficulty acquiring new teaching and technology skills, fear of losing control over the course, less positive student evaluations, and uneasiness about how this learning model fits into the university culture (Vaughan, 2007). Such factors were the reality we encountered as we embarked on this changed teaching approach.

> 'elearning *can provide significant opportunities for students to create and acquire knowledge for themselves*'

Teaching in new ways: The reality

The first challenge we faced in making the blended learning objective a reality was to redefine and redevelop our existing subject materials. This required new ways of thinking and modification of our content to be accessible through online access. In the early stages of the subject, we embedded an authentic learning experience which involved our student teachers participating in the organisation and implementation of an early childhood conference. Time constraints meant we needed to get student teachers working effectively in teams within two weeks. Despite the challenges of understanding teamwork and their immediate role in the event, the student teachers demonstrated positive attitudes, confidence, and skills in communication. This opportunity allowed them to relate the teamwork theory to a practical event.

Subsequent to this we presented a lecture that introduced the idea of a framework for leadership roles (Carter & Curtis, 1998) and an on-campus workshop on forming and writing a teaching philosophy. Student teachers were given a week to write the draft of their own emerging philosophy and regrouped to share and undertake some peer review. After mid-semester break, they undertook online learning modules for two weeks. These included set readings and references to digital resources to enhance their knowledge of leadership theory. This was supplemented by PowerPoint™ slides with voiceover to extend content. Although wikis and blogs were available, no students chose to use them during this stage. A lecture on financial management was followed by an optional workshop in a computer laboratory on the use of the Excel™ program for budgeting. Relationships with parents were introduced with an online reading and discussed through the use of an online chat.

The student teachers returned to the campus to have a workshop with the university careers advisor on the subject of preparation of a curriculum vitae and a job application. This was followed by a lecture and an optional workshop on advocacy and marketing, which included photographic and presentational skills required for documentation of children's learning. Both computer workshops were also used to assist students in their individual needs for compilation of their e-portfolios. All student teachers were required to develop an e-portfolio which included their teaching philosophy and curriculum vitae, a formal letter, job application, newsletter, documentation of children's learning, a budgeting task, reflection on the team experience of organising the conference, a reflection on their emerging ideas of leadership and finally, a reflective evaluation of their e-portfolio. Developing their e-portfolio proved challenging for many, particularly as our university does not have an established and supported portfolio format. Ultimately, students produced professional portfolios which represented significant learning and the ability to represent themselves to a professional audience.

The development of online programs demands we reconsider what it means to build and sustain effective learning and teaching relationships.

Editors

The final in-class aspect to the subject was individual presentations focusing on what leadership meant to each student teacher. Overall, these presentations were of an outstanding calibre and demonstrated that they had engaged in the leadership theory modules and were able to apply this to other experiences and articulate it to their peers. On the whole, they presented images of themselves as leaders relating theory to their life experiences both within and beyond the ECEC field. Most student teachers illustrated some engagement with the leadership theory and some a highly developed understanding of the complexities of leadership.

> 'students presented images of themselves as leaders relating theory to their life experiences both within and beyond the ECEC field'

The student teacher experience

Melanie, a student teacher in the programme, observes:

As a student in this subject I found that the blended learning experience was extremely valuable for a number of reasons. Firstly, the flexible delivery of the subject was valuable considering the busy semester that we had. I had placement commitments two days per week, classes the remaining three days and I worked both days of the weekend. Therefore, it was useful having a subject that I could work on at my own pace, whenever I found spare time.

Secondly, I found that the learning modules were focused and easy to understand. When I was engaging with the modules, I was learning information that was relevant to the topic. It saved 'wasted time' which can occur in some lectures when seemingly irrelevant information is discussed.

Thirdly, because I could work on the modules at my own pace, I could control my speed of learning and therefore understand the materials thoroughly. Finally, the subject seemed compatible with my learning style. I am an independent, self-motivated learner, which were attributes that seemed necessary for success in this subject.

> 'I am an independent, self motivated learner, which were attributes that seemed necessary for success in this subject'

Genna was also a student teacher in the programme. She comments:

As a student in this subject, I found that the blended learning strategies challenged my growth and learning as a preservice teacher. I am an independent learner and this subject provided me with the opportunity to develop a study schedule and complete the off-campus modules at my own pace. From conversations with others in the subject, those who were not independent learners did find it hard to complete the subject off campus.

> 'those who were not independent learners did find it hard to complete the subject off campus'

I particularly enjoyed the leadership module. The readings in this part of the subject challenged my thinking about traditional leadership roles. Although we were provided with the opportunity to use forums and chats to discuss the module, I feel that there could have been more of a discussion in class. This would have provided everyone with another opportunity to discuss concepts, especially if online access was a problem.

I also enjoyed the tutorials that were aimed at documentation and developing resumes. When reflecting on these tutorials, they were valuable for a number of reasons. Firstly, they were relevant to my future work in the early childhood field. Also, because we were able to choose which tutorials to attend, we were not attending a tutorial on something we were already competent in.

Overall, this subject suited my learning style and provided me with a supportive environment to develop my own understanding of leadership and management. I hope that with time students become more open to this style of teaching and embrace its possibilities.

This subject provided challenges for both the student teachers and staff involved. Student teachers responded to subject evaluations with mixed feelings. These included positive comments as:

This subject was delivered with flexibility which was great as we were on prac and it was good not to have to come in every week and complete tasks off-campus in our own time.

Fantastic way to approach a subject with a combination of online and on-campus lecturing.

I enjoyed learning about the aspects of leadership. I liked working through the leadership module at my own pace. I also found the tasks and readings relevant to the course.

There were contrasting comments as indicated in the following:

When we had the readings without having class, it was simply far too much work for the time that we had allocated. Would of preferred to be in class.

I did not like the tasks that we were to complete online rather than in class. I found that I was not stimulated to do this, compared to being in a class situation and doing them.

I felt like I never really knew what was going on. There were so many classes that were cancelled or not running. The study schedule helped, but the flexible learning idea of not having many actual classes did not support my learning.

Conclusion

The evaluative feedback presents dilemmas and contradictions which are still to be reconciled. The diversity and intensity of responses are surprising because some intimated a lack of understanding of how the subject was structured and the intention to provide flexible learning. This is noted in the literature where authors indicate the challenges faced by student teachers around self-regulation and the differing ability individuals have in this regard (Graham, 2006).

'some student teachers coped well and in fact enjoyed the challenge of independent learning while others articulated a need to be in class on a weekly basis and to have information provided to them directly'

It appeared that some students coped well and in fact enjoyed the challenge of independent learning while others articulated a need to be in class on a weekly basis and to have information provided to them directly. Others have encountered this difficulty of some students being *unprepared for the active learning role they must play in*

It is important to sell your product. What is in it for the student to click the link? Just as a bookstore promotes its books, we need to promote each learning experience, clearly outlining what the student will benefit from embarking n the experience.

Ishbel Macconnachie

In order to develop responsive and flexible online learning, students teachers' views on the meanings of both autonomous learning and blended learning can provide important insights.

Editors

a blended course (Vaughan, 2007, p. 86). This creates challenges for teacher educators as they need to be clear to student teachers about their responsibility in the process. It also makes evident that some of these third year student teachers needed to develop more autonomy in their learning. Perhaps our student teachers have not conceptualised what blended learning is or how it creates learning challenges and opportunities. However, it is evident that for some student teachers the online learning, conference work, and in-class presentation provided opportunities for them to engage in the subject effectively and in doing so develop their leadership capacities.

What was particularly heartening and demonstrated learning outcomes of a high level was the end of semester class presentations. These involved each student teacher making a five minute presentation to the class addressing the topic 'who am I as a leader?' They were asked to draw on the leadership modules in the subject and relate these to their practical involvement in the conference and other life experiences to present themselves as emerging leaders. These presentations were very well done and in many cases outstanding as student teachers effectively related theory to their developing leadership identity in a very professional manner. It is perhaps ironic that despite some of the criticism of the subject in the evaluative feedback the learning outcomes for this particular year were demonstrated to a much higher level than in previous years. Student teachers' self-directed learning on the topic of leadership was deeper and they made connections to practical realities. It seems that the nature of blended learning in this subject assisted students to develop skills in time management, organization, teamwork, self-motivation, and public presentation. There was evidence that student teachers now understood some of the complexities and challenges of leadership in the ECEC field.

The negative student teacher evaluations indicate to us the need to discuss roles and responsibilities at the commencement of the subject. In addition, we need to provide student teachers with more assistance to successfully navigate the online environment.

'negative student teacher evaluations indicate to us the need to discuss roles and responsibilities at the commencement of the subject'

It is also evident to us that the online environment needs to be attractive and well organised to assist student engagement. In addition, we recognise that optional tutorials with a focus on individual needs acknowledged student teacher abilities and provided strategic and timely learning. On reflection, we also see merit in sharing with student teachers our rationale for using this learning environment so they too can appreciate the outcomes a blended learning approach can achieve. For us as learners, the experiences (both positive and negative) have demonstrated that a blended learning approach can enhance management and leadership development in practical and theoretical ways. This illustrates the powerful potential for learning when content is matched with effective teaching strategies.

References

Carter, M., & Curtis, D. (1998). *The visionary director.* St. Paul: Redleaf Press.

Dziuban, C., Hartmann, J., Judge, F., Moskal, P., & Sorg, S. (2005). Blended learning enters the mainstream. In C. J. Bonk & C. R. Graham (Eds.), *The handbook of blended learning: Global perspectives, local designs.* San Francisco: Pfeiffer.

Ebbeck, M., & Waniganayake, M. (2003). *Early childhood professionals. Leading today and tomorrow.* Sydney: Maclennan and Petty.

Farrell, G. A. (2001). From tall poppies to squashed weeds: Why don't nurses pull together more? *Journal of Advanced Nursing, 35*(1), 26-33.

Garrison, D. R., & Vaughan, N., D. (2008). *Blended learning in higher education.* San Francisco: John Wiley & Sons, Inc.

Graham, C. R. (2006). Blended learning systems. In C. J. Bonk & C. R. Graham (Eds.), *The handbook of blended learning: Global perspectives, local designs.* San Francisco: Pfeiffer.

Hard, L. (2005). *How is leadership understood and enacted within the field of early childhood education and care?* Queensland University of Technology, Brisbane.

Hard, L. (2006). Horizontal violence in early childhood education and care: Implications for leadership enactment. *Australian Journal of Early Childhood, 31*(3), 40-47.

Holmes, B., & Gardner, J. (2006). *E-learning: Concepts and practice.* London: Sage Publications Ltd.

Offerman, M., & Tassava, C. (2005). A different perspective on blended learning. In C. J. Bonk & C. R. Graham (Eds.), *The handbook of blended learning: Global perspectives, local designs.* San Francisco: Pfeiffer.

Randle, J. (2003). Bullying in the nursing profession. *Journal of Advanced Nursing, 43*(4), 395-401.

Rodd, J. (2006). *Leadership in early childhood.* Berkshire: Open University Press.

Sinclair, A. (2007). *Leadership for the disillusioned: Moving beyond myths and heroes to leading that liberates.* Sydney: Allen and Unwin.

Vaughan, N. (2007). Perspectives on blended learning in higher education. *International Journal on E-Learning, 6*(1), 81-94.

Wheatley, M., J. (2005). *Finding our way: Leadership for uncertain times.* San Francisco: Berrett-Koehler Inc.

THE POWER OF RELATIONSHIPS ONLINE IN EARLY CHILDHOOD TEACHER EDUCATION

Judy Goth-Owens
United States

Judy Goth-Owens is on the faculty at Lansing Community College in Lansing, Michigan, in the Child Development and Early Education Program. She has a BSEd in Special Education from the University of Michigan, an MA in Human Development with a specialization in Leadership in Education and College Teaching/Teaching Adults from Pacific Oaks College, and has completed additional graduate work in Child Development and Family Studies at Michigan State University. In addition to her current faculty position she has held positions as a preschool teacher, a leadership trainer for Cooperative Extension, the director of an employer-sponsored NAEYC accredited child care center, a training coordinator for the local 4-C agency, and a parent educator. She has presented workshops and seminars at the local, state, and national level and written articles on topics including: infant-toddler programming, parent-adult communication, child care center administration, caring for children with behaviors that challenge adults, and diversity-inclusion. Her professional areas of strongest interest are infant-toddler programming, effective pedagogy in early childhood education, and online distance learning. She is a proponent of the Pikler Approach and has studied with Anna Tardos at the Pikler Institute in Budapest. She has adapted and developed numerous child development and early education courses for the online learning environment and taught extensively online.

Introduction

The relationships which adults nurture with children provide an underpinning for learning. If the relationships are built on trust and a secure attachment, children are more likely to explore and learn (Gonzalez-Mena & Eyer, 2007). Similarly, the relationships cultivated in early childhood teacher education can be a powerful catalyst for learning. If relationships are built on trust and reciprocity, student teachers will feel secure, be curious, explore and learn (Jones, 2007). These relationships are not just those between teacher educators and student teachers but, just as significantly, among student teachers within the learning environment, as well as student teachers' own relationships with themselves. Early childhood teacher educators appreciate and cultivate these important relationship elements when teaching classes face-to-face, but may view the online learning environment as too impersonal, and unlikely to create affiliations and connections.

> 'if relationships are built on trust and reciprocity, student teachers will feel secure, be curious, explore, and learn'

Yet teaching online using a discussion-based approach to early childhood teacher education can harness the power of relationships to create significant learning opportunities for student teachers. Online teacher educators who respect the potential inherent in these relationships can purposefully structure a discussion-based online learning community for early childhood student teachers that is learner-centered, promotes self-reflection, and supports student teachers in building the kind of relationship-focused strategies that are central to early childhood education.

'teaching online using a discussion-based approach to early childhood teacher education can harness the power of relationships to create significant learning opportunities for student teachers'

Identifying a foundation for learning and teaching online

Building an effective Early Childhood Education (ECE) online community for learning begins with respecting the dynamics of relationships between teacher educators and student teachers. While acknowledging that teacher educators are the only ones who can report grades in courses for college credit, we must clearly know that what student teachers learn ultimately rests with them. Teaching strategies that empower student teachers and offer them a genuine shared responsibility for learning, create an atmosphere that is less teacher-directed and more learner-centered—a relationship paradigm unfamiliar to some learners.

'teaching strategies that empower student teachers and offer them a genuine shared responsibility for learning create an atmosphere that is less teacher educator-directed and more learner-centered—a relationship paradigm unfamiliar to some learners.'

However, student teachers may come to online community learning environments with previous learning experiences that have left them feeling powerless, unsuccessful ,or even suspicious. As a result, the concept of shared responsibility may be mistrusted and resisted by student teachers. A teacher educator, therefore, must give patient attention and encouragement to create and sustain this kind of relationship. Such attention begins with acknowledging that all student teachers bring life experiences with them. Early childhood student teachers, even those who have never enroled in a course before, come with their own working theories about how children grow and develop. In order to help student teachers make sense of the new information which we are inviting them to explore, our teaching has to acknowledge and integrate this pre-existing knowledge. Respecting deeply held beliefs, while encouraging new and different understandings, may present challenges. Respectful teacher educators demonstrate appreciation for student teachers' personal beliefs while proposing new perspectives. At the same time, student teachers ought to be challenged in the learning environment to be willing to learn new and different understandings that may dispute their own deeply held beliefs.

Knowledge is constructed when information is handled, turned around, examined within the framework of prior knowledge and experiences, and in new situations. This is the fundamental premise of constructivism, an influential theory about knowledge and learning (see, for example, Dewey, 1966; Piaget, 1973). Constructing meaning is learning. We want student teachers to make information their own by using it to appreciate and understand in new ways what one sees happening in the world—in this case children's behavior—so that information becomes knowledge. Just as children's constructivist classrooms are characterized by mutual, or two-way, respect between teachers and children (DeVries & Zan, 1995), the online learning environment for early childhood teacher educators should support the interactive and reciprocal nature of learning.

Discussion-based approaches promote student teachers' own construction of knowledge. Research clearly points to discussions instead of lectures as a preferred method of instruction:

In order to have a shared responsibility for learning, both teacher educators and student teachers ought to reflect on how a 'learner' is constructed, particularly given the dynamics of online relationships.

Editors

On-line learning could be a good system to mentor student teachers. However, there are some older teachers who are not comfortable using computers

Carla Scalia

Yes, reciprocity and interaction are important. But they might also be different in some regards to face-to-face teaching situations. We are interested, then, in how one experiences reciprocity and interaction in various learning contexts or environments.

Editors

when the variables studied are retention of information after a course is over, transfer of knowledge to novel situations, development of skill in thinking or problem-solving, or achievement in affective domains, such as motivation for additional learning or change in attitudes—in other words, the kinds of learning we care most about. Gardiner, 1994, p. 39

Online learning is an ideal format for a discussion-based approach in which a shared learning community is built through trusting relationships. Elizabeth Jones calls this 'making friends', a process of building a community for shared learning that is an essential part of participation in the social construction of knowledge (Jones, 2007).

'Elizabeth Jones calls this 'making friends', a process of building a community for shared learning that is an essential part of participation in the social construction of knowledge'

In the early childhood teacher education online learning community, the communication is textual and student teacher initiated. This allows the learner flexibility in responding, and may provide more opportunity for contemplation than the immediacy required in responding to questions face-to-face. Since responses are read, the thinking of student teachers may become more visible to the teacher educator. This setting also provides opportunities for transformative learning, a process based on critical reflection and questioning of prior experiences, ideas, and assumptions (Mezirow, 2000).

Student teachers in the discussion-based online classroom engage with the course content by exploring new information in the context of their own experiences through deliberation and collaboration with others. In early childhood teacher education, for example, student teachers may be given information about current brain research and the significant impact of touch and primary care on a child's healthy brain development. Student teachers are asked to reflect on their own experiences with touch, and the reactions to touch they may have seen in young children, and link these reflections to this research. A dialogue proceeds from individual stories that reflect each person's cultural and contextual experiences. Together, student teachers acknowledge and respond to each other and teacher educators. A relationship-building process is created through these interactions as student teachers validate and challenge each other's attempts at understanding and explaining. Student teachers may then develop new ways of understanding and explaining the topics or ideas on which they are collaborating. In this way, an online learning community supports and encourages knowledge acquisition as it creates a sense of excitement about learning together (Palloff & Pratt, 1999).

'student teachers in the discussion-based online classroom engage with the course content by exploring new information in the context of their own experiences through deliberation and collaboration with others'

Designing an online learning community

An effective online learning community should provide a predictable structure that feels safe and invites learners to take risks, try new things, and grow. Online learning, and the use of continually changing technology, may be new to student teachers. It may feel risky to communicate with others using only text. Creating a safe learning environment online for relationships to thrive has to happen from the first encounter and may be cultivated by the following practices:

Information on the course

Provide information for student teachers about how the course will work in advance of when the course begins. Create a Frequently Asked Questions (FAQ) online discussion forum that remains open for the duration of the course for student teachers to ask questions. If student teachers are in the same geographic area, a face-to-face orientation session may provide a bridge for them to what may be a new and challenging learning environment.

Sharing your ways of teaching

Tell student teachers why you teach the way you do. Student teachers are developing their own philosophy of teaching and learning. By making your philosophy transparent, student teachers get to know more about who you are as you model your philosophy.

'tell student teachers why you teach the way you do'

Create rules of engagement

Some rules may be made collaboratively with student teachers. The experienced teacher educator can propose suggestions and specify some rules, such as those about confidentiality, as non-negotiable. Although the teacher educator may provide rules for behavior in this setting, much of the content will emerge from the dialogue among the community members (Jones, 2007).

A space for introductions

Create an initial discussion forum that is designed as a place for introductions. Providing suggested questions to answer as a way of introduction helps get student teachers engaged. It is also an experience that can make student teachers feel exposed, so it is a good place to begin offering them choices, about what and how much to share.

Address cultural and geographic issues

The online classroom has no physical boundaries. It is not based on place, but it is a community formed around similar interests and goals. Student teachers may be in different time zones or on different continents. They may be more comfortable communicating in a language other than the one the class is being taught in. There may be different norms for communication that can impact discussions and the relationships among student teachers. For example, what is or is not a timely response, or a standard for meeting a deadline may be open to interpretation. Openly acknowledging and discussing the sociocultural implications of a diverse group communicating online can at times be uncomfortable but will likely contribute to a welcoming atmosphere, dissolve barriers, and add to everyone's growth.

Monitor responses for inappropriate behavior or conflict

The teacher educator must be ready to facilitate the resolution of conflicts and intervene in situations that may be hurtful or destructive.

Setting assignments which empower student teachers

Teacher educators should provide choices and options for assignments to empower student teachers and respect individual differences. Online communities

On the ground mentors are always needed to support online learning.
Relinde Tap

Don't expect student teachers to remember everything.
Bambi McLean

The basis of relationality is this personal narrative—a willingness to share one's own stories, and to show how each narrative and philosophy of education are deeply intertwined.
Editors

only work when student teachers sustain interactions with each other, so specific expectations for participation in the discussions should be required. Opportunities for student teacher choice can be offered for individual assignments or projects.

Balance your presence online as the teacher educator

Balance your own presence as a teacher educator online with techniques that promote student teacher empowerment. Just as teacher educators discover becoming comfortable with silence in face-to-face classrooms, online teacher educators who step back from being the primary source of knowledge also realize that student teachers then find opportunities to take on new roles and responsibilities.

'online communities only work when student teachers sustain interactions with each other, so specific expectations for participation in the discussions should be required'

Facilitating online discussion-based learning

Since most learning in online discussions happens when student teachers interact with each other and teacher educators, teacher educators must actively promote discussions. Student teachers engaged in discussion-based early childhood teacher education online have opportunities to explore, question, collaborate, and reflect. Online discussions may encourage growing relationships, while providing multiple opportunities for student teachers to construct knowledge. The following are some practices and strategies which may promote this kind of discussion:

Consistency and predictability

Use a consistent and predictable course structure, with a familiar pattern of expectations and due dates that helps relieve anxiety about practical matters, and allows student teachers to focus more on the discussions.

Acknowledging online participation

Designate a significant portion of the course grade to participation in online discussion. This makes transparent to student teachers the value you place on this activity, and helps them shift from traditional thinking about learning and grades. Because of this shift, student teachers may need clear guidelines about the frequency, regularity, and content expected in the online discussions.

'student teachers may need clear guidelines about the frequency, regularity, and content expected in the online discussions'

The use of questions

Design discussion questions that add depth and value by providing an informational foundation, and challenge student teachers to consider this new knowledge in light of their own previous or current experiences. Asking questions that invite reflection on personal experiences establishes connected knowing (Belenky, Clinchy, Goldberger, & Tarule, 1986). Encouraging student teachers to tell stories facilitates the formation of personal connections to understanding, and the creation of stories they can recognize as their own (Jones, 2007). For example, after completing a required reading on various approaches to teaching early literacy in kindergarten, student teachers might be asked:

This opens conversations about presence and silence during online learning.
Editors

Which of the approaches to reading discussed in the book were strategies that you were used to reading?

How did that work for you?

If you were a kindergarten teacher today, which of the approaches do you think you would use? Why?

'encouraging student teachers to tell stories facilitates the formation of personal connections to understanding, and the creation of stories they can recognize as their own'

Small group online discussion

Assign small groups of six to eight student teachers for online discussions. This intimate environment provides interaction with fewer people than in an entire class, and can generate a deeper level of meaningful discussion.

Model responses and pose questions that promote further discussion

As teacher educators, we can model responses and pose questions in ways that promote further discussion. *Tell us more about how that experience changed your thinking about... What do you think might have kept you from...? How did your strong feelings impact...?* When student teachers see which kind of questions stimulate conversation, they will learn this skill (Finkel, 1999).

'when student teachers see which kind of questions stimulate conversation, they will learn this skill'

Keeping focused and connected

Help groups stay focused and productive by staying in touch with each group. At the same time resist the temptation to jump in immediately to answer questions. When you provide space for another student teacher to respond, or ask if anyone else in the group can answer the question, you contribute to the empowerment process.

Encouraging self-reflection and self-assessment

Incorporating self-reflection and self-assessment into online learning experiences reinforces for student teachers a sense of shared responsibility in the learning environment, and reminds them that assessment and feedback are important factors in learning. Practices included throughout the course that expect the learner to reflect on and assess their own learning, as well as providing feedback, may include:

- Creating grading criteria, expectations, or rubrics that help define for student teachers your expectations of quality work. Expect student teachers to use these tools for self-assessment.
- Expecting student teachers to regularly post lessons learned as a way to enable them to reflect on and analyze their learning. Although this should be designed primarily to benefit student teachers, it can also be an important assessment tool for the teacher educator.
- Encouraging student teachers to reflect not only on their understanding of course content, but also on their own learning processes. Early childhood

education student teachers are learning about their own learning and can be challenged to explore how they see themselves as online learners.

> 'student teachers are learning about their own learning and can be challenged to explore how they see themselves as online learners'

Recognizing student teachers' relationships

The power of relationships in early childhood teacher education online extends beyond student teachers' engagement in course content. They may be parents, older than the traditional college age, and working at full- or part-time jobs. They may be the first person in their family to go to college, or they may already have a degree in another field and have found a passion in working with young children. Some are young adults recently out of high school, too.

> 'the power of relationships in early childhood teacher education online extends beyond student teachers' engagement in course content'

This creates a diverse online learning community. While working together online, student teachers build personal relationships and connections that are helpful as they support and encourage each other through the complexities of daily living. These affiliations are often sustained over time and can keep student teachers from becoming discouraged and abandoning educational goals that can at times seem overwhelming.

> 'While working together online, student teachers build personal relationships and connections that are helpful as they support and encourage each other through the complexities of daily living.'

In online discussions the dialogue is not a once a week event, but is an ongoing and continuous process. Student teachers who are currently working in the early childhood field regularly post stories such as:

I was talking with my co-teacher at work today about the online discussion we've been having this week. I discovered she also thinks our room could use some rearranging and wants to hear more about what my group suggested.

After our online discussion last night about staff evaluations, I asked my director today if our program has a process for this. She told me no, but she wants to start one. She asked ME to help her get this off the ground! Can you guys give me some ideas of what's worked for you?

These professional and collegial relationships are enhanced when online student teachers integrate their discoveries into their daily work lives.

Demonstrating the parallels in practice

Teacher educators who respect the power of relationships and construct online learning with intentions of promoting trust and a shared responsibility for learning and fostering self-reflection, create prime experiences for adult learners.

As teacher educators, we can use the time in which we work with student teachers to encourage collegiality and peer support which, in turn, models working with others.

Editors

'teacher educators who respect the power of relationships and construct online learning with intentions of promoting trust and a shared responsibility for learning and fostering self-reflection, create prime experiences for adult learners'

They also demonstrate dispositions and strategies that student teachers may be expected to implement in their own work as early childhood educators. As teacher educators preparing early childhood professionals in the online learning community, we can include practices that demonstrate these dispositions. The following are some such practices:

Diversity of learning and teaching

We need to respect different learning styles and use a variety of teaching techniques to reach all learners. If we want our students to eschew a cookie-cutter approach to teaching young children, the learning experiences we provide our student teachers should reflect a variety of methods and options. Although the core of online learning is textual, and the ability to fully participate in online discussions requires verbal and literacy skills, there may be adaptations or adaptive devices that can contribute to an inclusive environment. In addition, interactive games, guest speakers, electronic audio and visual media, and field experiences are feasible methods for online teaching.

User-friendly format

We ought to organize and present a well planned user-friendly format for the class in order to provide student teachers with the best possible learning experiences. If we want our student teachers to approach their work with children with intention, the learning environment we create should demonstrate our own intentional design. Intentional teaching is acting with a purpose and a plan, and involves continual assessment and adjusting strategies based on that assessment (Epstein, 2007).

'intentional teaching is acting with a purpose and a plan, and involves continual assessment and adjusting strategies based on that assessment'

Professionalism

As teacher educators, we must demonstrate professional behaviors in the areas of confidentiality and upholding ethical conduct. If we want our student teachers to take seriously a code of ethics, the rules we set in the classroom must be taken seriously. We can gently remind them about the importance of confidentiality as they tell their stories in online discussion. We can help them shape their stories to be told respectfully, while at the same time not distorting truth. This provides a powerful model of professionalism in real life situations.

Compassion and respect

Demonstrate compassion and respect for each individual, while defining and implementing clear and consistent limits. If we want our student teachers to be able to establish and communicate limits to children, and guide children's behavior by practicing developmentally appropriate guidance techniques, teacher educators must be able to demonstrate that fairly and consistently

Many teachers share that their most powerful teaching moments are unplanned, and without seeming to involve continual adjustment based upon assessment. Rather they are responsive to their intuitive professional sense of what will bring forth new learning.

Editors

enforcing rules helps everyone know where they stand. Teacher educators do this when they listen with respect to differing opinions of student teachers, while maintaining a safe place for all views. Teacher educators who respectfully enforce agreed upon rules and deadlines show student teachers how this can be done assertively, but compassionately.

Demonstrate risk-taking and innovation

As teacher educators we should demonstrate the interactive and reciprocal nature of learning, and take risks to try new things and grow. If we want our student teachers to create learning environments for children that respect children's curiosity and capacities, then the learning communities we help create should give our students multiple opportunities to experience this for themselves.

Everything we do as educators tells our student teachers what we value and is a reflection of our beliefs and philosophy. Learning does not happen only online, in a classroom, or when someone is directly teaching someone else. If we believe that learning is an on-going lifelong process, we will continue to learn and grow ourselves as we teach while providing our student teachers with dynamic examples.

> 'everything we do as educators tells our student teachers what we value and is a reflection of our beliefs and philosophy'

According to Elizabeth Jones (2007, p. 26):

Early childhood education should be relationship-based. Trusting, making friends, and reflecting with one's friends on one's experiences are the foundation for the rest of education and life. We will most effectively prepare teachers of young children by teaching them in the way we would like them to teach young children—by modeling developmentally appropriate practice of all the skills needed by the children and by their teachers and caregivers.

The relationships we create and facilitate are not by-products of our teaching, but are the essence of teaching.

> 'relationships we create and facilitate are not by-products of our teaching, but are the essence of teaching'

An important message shared at the Working Forum for Teacher Educators has been: *It is through the sharing of stories that our collective understandings grow.* Sharing stories happens in learning settings which respect and nurture each individual's contributions, understandings, and growth. This prime environment is not limited to classrooms where student teachers and teacher educators meet together face-to-face. In the context of a discussion-based approach, the online learning environment can be just such a space. Early childhood education online has emerged as a significant tool we can use to build relationships, and give ourselves and our student teachers a place to share stories and grow.

> 'it is through the sharing of stories that our collective understandings grow'

References

Belenky, M. F., Clinchy, B. M., Goldberger, N. R., & Tarule J. M. (1986). *Women's ways of knowing: The development of self, voice, and mind*. New York: Basic Books.

DeVries R., & Zan, B. (1995). Creating a constructivist classroom atmosphere. *Young Children, 1*(1), 4-13.

Dewey, J. (1966). *Democracy and education*. New York: Free Press.

Epstein, A. S. (2007). *The intentional teacher: Choosing the best strategies for young children's learning*. Washington, DC: NAEYC.

Finkel, D. L. (1999). *Teaching with your mouth shut*. Portsmouth, NH: Boynton/Cook.

Gardiner, L. F. (1994). *Redesigning higher education: Producing dramatic gains in student learning. Report No. 7*. Washington, DC: Graduate School of Education and Human Development, George Washington University (an ASHE-ERIC Higher Education Report).

Gonzalez-Mena, J., & Eyer, D. W. (2007). *Infants, toddlers, and caregivers: A curriculum of respectful, responsive care and education*. New York: McGraw-Hill.

Jones, E. (2007). *Teaching adults revisited: Active learning for early childhood educators*. Washington, DC: NAEYC.

Mezirow, J. (2000). *Learning as transformation: Critical perspectives on a theory in progress*. San Francisco: Jossey Bass.

Palloff, R. M., & Pratt, K. (1999). *Building learning communities in cyberspace: Effective strategies for the online classroom*. San Francisco: Jossey-Bass.

Piaget, J. (1973). *To understand is to invent*. New York: Grossman.

MOVING FORWARD BY LOOKING BACK: PILOTING A WEB-ENHANCED TEACHER EDUCATION PROGRAM

Julie Whittaker
New Zealand

Katrina Ludeman
New Zealand

At the time of the Working Forum for Teacher Educators, Julie Whittaker was a lecturer (eLearning) at New Zealand Tertiary College (NZTC)—a specialist early childhood teacher education provider. She was involved in the development of web-enhanced distance learning programs within NZTC as well as participating in a national project on maturing e-Learning guidelines with a particular emphasis on staff development.

Katrina Ludeman, BTchg (ECE), is the Centre Supervisor for Kindercare Learning Centre, Hilltop, Auckland, New Zealand. As a student teacher, she was involved in the New Zealand Tertiary College degree program pilot study which was delivered through a web-enhanced distance learning mode. Katrina is actively involved in the everyday teaching of young children. She is the centre curriculum support person and a field practice associate tutor for student-teachers.

Introduction

What is it like to be an online student? What is it like to learn without desks, chairs, whiteboards, pens, paper, clocks, bells, chatter, or laughter? What do online students find challenging? What does an online environment provide for student teachers that is not available in a traditional classroom?

> 'what does an online environment provide for student teachers that is not available in a traditional classroom?'

The literature employs a range of lenses through which various educational stakeholders view the benefits, challenges, scope, and risks of online learning and teaching in general. While Bredekamp (2002) and others emphasize the immense potential of web-based technologies for early childhood teacher education, little has been published from the perspective of student teachers. The New Zealand Tertiary College (NZTC) Web-Enhanced Distance Learning (WEDL) Pilot Project addresses that gap by recognizing student teachers as important stakeholders and acknowledging their voices in influencing the development and research of pilot projects and the ongoing design of *ecelearn*—an online learning environment for early childhood teacher education.

This paper reflects the voices of student teachers while also acknowledging that any review of pilot study data ought never be a simple, linear process. Drawing upon student teachers' reflections helps us as teacher educators to engage with the design and implementation of an innovative web-enhanced program, *ecelearn*. The very nature of teaching and learning in early childhood contexts requires that teacher educators reflect upon what has happened in the past with a view to informing future practice. The same reflective process was used to guide the decisions and actions of the WEDL pilot project and the *ecelearn* development team.

> 'the very nature of teaching and learning in early childhood contexts requires that teacher educators reflect upon what has happened in the past with a view to informing future practice'

This paper shares a simple reflective model entitled *What?, So what?, Now what?* to frame the presentation of the WEDL pilot process in terms of the student teachers' and College's perspectives.

What? represents learners' voices—student teachers' personal experiences of learning online. *So what?* is NZTC's voice—a sharing of perspectives on the findings from the pilot version 1.0 research report, and how this report impacts on decisions and actions leading to the subsequent pilot version, WEDL 1.5, informing the design and development of *ecelearn*. Finally, this paper focuses on the *Now what?*, reflecting upon what NZTC has learned from the process, and the next steps and challenges in delivering a high quality web-enhanced distance learning experience for College student teachers and teacher educators.

WEDL and ecelearn

The New Zealand Tertiary College *ecelearn* development project commenced with the pilot study WEDL 1.0 and was followed by the subsequent pilot WEDL 1.5 involving its key users—administrators, teacher educators, and student teachers. The pilot projects were undertaken to develop the learning tools and features to support our early childhood teacher education profession and to ensure from the conception of the project that it was developed by and for its key users. Administrators, teacher educators, and student teachers were involved in extensive use of the learning platform alongside developers and researchers to inform every aspect of the design, development, and delivery of effective and engaging web-enhanced distance learning for early childhood students and teacher educators. The outcome is *ecelearn*—a specialist online learning environment for the early childhood profession.

What? Student teachers' perspectives of web-enhanced distance learning

Access, flexibility, technology, support, motivation, and communication are just some aspects of online learning that may be considered benefits or challenges by student teachers. However, their perceptions may change according to their evolving life experiences and needs.

> 'access, flexibility, technology, support, motivation, and communication are just some aspects of online learning that may be considered benefits or challenges by student teachers '

So what were the realities of access, flexibility, technology, support, motivation, and communication for NZTC WEDL student teachers? We asked one student, Katrina, to discuss her experiences of learning online with *ecelearn*:

The prospect of learning online was new to me. I hadn't previously had the opportunity to experience early childhood teacher training delivered via web technology. I had completed my Diploma of Teaching in 2001 beginning with NZTC's College-based mode of learning but, when I began to work full time in an early childhood centre, the College's flexibility of delivery meant that I could change to their field-based mode. Then in 2007 I began the journey of gaining my Bachelor of Teaching (ECE) via a web-enhanced distance learning mode. I was a little anxious about studying without attending classes, but excited about the prospect of being part of this new mode of learning.

Access

Just after the beginning of my course I went to London. I was away for a whole month which was a substantial amount of time taken from the six-month course. However, as the degree was via web-enhanced distance learning, all I had to do was have access to a computer and the Internet and I was able to continue completing the various requirements of the degree course. I only took one textbook with me to London, everything else was available online. At times I used Internet cafes after sightseeing. At other times, I was able to utilize computers and Internet connections whilst staying with family and friends. No matter what time it was anywhere in the world, I was able to log onto the NZTC ecelearn site and have complete access to everything I needed.

'no matter what time it was anywhere in the world I was able to log onto the NZTC ecelearn site and have complete access to everything I needed'

Flexibility

The flexibility of online learning was a major advantage for me. I was able to study when it was convenient for me. I work full time in an early childhood centre and have other commitments which must be met at specific times of the day. The WEDL mode of delivery allowed me to study late in the evenings and at any time throughout the weekends. If I had a question in the middle of the night, I was able to send it through then and there. I didn't have to wait to make contact by phone the next day and generally the answer to my question was waiting for me when I next logged in. I wasn't restricted to attending lectures at certain times or dealing with traffic and parking issues. Convenience and flexibility is needed in the busy lives that we all lead.

Technology

Before I began learning online I had some knowledge of how to use a computer—a basic knowledge, but enough to access the Internet and generally find what I was looking for. Once I began, my knowledge increased immensely because the first online task was a guided exploration of the WEDL website and all its features. The site was user-friendly and only required a minimum of technological ability. The login page was simple and it provided me with unlimited access to everything that was needed to complete the degree. The site was easy to navigate and included a section where I could have contact with other students and another for direct contact with my lecturer. The course content was easy to find and detailed, including plenty of reflective questions. There were links to education search engines and to other sites of interest, and the site allowed me to change easily between screens when researching information, rather than searching through a mountain of paper.

'there were links to education search engines and to other sites of interest, and the site allowed me to change easily

Young people are so savy in terms of ICT and access knowledge easily. A student room with ICT can become their classroom.

Chris Naughton

between screens when researching information, rather than searching through a mountain of paper'

Support

IT help was always available via the dedicated helpline. And I did need it when my broadband wasn't available and I had to try and submit my assignment via a dial-up connection. The IT team responded efficiently. They were helpful, friendly, and used basic computer language that I was able to understand.

Motivation

Self-motivation is essential for web-enhanced distance learning. Without such things as effective time management skills, I would not have been able to complete the qualification. Although there was plenty of support continuously available from College, I realized that I was my own greatest support and ensured that I kept my motivation to succeed at a high level.

Communication

The discussion forum was intended to allow us to communicate with fellow students and to discuss different aspects of the course. I wasn't very familiar with online forums and didn't feel overly confident using them. This resulted in me hardly using it at all. I only participated once or twice and, from what I did see in the discussion forum, most of the other students also participated infrequently. The forum posed in-depth academic questions which appeared to be encouraging deep discussion and thought around topics relating to the individual course assignments. I feel that a more casual forum, with set guidelines, would have possibly promoted more discussion between students. It would have been useful for me to know what the other students' thoughts were about the assignments and how they were feeling and coping with learning online.

New Zealand Tertiary College's research of the initial WEDL 1.0 pilot indicates that, consistent with Katrina's reflections, the participating student teachers considered online learning to be an enjoyable experience, with flexibility and convenience being the primary advantages (Walker & du Plessis, 2007). These results, additionally, appear to reflect a wider knowledge of the benefits of web-enhanced learning (see for instance Kelly & Schorger, 2002).

'student teachers considered online learning to be an enjoyable experience, with flexibility and convenience being the primary advantages'

Student teachers were generally supportive of the initial 'Learning Online' course, deeming it to be *clear and well organized, and a useful introduction to the ecelearn platform* (Walker & du Plessis, 2007, p. 47). They considered it enabled them to experience the learning environment and develop through various levels of computer competence. The research also found that lecturer contact was *supportive, timely, and helpful* (p. 9).

One concern reflected above, is that peer to peer communication occurred infrequently. This issue led to the suggestion that discussion forum participation should have a minimum requirement of involvement in order to build online *communities of practice* (Wenger, 2000) and encourage student teachers to engage meaningfully in this powerful collegial opportunity.

Motivation is often perceived as being the responsibility of the learner. But it is more than this. It encompasses teacher educators, programs, and pedagogy, as well as the aesthetics of learning.

Editors

For the younger generation computers are a familiar tool which eases their transition to online technology. There is a challenge of motivation though. With online delivery, phone support can enhance personal connection—it is important to have human contact.

Donna Wrack

'discussion forum participation should have a minimum requirement of involvement in order to build online *communities of practice* and encourage student teachers to engage meaningfully in this powerful collegial opportunity'

Much of what Katrina and her student teacher peers have voiced appears congruent with the ongoing reflections of the WEDL teacher educators (Walker & du Plessis, 2007). The next section explores the insights that were developed by the College from these shared reflections.

So what? Implications for a teacher education provider

Some important lessons may be learned from Katrina's perception of her WEDL experience. The College sees key responsibilities for effective online teaching and learning to include:

- listening to student teachers
- knowing the early childhood student teachers
- appreciating the importance of instructional design in learning experiences
- designing a specialist learning platform for student teachers, and
- facilitating professional development for online teacher educators.

Listening to student teachers

Awareness of students' perceptions can increase the lecturer's ability to design more effective learning experiences and help individuals through understanding and alleviating barriers to learning. Muilenburg & Berge, 2005, p. 29

'students' perceptions can increase the lecturer's ability to design more effective learning experiences and help individuals through understanding and alleviating barriers to learning'

The strong student teacher voices amplified the success of the WEDL 1.0 program for early childhood education student teachers. The College's commitment to *providing comprehensive and professional programs [that] empower people to become effective early childhood teachers* (NZTC, 2008, p. 2) required that student teacher voices and recommendations be carefully listened to, seriously reflected upon and used to drive the evolution of *ecelearn*. Student teachers' perceptions of learning in a web-enhanced environment along with their recommendations fully supported the conceptual enhancements considered for the subsequent WEDL 1.5 project.

Knowing the early childhood student teachers

Listening to student teachers is a pathway that leads to understanding who they are as people, as learners, and as early childhood practitioners. Listening to the WEDL student teachers provided indicators of their individual and collective learning needs. Although it could never be said that early childhood student teachers are a homogenous group of learners (Twigg, 2001), they are nevertheless adult learners and, as such, have particular characteristics that impact on the experience of learning. For instance, they tend to have a depth of life experience and knowledge to support their learning, and specific reasons for enrolling in a qualification (McVay-Lynch, 2002). In addition, it is often assumed that, as adult learners, student teachers are motivated to learn (Knowles, 1980). However, these characteristics are not always immediately evident. Hence, motivation, life-experience, and personal interests can only be effectively addressed by getting to know the student teacher. In this way, institutions are able to avoid making inaccurate assumptions about each student teacher's nature as an adult learner.

'although it could never be said that early childhood student teachers are a homogenous group of learners, they are nevertheless adult learners and, as such, have particular characteristics that impact on the experience of learning'

As NZTC holds relationships central to teaching and learning, initial strategies to support new relationship building in the online learning environment were seen as critical. Strategies included the posting of introductions and biographies by student teachers and teacher educators, along with ongoing dialogue in order to gain greater understanding about what leads their learning and practice.

Underscoring the importance of getting to know the learner, NZTC online platform developers have paid close attention to the ways in which the online design process contributes to strong learning relationships, and an effective web-enhanced program. Creating a learning environment that encourages relationship building through an intuitive, user-friendly environment was fundamental to ensuring that the benefits of online technology enhanced community building and individual learning.

Appreciating the importance of instructional design in learning experiences

Instructional design (ID) is a systematic approach to designing and developing course content and activities to promote learning. It should be based on sound pedagogical theory and often follows a traditional process of Analysis, Design, Development, Implementation and Evaluation, usually referred to as the ADDIE model of instructional design (Dick & Carey, 1996).

Slater (2007) believes that effective instructional design is contingent upon the front-end analysis. In particular, before a course can be designed the needs and goals of the learners, their learning characteristics, the learning context, and the learning outcomes have to be analysed in order to make informed decisions about the delivery of instruction. Slater suggests:

it is not the technology that determines the effectiveness of learning but, rather, how the learning is designed and implemented. Slater, 2007, p. 2

'it is not the technology that determines the effectiveness of learning but, rather, how the learning is designed and implemented'

With the massive growth of online social networking, both student teachers and teacher educators may be familiar with techniques of knowing others. However, how one gains knowledge of another person online might be fundamentally different to that gained in face-to-face encounters.

Editors

Ballard, Stapleton, and Carroll (2004) suggest that in order to design effective learning experiences designers must first understand *the features that students actually use and those that they find helpful in their coursework (p. 198)*. This factor has been central to NZTC's research and subsequent design process with the development of *ecelearn*.

Designing a specialist learning platform for students

The College's decision to intentionally design *ecelearn* was an innovation which has proved to be very successful. The initial pilot WEDL 1.0 project research revealed that the original platform was successful for both student teachers and teacher educators. For instance, both groups acknowledged the ease of navigation, the consistent placement of buttons and icons, and the easy to read text. As Fox and Donohue (2007) explain when describing the initial pilot WEDL version 1.0:

we have been intentional in creating a user interface that is friendly, inviting, accessible, simple to use, easy to navigate, hard to get lost in, and with help functions that are designed specifically for new online learners. Fox & Donohue, 2007, p. 4

> 'we have been intentional in creating a user interface that is friendly, inviting, accessible, simple to use, easy to navigate, hard to get lost in, and with help functions that are designed specifically for new online learners'

Further improvements were identified as outcomes of WEDL 1.0 that led to the second WEDL 1.5 pilot. Enhancements to the learning environment included a look and feel review, course template and instructional design review, and enhanced functionality considerations. Improvements developed to be tested in WEDL pilot version 1.5 include:

- adding images and diagrams that highlight the concepts presented to support learning
- refining the color schemes to be engaging yet easy on the eye
- giving more prominence to progress bars, without them being too distracting to the eye
- including more self-review assessment questions that provide immediate feedback to student teachers
- adopting discussion forum questions that more intentionally promote peer interaction online and provide naturalistic learning opportunities where student teachers can collaborate
- initiating a minimum requirement for student teachers for discussion forum involvement.

These strategies are supported by Smith and Brown (2005) and Jonassen, Peck and Wilson (1999), who consider that learning is enhanced by focusing on designing active and interactive engagement with content, tasks, and formative assessment.

> 'learning is enhanced by focusing on designing active and interactive engagement with content, tasks, and formative assessment'

Overall, many improvements to support student teachers' WEDL experiences were identified and acted upon. The next step was to enhance the online experience of teacher educators who, in effect, were also learners and new to the online environment. A decision was made to provide further professional development in online teaching and learning before commencement of WEDL 1.5.

Facilitating professional development for online teacher educators

Prior to engaging in the first pilot WEDL 1.0, the College identified the importance of online orientation for student teachers who might be unsure of, or unfamiliar with, the technology and who could practice and have their initial questions and concerns answered (Mackeracher, 2004; McVay-Lynch, 2002). In addition, it was recognized that the professional development of teacher educators is essential to the success of the pilot, and therefore they were enrolled in an online teaching course.

The pilot research indicated that teacher educators new to the online environment *should be familiar with netiquette and online pedagogy* (Walker & du Plessis, 2007, p. 9) and identified the importance of teacher educator online facilitation skills when participating with student teachers in discussion forums. Guided by contemporary literature (for instance, Palloff & Pratt, 2005; Conrad & Donaldson, 2004) and the College's research (Walker & du Plessis, 2007) on the facilitation of discussion forums, professional development has underscored the value of supporting student teacher interaction and collaborative knowledge construction.

'teacher educators new to the online environment *should be familiar with netiquette and online pedagogy*'

Drawing upon the data from research of WEDL 1.0, the College developed an in-house orientation program for teacher educators to include in WEDL 1.5. The focus of the orientation is both on teaching online, and on how student teachers learn online. The emphasis throughout was on the importance of online learning relationships and the benefits these relationships potentially have in supporting student teachers in their online learning endeavours.

McVay-Lynch (2002, p. 67) notes:

it is only by experiencing the online environment as a student that teachers finally understand student fears, stress, frustrations, and joys in learning in the web-based environment.

'it is only by experiencing the online environment as a student that teachers finally understand student fears, stress, frustrations, and joys in learning in the web-based environment '

In the College's newly developed professional development program, teacher educators are introduced to key literature on online pedagogy, the characteristics of adult learners, and online netiquette, prior to their first online experience. An online questionnaire allows them to articulate their expectations of learning and teaching online. Support is provided through their early online experiences, with an exploration of the *ecelearn* teaching and learning platform within the contexts of working with course content, communicating with peers, and employing relevant, 'just in time' and individual IT helpdesk support.

The final aspect of the professional development program is the opportunity to put the theory of online teaching into practice. Discussion forum facilitation skills learned online were introduced and practiced asynchronously in the safe, non threatening environment of a small group of online peers where initial experience was gained and confidence built before engaging with student teachers.

Now what? The future of web-enhanced learning at NZTC

The student teachers have reflected and made recommendations. NZTC has listened and taken action based on their voices. The learning platform has been reviewed, modified, and enhanced. The teacher educators have undergone professional development. What, therefore, has been learned through this process and where does NZTC go upon the completion of the pilot version 1.5?

'What, therefore, has been learned through this process?'

Preliminary reports from WEDL version 1.5 suggest that student teachers, teacher educators, and instructional designers have experienced a significantly enhanced platform through the student led feedback and subsequent enhancements inspired by WEDL 1.0. On reflection, NZTC has learned that its decision to tailor the platform and delivery specifically to early childhood is a major innovation—an innovation that includes aspects of learning online, such as effective facilitation and interaction among student teachers and teacher educators through discussion forums that are universal to any platform or delivery mode. The complex task is to continue to gain insight into the needs of student teachers and teacher educators, to weave this with that latest online best practice research and emerging eLearning standards, and to continue to develop an effective and engaging online learning environment using latest technology tools, while remaining focused on our early childhood teaching and learning requirements.

New Zealand Tertiary College's response to the research findings has been multifaceted. Most importantly the College has ensured that the development of *ecelearn*, from design, development, processes of administration, course content, professional development, and ongoing help systems is embedded within the culture and framework of the College mission statement of *empowering people to become effective early childhood teachers*.

Feedback on the design and effectiveness of online programs increases our understandings. An essential finding emerging is the need to ensure that programs are tailored to meet the needs of student teachers. In other words, the honoring of diversity.

Editors

References

Ballard, S., Stapleton, J., & Carroll, E. (2004). Students' perceptions of course web sites used in face-to-face instruction. *Journal of Interactive Learning Research, 15*(3), 197-211.

Bredekamp, S. (2002, July). *Using technology in early childhood professional development. In Technology and Early Childhood Professional Development: A Policy Discussion.* Education Commission of the States, Los Angeles.

Conrad, R. M. & Donaldson, A. (2004). *Engaging the online learner: Activities and resources for creative instruction.* San Francisco: Jossey-Bass.

Dick, W., & Carey, L. (1996). *The systematic design of instruction* (4th ed.). New York: Harper Collins College Publishers.

Fox, S. & Donahue C. (2006). Trends and promising practices in early childhood teacher education online: The view from New Zealand. *He Kupu, 1*(1), 29-34.

Jonassen, D. H., Peck, K. L., & Wilson, B. G. (1999) *Learning with technology: A constructive perspective.* New Jersey: Prentice Hall.

Kelly, K. L., & Schorger, J. (2002). *Online learning: Personalities, preferences, and perceptions.* (Report No. 143). (ERIC Document Reproduction Service No. ED 470 663)

Knowles, M. S. (1980) *The modern practice of adult education.* Englewood Cliffs, NJ: Cambridge.

Mackeracher, D. (2004). *Making sense of adult learning* (2nd ed.). Toronto, Canada: University of Toronto Press.

McVay-Lynch, M. (2002). *The online educator: A guide to creating the virtual classroom.* London: Taylor & Francis.

Ministry of Education, New Zealand. (2006). *e-Learning guidelines—Guidelines for the support of e-Learning in New Zealand tertiary institutions.* Retrieved from http://elg.massey.ac.nz/Guidelines-question.pdf.

Muilenburg, L. Y., & Berge, Z. L. (2005). Student barriers to online learning: A factor analytic study. *Distance Education, 26*(1), 29–48.

New Zealand Tertiary College. (2008). *New Zealand Tertiary College Prospectus 2008.* Auckland: New Zealand Tertiary College.

Walker, L., & du Plessis, K. (2007). *Executive summary report on results of web-enhanced distance learning pilot project.* Auckland: New Zealand Tertiary College.

Palloff, R., & Pratt, K. (2005). *Collaborating online: Learning together in community.* San Francisco: Jossey-Bass.

Smith, J., & Brown, A. (2005). *Building a culture of learning design: Reconsidering the place of online learning in the tertiary curriculum.* Retrieved from http://www.ascilite.org.au/conferences/brisbane05/blogs/proceedings/71_Smith.pdf

Slater, J. (2007). *Jottings by Janis.* Retrieved from http://jottingsbyjanis.blogspot.com/2007_03_01_archive.html

Twigg, C. A. (2001). *Innovations in online learning: Moving beyond no significant difference.* Troy, NY: Rensselaer Polytechnic Institute Center for Academic Transformation.

Wenger, E. (2000). Communities of practice and social learning systems. *Organization, 7*(2), 225-246.

Continuing the conversations

This final chapter of conversations on early childhood teacher education continues with the theme of nourishing the self. Each conversation has identified the importance of student teachers' voices, and of providing spaces for these. And in an online environment, such sharing is possible across traditionally insurmountable borders. Now, it may have seemed inconceivable two decades ago to suggest that an electronic medium for teacher education would be perceived as a viable option for supporting a student teacher in studying early childhood theory and practice. Yet not only has flexible, web-enhanced or online learning become possible, it is increasingly popular, suggesting merit to the visions of the early proponents of online early childhood teacher education.

The German philosopher Martin Heidegger claimed that technology gives presence to who we are. It follows that the online learning environment will not simply widen the scope for early childhood teacher education; it will have an impact on what it means to be a student teacher or a teacher educator. The increasing use of electronic media will affect the way we think about education, its nature and purpose, about communication, about assessment, about relationships, standards, collaboration, ethics, professionalism, culture, research and so on. That online learning will have such an impact is not surprising—the classroom, the printing press, the picture book, the personal computer, all had similar impact on these aspects of human life.

Three philosophical positions are important to consider: questioning (Heidegger, 1977), keeping questions permanently open (Foucault, 1989), and the celebration of difference (Lyotard, 1988). What do these philosophies mean for conversations on teacher education, online learning, and early childhood education more generally?

Lilian Katz notes in this book's opening address that early childhood teacher educators are constantly engaging with complex theoretical and practical dilemmas. Being confronted with a dilemma is not a problem, in the negative sense of a problem. The presence of a dilemma, in other words, is not an indication of a lack of quality in our teacher education practices.

Given the reality of diverse, heterogeneous social and cultural communities, we would be naive to expect our working lives to be dilemma-free zones. What does perhaps indicate the quality of our teacher education programs is the way in which we respond to dilemmas. How do we welcome differences in learning styles, technological capabilities, beliefs about education, and early childhood teaching practices? Are we permanently open to new ideas, and to revisiting our assumptions about education and learning? And in what ways do our online teaching practices celebrate, and protect, difference as an essential quality of being human?

In the spirit of conversation, these are very open questions, and very open conversations. We believe that teacher educators who continue to engage with these questions will positively and constructively influence the lives of student teachers in ways that nourish their sense of being authentic teachers (Gibbs, 2006) both in, and out of, the worldwide web.

References

Education Commission of the States. (2002). *Technology and early childhood professional development: A policy discussion*. Denver, CO: Education Commission of the States.

Foucault, M. (1989). The masked philosopher. (J. Johnston, Trans.). In M. Foucault, *Foucault live, Interviews 1966-84* (pp. 193-202). New York: Semiotext(e).

Gibbons, A. (2006). Distance learning and early childhood education: Retrospectives and future directions. *He Kupu 1*(1), 1-10.

Gibbs, C. J. (2006). *To be a teacher: Journeys towards authenticity*. Auckland, New Zealand: Pearson Education.

Heidegger, M. (1977). The question concerning technology. (W. Lovitt, Trans.). In M. Heidegger, *The question concerning technology and other essays* (pp. 1-49). New York: Harper & Row.

Lyotard, J-F. (1988). *The differend: Phrases in dispute*. (G. Van Den Abbeele, Trans.). Minneapolis, MN: University of Minnesota Press.

CHAPTER 6

FUTURE DIRECTIONS FOR EARLY CHILDHOOD TEACHER EDUCATION: TEN CONCERNS AND TEN PRINCIPLES

Colin Gibbs
New Zealand

 *Colin Gibbs is an educational consultant and Professor of Education and Teacher Education. He most recently taught at AUT University, Auckland, New Zealand. Over the last decade or so, he has focussed particularly on the personhood of teachers, teachers' beliefs, developing authenticity as teachers, and the value of the arts and spirituality as means to enrich teaching and learning. He promotes examining approaches to education which celebrate diversity in pedagogies and beliefs. As such, he was instrumental in establishing the first dual mainstream-Steiner and mainstream-Montessori teacher education degree programs. Colin presents papers and workshops nationally and internationally. He has over 100 publications including the book entitled* To be a Teacher: Journeys Towards Authenticity. *(Pearson Education, New Zealand) and is presently writing a book tentatively entitled* A Heart to Teach: Moments of Abundant Teacher Presence.

Introduction

This Working Forum has been about conversations from multiple perspectives, all of which have focussed on our central topic: early childhood teacher education.

My task is to draw together some themes that are emerging from our conversations. In doing so, I am mindful of not forcing conclusions, but rather allowing the space for us to keep on dwelling in the questions so that, as Michel Foucault (1989) nicely puts it, the questions remain permanently open so that the conversations may continue. Thus, I wish to ask some new questions within the same conversations while at the same time begin fresh conversations about future directions, and about what I believe really matters in early childhood teacher education. To position this conversation I shall identify ten concerns regarding early childhood teacher education in the future, and then propose ten principles which I value in early childhood teacher education programs.

'I wish to ask some new questions within the same conversations while at the same time begin fresh conversations about future directions, and about what I believe really matters in early childhood teacher education'

Some reflections on our Working Forum

This Working Forum has been about conversations; important conversations about early childhood teacher education. If conversations are to have life, then there need to be people willing to share and listen to ideas. This means pondering, reflecting, postulating, and even perhaps contemplating. Conversations cause connections as new understandings and appreciations arise—but conversations are made even richer when those who are engaged in them are connected by their mutual interests. Such is the case for this forum—our conversations center on our mutual interest and that is in early childhood teacher education.

These conversations have been, and no doubt will continue to be, rich in content and diverse in scope. They cause us to make connections as well as reconnections, sometimes new, other times affirming what we already may have accepted or believed. I am reminded that the power of words is greater than that which is spoken—the power of words is the source of creating something new. And therein lies the excitement of on-going conversations. Our conversations serve not only to connect and affirm—they also serve to create new possibilities. The future of early childhood teacher education, in this sense, therefore depends on our conversations.

'our conversations serve not only to connect and affirm—they also serve to create new possibilities. The future of early childhood teacher education, in this sense, therefore depends on our conversations'

Ten concerns for early childhood teacher education

At the commencement of the Working Forum, Lilian Katz (2008) asked us: *What are the problems that as early childhood educators, we are trying to answer?* I like the biblical principle of watching out for the signs. It helps me to contemplate and understand what has happened, and what may yet very well happen. My sense is that there are signs both nationally and internationally in early childhood teacher education. And these signs raise questions which deserve our attention, for much of the course of the future is in our hands.

So, I asked myself, *What are my ten concerns for early childhood teacher education in the future?* My concerns which follow are neither prioritised nor exclusive. Nevertheless, I trust that they will help us with our on-going conversations.

1. A concern about policy makers' pottery wheels

Let me begin by saying that we need policy makers. Policy makers can and should enable fair and equitable systems for the provision of early childhood teacher education. My concern relates to who may be seen as the potter, and who may be seen as the clay when it comes to early childhood teachers, teaching, and learning.

'policy makers can and should enable fair and equitable systems for the provision of early childhood teacher education'

As an example, consider the achievement of Māori (the indigenous people of Aotearoa-New Zealand) which is reported as being lower than that of non-Māori students. Not surprisingly there is great concern about rectifying this situation, as there ought to be. So, the recently released Aotearoa/New Zealand curriculum document *Ka Hikitea—*

Managing Success: The Māori Education Strategy 2008-2012 (2008) emphasizes enabling the educational systems to function effectively so that Māori students' achievement will increase. Such an argument is seductive in that it proposes that if systems are effective, then achievement will increase. A good and desirable outcome, except that when and if there are increases in achievement, they are inevitably attributed to policy makers who correctly orchestrated education systems. If, however, Māori students fail to make the achievement gains expected, then teachers are to blame. After all, the policy makers addressed the system. Thus, teachers become the blame for failure, but are absent when the praise is given.

> 'teachers become the blame for failure, but are absent when the praise is given'

My concern is that such reasoning places teachers as clay in the hands of potters—the policy makers at their system's wheels generating policies. So, sadly, the argument is not as simple as first seems, for we know that well-designed systems do not necessarily lead irrevocably to achievement gains. They may, but teaching and learning are about people and relationships, in the first instance, not policy. Policy does matter, but what matters most in teaching and learning is people. As early childhood teacher educators, we must be vigilant to protect what is valued.

> 'policy does matter, but what matters most in teaching and learning is people'

Let me take another instance. As part of the *No Child Left Behind Act* of 2001 in the United States, all states are required to measure student academic achievement. They use methods that analyse *gains, growth in scores, or the amount of knowledge added from year to year as students progress through school* (Amrein-Beardsley, 2008, p. 65). Not surprisingly, such methods are popular among policy makers (Olson, 2004a). After all, as Amrein-Beardsley (2008, p. 66) points out, such a system, which is:

built largely on algorithms calculated by computer, permits large scale analyses of student achievement data from which determinations may be made about growth in student achievement and the effectiveness of districts, schools, and teachers over time
(Sanders & Horn, 1994; Sanders, Saxton, Schneider, Dearden, Wright, & Horn, 2002).

In short, *good* teachers can be statistically identified as those who produce the most academic achievement gains in students.

> 'the argument becomes, *good* teachers can be statistically identified as those who produce the most academic achievement gains in students'

Not surprisingly, such methods are proving popular with those who make and market tests. These companies stand to gain from the financial investment in the testing industry of between $US1.9 billion and $US5.3 billion from 2004 through to 2010 (Olson, 2004b).

Furthermore, some of these testing methods are claimed to be *unimpaired by students' backgrounds (race and levels of poverty), which* [are seen to] *distort all other analyses of test score data* (Amrein-Beardsley, 2008, p. 66). In short, the testing regime has ethnically and socially cleansed the performance of students' backgrounds.

What we are seeing is that the testing business in education has become what the pharmaceutical business is to health. The commercial enterprise of the pharmaceutical business has often been accused of profiteering from producing 'more' and 'better' drugs for consumers, namely patients. We need to be vigilant to ensure that testing companies do not continue to produce 'more' and 'better' tests for consumers, namely students.

> 'we need to be vigilant to ensure that testing companies do not continue to produce 'more' and 'better' tests for consumers, namely students'

What does this mean for early childhood education, children, and teachers? Put simply, when policy makers, curriculum developers and test makers run away with such ideas, we need to ask the question—what are you doing to our children? And… what are you doing to our teachers? Will it be but a matter of time before early childhood centres become centres for value-added assessment systems? We protect our children from unsafe environments. We need also to protect our children from such unsafe policy excesses.

> 'we protect our children from unsafe environments. We need also to protect our children from such unsafe policy excesses'

2. A concern about 'white shoe' education evangelists

I have a concern about 'white shoe' education evangelists. Education is not exempt from profiteers who claim quick fix solutions designed to appeal to the immediate needs and wants of teachers, and who then take the money and run.

Teaching is complex—simple solutions rarely satisfy such complexity. In fact, I think it was the newspaperman H. L. Mencken (source unknown) who said, *for every complex problem there is an answer that is clear, simple, and wrong.*

Teaching and learning are relational and therefore need time and personal investment to nurture. My concern is for us to beware of such education evangelists who promote the ultimate all-in-one solution at a financial cost for early childhood education centres, for their shoes gather no dust.

> 'my concern is for us to beware of such education evangelists who promote the ultimate all-in-one solution at a financial cost for early childhood education centres, for their shoes gather no dust'

3. A concern that increasing control may cripple autonomy and build distrust

Control, by its very definition, serves to limit or even close down. It reduces risk of failure and an increase of certainty that a predetermined pathway will be adhered to. But more than this—control is often (but not necessarily always) associated with distrust—that is, when we consider that we are being controlled, we are likely to also perceive that we are not trusted to act in ways that will bring about what others want. Such control restricts our scope of activity so that we have fewer opportunities to be distracted from that task so that we might then perform in expected ways. Climates that cultivate 'conform and perform' policies cripple autonomy and build distrust.

As we meet the needs of students previously excluded from accessing teacher education, there may well still be a remaining group, or indeed a new group, of potential candidates who remain excluded for a variety of reasons—e.g., connectivity, access to computers. However, while we may wish to give computers to the unconnected, this does not mean that we necessarily should.

Editors

'climates that cultivate 'conform and perform' policies cripple autonomy and build distrust'

Perceptions of autonomy, on the other hand, generally enable the opening of opportunities to explore, to experiment, and to give things a go. Innovativeness, creativity, and risk-taking thrive in situations where people perceive a genuine sense of responsible autonomy. When teachers believe they are trusted to be responsible in exercising that autonomy, then they will be more innovative (Locke, Zubritzky, Cousins, & Bobko, 1984), they will take on new educational practices and teaching approaches (Stein & Wang, 1988), they will be more resilient, and they will be more likely to take chances even if it means failing (Guskey, 1988; Smylie, 1988). But furthermore, they will also be more likely to be satisfied with their job, and less likely to be absent from work (Farber, 1991; Friedman & Farber, 1992).

Ackerman (Lawson, 1972, p. 242) posed the question: *shall a child be governed from the head down or from the heart up?* Likewise, I ask, shall a teacher be governed from the head down or from the heart up? In short, early childhood teacher educators need to be vigilant to ensure that they retain genuine professional autonomy in their decisions about teaching and learning.

'shall a teacher be governed from the head down or from the heart up?'

4. A concern about producing products rather than nurturing people

The political zeal for measurable standards of performance, although honourable in intent, may have undesirable side effects. I think a robust general principle in education is that 'what we emphasise in education is often what we get'. When we emphasise achievement outcomes above all else, then we are likely to produce achievement outcomes above all else. High achievement is desirable. But at what cost? When education becomes focussed on the mass production of products—namely, evidence of demonstrable achievement—then we have lost what it means to be educated. Teaching and learning is not just about achievement and standards of performance; it is not simply the production of quality assured products. It is about care, compassion, love, hope, joy, passion, grace, relationship, and more. It is about people and how we nurture and are nurtured on our learning journeys.

'what we emphasise in education is often what we get'

So, when we consider what the signs are showing us, it begs us to ask:

What do we value in early childhood education?

What is it that we wish to emphasise?

And how might we make this authentic in our early childhood teacher education curricula and pedagogy?

5. A concern about compulsory school creep

Perhaps many of the former points I have made may be seen as relating in the first instance to schooling. But I suggest they also have much to do with early childhood education, for they reveal signs. Let me explain.

Though some may disagree, it is my view that many of the new school curriculum initiatives in Aotearoa/New Zealand have been driven by the political aspirations to increase secondary school achievement in the first instance. The result has been that much of the innovative practice that has traditionally been rich in the primary schooling years has become lost or submerged under the pressure to produce demonstrable performance on specified learning outcomes—a consequence of the backwash from the political tinkering with secondary education.

> 'much of the innovative practice that has traditionally been rich in primary schooling years has become lost or submerged under the pressure to produce demonstrable performance on specified learning outcomes—a consequence of the backwash from the political tinkering with secondary education'

This contrasts to some decades ago when the free play philosophy of early childhood education flourished, and indeed, permeated into the early years of primary schooling, creating as it were innovative, exploratory-based programs such as the one called 'developmental' in Aotearoa/New Zealand. It is true that such play philosophies are now subject to some questioning as to their real effects on learning, but the point is that they made a substantial upward influence on schooling. Put simply, programs and practices in early childhood influenced programs and practices in the early years of schooling—a 'push up' effect if you like. Our conversations at this forum help us. Lily Wong (2008), for instance, gave us warning signs—she spoke of the 'push down' effect where in Singapore children do a preparatory year in reading and writing before entering school.

My concern is that compulsory school initiatives, driven by government's desire to increase performance and achievement, will experience downward creep into early childhood education causing programs, curriculum, and pedagogy to trade many innovative and flexible practices for those which are narrowly focussed on endpoint rather than in-process performances.

6. A concern about dependence on educational myths and fads

Education has its share of myths and fads, and unfortunately early childhood is not exempt. Many of these have now become enshrined in the professional dialogue and literature as 'given truths' in spite of often dubious research support. For example, Ivan Snook (2007) provides an excellent philosophical critique of learning styles (and what he terms as other modern educational myths such as multiple intelligences, and emotional intelligence) and rightly suggests that in our role as critic and conscience of society, and of our own teacher education profession, we ought not uncritically accept *fashionable concepts which often serve ideological purposes* (p. 8).

> 'we ought not uncritically accept *fashionable concepts which often serve ideological purposes*'

7. A concern about undervaluing families

Early childhood education values families. It is generally accepted that governments wish to support families, as well as early childhood education. Yet, there is always a tension as to when government activity becomes akin to over-regulation or even political interference for that matter, especially when it concerns families. And when this occurs, there are often unintended messages conveyed.

Take, for example, New Zealand's current policy of increasing participation rates in early childhood. Many would see this as a laudable goal—after all, we want our children to participate in quality care settings where there are rich experiences in education. But consider this. Does this also convey an unintended message that early childhood centres are 'more' valuable environments for children than those provided by families? Clearly, parents, and especially mothers, are encouraged to return to the workforce, for it is said that politically we value a highly productive economy. But remember the welcoming words of our kaumatua, the Māori elder, at this Working Forum who reminded us of grandmothers being the first teachers; Lily Wong (2008) who shared that Singaporeans viewed grandmothers as the preferred first teachers. And Andrew Gibbons (2008) who came to the conclusion, *I would say to your child, stay at home with your grandmother. She is far more important to your education than I.*

'early childhood education programs are not always the panacea for all children's educational, social, emotional, physical, and spiritual circumstances'

We need to realise that early childhood education programs are not always the panacea for all children's educational, social, emotional, physical, and spiritual circumstances. Yet, they may be for some, perhaps many. If we value parent and family participation in early childhood programs as well, then we ought to enable such access and participation to be able to happen. Then the environments of families and early childhood centres may both be seen to be valued in their similarities as well as their differences.

'if we value parent and family participation in early childhood programs as well, then we ought to enable such access and participation to be able to happen'

8. A concern about living in unquestioned rhetoric

Early childhood teacher education has its linguistic code—professional jargon if you like—which serves to not just communicate especially between its members, but also results in including and excluding people. Much of this linguistic code derives from familiar theoretical literature. Thus, we hear of *scaffolding, constructivist, social constructivist, critical reflectivity, teacher as reflective practitioner,* and so on. Interestingly, as I discussed this with Lilian Katz we agreed that the term 'scaffolding' probably is used inaccurately—from an engineering point of view the term is better translated as bracing rather than scaffolding. And builders know that bracing and scaffolding have different meanings and functions—one holds the structure together; the other provides access to the structure.

My concern is that such technical talk, however, may fall victim to becoming unquestioned rhetoric—that is, language seemingly based upon an 'appeal to authority' which is used to persuade or impress others. I need to constantly remind myself of this too! When language is used this way, it no longer becomes part of meaningful communications, but rather serves as emblems of membership. If we teach out of who we are (Palmer, 1998), then clearly how we communicate must reflect the integrity of that personness (Gibbs, 2006). As teachers, then, the language we use must reflect our commitment to inclusive, not exclusive, communication.

9. A concern about the stifling of special character

In the drive to increase achievement, my concern is that diversity of special character programs in early childhood may be repressed. We know that there are many expressions of special character in early childhood—Montessori, Steiner, Christian, Islamic, Buddhist, Baha'i, as well as the numerous forms of indigenous language early childhood centres, to name just a few.

Special character education contributes an important dimension to early childhood education. It challenges us to reconsider our positions which we may hold with a presumed certainty, and to remember that there is not just the one way to teach. It challenges us to consider new possibilities for learning and teaching. We have much to learn from special character early childhood education, and therefore we must resist any attempts to stifle their presence, or to standardise their practices.

> 'special character education challenges us to reconsider our positions which we may hold with a presumed certainty, and to remember that there is not just the one way to teach. It challenges us to consider new possibilities for learning and teaching'

10. A concern about resisting the new and devaluing the old

Living in the status quo leads to a place of either complacency or powerlessness. So, too, does resisting the new and devaluing the old. I must say that this notion resonates for me as in recent times I have become even more interested in the ideas of the great philosophers such as Plato, Rousseau, and so on. I have also returned to those who tried out new ideas in their time—Elwyn Richardson, Gordon Tovey, Sylvia Ashton Warner, Clarence Beeby—as well as educational experimenters such as A. S Neill, Rudolf Steiner, and Maria Montessori. I am finding that they are teaching me much about how I might teach in the future. And I am finding new insights through the teachings of people such as Parker Palmer, Saint Aquinas, Māori Marsden, Kristnamurti ,and the Dalai Lama. That is my journey and I know others seek out others to glean new insights about themselves as teachers, and about teaching and learning.

The ways of old provide insights into the ways of the future. Likewise, the new provides ways of re-interpreting the ways of old. Technological advancements, for example, open many possibilities to both enrich as well as restrain early childhood education. This becomes clear as we read the many papers in this book on the implementation and effects of online early childhood teacher education. By valuing the wisdom of old, we may better appreciate the potential of the new.

> 'the ways of old provide insights into the ways of the future'

Ten principles to underpin early childhood teacher education

When we think about early childhood teacher education, it is good to ask ourselves the question—*what are the essential principles upon which we will build robust programs?*

I suggest that regardless of whether we are building curricula for initial teacher education, induction and the early years of teaching, or inservice and professional development, there must be a set of principles to guide us. Principles keep us grounded. And so here are ten of the principles which I value in early childhood teacher education programs. They are not intended to be comprehensive, nor are they necessarily prioritised.

1. Early childhood teacher education honors the whole person

Perhaps more so than any other education sector, early childhood education espouses the importance of attending to the whole person. Usually this refers to the baby, infant, and child. But it goes further than this. For our purposes, to honour the whole person means beginning with the whole teacher—appreciating, valuing, and nurturing. An important task we have as teacher educators is to ensure that our student teachers are honoured as people who have different beliefs, dispositions, values, interests, and experiences. When we begin by honoring who they are as 'whole' people, then we can allow them the grace to be who they are as teachers, and not who we want to shape them into being.

2. Early childhood teacher education welcomes the full expression of diversity

Diversity manifests itself in many ways. It obviously encompasses gender, but also includes appreciating the fullness of ability and capability, as well as ethnic diversity, and of allowing for the full unimpeded expression of one's cultural identity.

Diversity also refers to the range of early childhood education programs, pedagogies, and philosophies. There is richness in diversity especially where these are entitled to be freely expressed. When such freedom is achieved, then we will less likely say that we have mainstream early childhood education and alternative early childhood education. Each is another expression of the other; sometimes in harmony, sometimes in difference. As teacher educators, we have an important role to play in ensuring that we welcome the full expression of diversity.

> 'as teacher educators, we have an important role to play in ensuring that we welcome the full expression of diversity'

3. Early childhood teacher education nurtures individual teachers and their journeys toward increasing authenticity

Teachers are individuals with their own beliefs, values, dispositions, and personalities. When there is harmony between what teachers believe and value, and how they come to teach, then there is a place of power (Gibbs, 2006). Powerful teaching occurs when there is synergy between the self-as-person and how the person teaches. Parker Palmer (1998) sees this as teaching out of an undivided self. Teacher education programs, therefore, need to be centred on what I refer to as teachers' and student teachers' individual journeys towards authenticity (Gibbs, 2006).

Parker Palmer goes further and speaks of authentic spirituality as an essential part of the person who is teacher, and that which must be nurtured. He says:

Authentic spirituality wants to open us to truth—whatever truth may be, wherever truth may take us. Such spirituality does not dictate where we must go, but trusts that any path walked with integrity will take us to a place of knowledge. Such a spirituality encourages us to welcome diversity and conflict, to tolerate ambiguity, and to embrace paradox. By this understanding, the spirituality of education is not about dictating ends. It is about examining and clarifying the inner sources of teaching and learning, ridding us of the toxins that poison our hearts and minds. Palmer, 1993, p. xi

Our journeys as teachers see us reaching out for more—reaching further to grasp new ideas, concepts, and possibilities, but also reaching inwards to nourish and reveal more of who we are as people and as teachers. Our inward journey takes hold of the authenticity of our life that feeds the life of our teaching.

> 'our journeys as teachers see us reaching out for more— reaching further to grasp new ideas, concepts, and possibilities, but also reaching inwards to nourish and reveal more of who we are as people and as teachers'

Given this, I guess we may ask the question:

What space do we create in our teacher education programs to nurture individual teachers and their journeys toward increasing authenticity?

> 'what space do we create in our teacher education programs to nurture individual teachers and their journeys toward increasing authenticity?'

4. Early childhood teacher education values teachers' beliefs as being instrumental in understanding their motivation and actions

Over the last two decades we have learned much about motivation. Sadly, some of these lessons are yet to be learned in teacher education. For example, social cognitive theory shows us that knowing how to teach, and even being able to demonstrate such knowledge, does not mean that we are likely to teach in those ways. What matters are teachers' beliefs about themselves, and those of their students. For instance, research shows that teachers who have strong self-efficacy are more resilient, more innovative, and more effective as teachers (Gibbs, 2006). While our emphasis needs to be on skills and attitudes, in themselves these are insufficient. We need to address the central task of ensuring that teachers' self-efficacy is enhanced—that is, their beliefs. Then we will see increased motivation as well as more innovative practices in our early childhood teaching.

> 'social cognitive theory shows us that knowing how to teach, and even being able to demonstrate such knowledge, does not mean that we are likely to teach in those ways'

5. Early childhood teacher education nourishes the fullness of teacher presence

Conversations about the sense of presence of teachers is absent from most of our literature about teaching. Yet, I am convinced that teachers' presence is perhaps the most persuasive and endearing aspect of teaching. When we talk with teachers about teacher presence—especially those who show what I call 'abundant teacher presence' (Gibbs, 2009)—we glean exciting revelations about the depth of who teachers are. Let me give you an example. Following is a conversation with a teacher who has taught children of all ages. Listen as he talks about what teacher presence means to him as a teacher:

Presence is a space that must be felt. It is a feeling that makes another feel warm, cared for, attended to, listened to, and heard. It is a feeling that this person is putting their focus and heart into you at that time. They want to know you. It is in their eyes too, sparkle, smile, and lots of asking you about you… not about telling you about them.

Presence is about creating a real relationship. It is about laughter and about noticing when others have trouble or sadness on their face. Presence is when you can feel they care. They are genuine. They want to connect for real. Presence is there when, after the exchange, that person remains with you... their words... their smile...their touch... their genuineness... their energy has been positive.

Presence is an energy... you can feel it. You can see it on a person's face. It is in their eyes and in their smile. They interact with you lots and it is not always verbal... a smile... a shared joke... a touch... a wink... a comment. It is when the teacher is there with the kids... fully there.... It is about face-to-face, eye to eye. It is about doing lots of activities together. It is there when laughter is heard and real interactions of the human kind are heard... when the teacher is there for their kids... tears... laughing... listening with heart. Teachers who have this presence are easily recognisable... they are those who have great mana and authority, but it is theirs because young people have given it to them. It has been earned, not demanded. It is not authority taken, because that sort of authority is never freely given. These special teachers earn their influence by service and duty of care to others. Gibbs, 2009.

What does this all mean? Well, simply it asks the question: *How does my teacher education programme allow for, respect, and nurture each teacher's sense of teacher presence?*

> 'how do teacher education programmes allow for, respect, and nurture each teacher's sense of teacher presence?'

6. Early childhood teacher education honors emotions, dispositions, and personality as reflecting the humanness of teachers—this includes, for instance, joy, love, compassion, grace, humility, and passion

Many of our teacher education programs have become entrenched in academic institutions where the essential capacities of the emotional, affective, and spiritual have been depreciated. Thus emotions, dispositions, and personality are less valued while the cognitive and academic are honoured. Yet we know that the heart of teaching is in relational connectedness—with self, with others, and with the world in which we live (Gibbs, 2006). Joy, love, compassion, grace, humility, and passion portray an essence of life and living, and as such convey much about the 'personness' of the teacher. This means that the fullness of becoming a teacher must encapsulate not just the head, but all aspects concerned with the significance of living.

> 'we know that the heart of teaching is in relational connectedness—with self, with others, and with the world in which we live'

Kristnamurti (1953, p. 13) says that:

Education is not merely a matter of training the mind. Training makes for efficiency, but it does not bring about completeness. A mind that has merely been trained is the continuation of the past, and such a mind can never discover the new. That is why, to find out what is right education, we will have to inquire into the whole significance of living.

7. Early childhood teacher education values freedom to initiate, as well as to exercise autonomy with responsibility

Sadly, when we consider many of our teacher education programs and practices, it is seldom that we see the full outworking of the valuing of freedom to initiate coupled with the exercising of autonomy with responsibility. I make this point for I believe that a fundamental purpose of education is enabling students to learn to act autonomously, when appropriate, but always with a genuine sense of responsibility. The balance is delicate for it is somewhere between, on the one hand, the strict unquestioning adherence to law-boundedness, as contrasted on the other hand with acting without due regard for others.

'a fundamental purpose of education is enabling students to learn to act autonomously, when appropriate, but always with a genuine sense of responsibility'

Early childhood education settings are important sites for learning how one can freely exercise autonomy with a deep sense of responsibility. Inevitably, responsibility involves both care and compassion, and these, therefore, become necessary dispositions in early childhood teachers. It also requires environments that create spaces for meaningful relationships through which there is freedom to act with responsibility. Early childhood teachers are instrumental in enabling these spaces. The Dalai Lama encapsulates this thought when he says:

If you approach others with the thought of compassion that will automatically reduce fear and allow openness with other people. It creates a positive, friendly atmosphere. With that attitude, you can approach a relationship in which you, yourself initially create the possibility of receiving affection or a positive response from the other person… that kind of openness at least allows the possibility of having a meaningful conversation with them. Cutler, 1998, p. 69

This speaks to me of early childhood teachers and teacher educators who are committed to the valuing of freedom to initiate while at the same time allowing the exercising of autonomy with responsibility and that this is expressed through their life, and through the life of their teaching.

8. Early childhood teacher education enables teachers to critically reflect, self-reflect, contemplate, and to nourish their souls

Much has been written about teachers as reflective practitioners. Reflecting on one's practice has been shown to bring about positive changes in how teachers teach. Unfortunately though, in many teacher education programs critical reflectivity has been loosely interpreted as 'evaluation' (of lessons, of teaching technique, and so on). Furthermore, it often misses focusing on what is the heart of the teacher. Thus, the true essence of the reflective process is lost. If teaching is about teaching from within—that is, teaching which draws from the person you are—then there is also a need to reflect on the person who is teacher.

'if teaching is about teaching from within—that is, teaching which draws from the person you are—then there is also a need to reflect on the person who is teacher'

For some teachers, this means some form of contemplation; for others it might mean daily quiet times where one can 'connect with the innerness of oneself'. Whatever teachers do, when they focus on the person who is teacher, inevitably it leads to changes in the self. When changes occur, they affect the presence of the soulness of teachers.

'whatever teachers do, when they focus on the person who is teacher, inevitably it leads to changes in the self. When changes occur, they affect the presence of the soulness of teachers'

In this regard, Steiner provides an interesting perspective. He suggests there are three aspects to the human soul, namely, thinking, feeling, and willing. The thinking aspect of soul is associated with ideas and knowledge, and Steiner suggests it is therefore linked to freedom. Teachers ought to reflect in order to nourish the thinking component of their soul. The feeling aspect of soul is associated with the rhythmic system, and in particular, breathing. It follows that teachers ought to consider forms of relaxation or perhaps meditation where they may become more attuned to their bodily rhythms such as breathing, for this nourishes their soul. Steiner also says there is a third dimension to soul, namely that of willing. Willing is the least conscious, and includes instinct, drive, desire, motive, wish, intention, and resolve. Steiner's advice then would be that as teachers and teacher educators we ought to also nourish our souls by contemplatively attending to these three aspects—thinking, feeling, and willing.

> 'as teachers and teacher educators we ought to also nourish our soul by contemplatively attending to these three aspects—thinking, feeling, and willing'

If we are convinced that teacher education is not simply technical reproduction, then it poses the question:

To what extent do our teacher education programs enable teachers to critically reflect, self-reflect, contemplate, and to nourish their soul?

9. Early childhood teacher education encourages teachers to be wise and to grow in wisdom

Teachers—especially spirit-aware teachers—reflect, contemplate, reason, seek intuition, and wisdom (Gibbs, 2006). Wisdom requires an inner searching and an outer reaching, a preparedness to transcend the present and known, and to take hold of new revelations and insights. Let me stress that each teacher has her or his own ways of seeking and revealing wisdom and it would be unwise for me to insist on one way. But let me share some insights from two perspectives.

The Reverend Māori Marsden sees meditation as the key to transforming knowledge into wisdom. He writes:

By meditation in the heart, the centre of one's being, illumination comes suddenly in a moment of time, and the unorganised sets of ideas suddenly gel together to form an integrated whole in which the tensions and contradictions are resolved. Knowledge is transformed into wisdom. This is essentially a spiritual experience. Royal, 2003, p. 59

The pathway to wisdom is also reflected in Buddhism.

In Buddhism, wisdom is sometimes called 'self-secret'. We have it, but we don't know that we have it. The secret is not a secret kept from someone else. It's a secret that we ourselves don't know yet! Rinpoche, 1999, p. 56

Undoubtedly, many teachers are wise and many show remarkable measures of wisdom. Sadly, however, few early childhood teacher education programs seem to explicitly commit themselves to nurturing teachers who are wise, and who genuinely pursue wisdom.

> 'sadly, few early childhood teacher education programs seem to explicitly commit themselves to nurturing teachers who are wise, and who genuinely pursue wisdom'

And few teacher educators speak openly about fostering wisdom. Maybe this is because as teacher educators we may not be sure how we might help teachers to be wise, and to develop wisdom. But maybe that is the place to begin.

10. Early childhood teacher education upholds and practises social justice

Rabbi Michael Lerner (n.d.) said this:

By social justice I mean the creation of a society which treats human beings as embodiments of the sacred, supports them to realize their fullest potential, and promotes and rewards people to the extent that they are loving and caring, kind and generous, open-hearted and playful, ethically and ecologically sensitive, and tend to respond to the universe with awe, wonder, and radical amazement at the grandeur of creation.

> 'teachers have a responsibility to demonstrate social justice. It begins with who they are, and it extends into their communities of learning which they share with their students'

Teachers have a responsibility to demonstrate social justice. But to have such a commitment must begin with who they are, what they believe and live by, which in turn extends into their communities of learning that they share with their students. Such teachers believe and work in ways that promote fairness and equality, and eliminate discrimination. They convey deep commitment to the principle of fairness being valued in actions and thinking (Gibbs, 2006). Marilyn Cochran-Smith puts it this way:

We need teachers who regard teaching as a political activity and embrace social change as part of the job, teachers who enter the profession not expecting to carry on business as usual but prepared to join other educators and parents in major reforms. Cochran-Smith, 1995, p. 494

Marilyn Cochran-Smith rightly challenges us to think about how teacher education upholds and practises social justice. Likewise, I cannot help but feel that our conversations must surely spend more time considering what this means for our teacher education programs.

Final comment

What does it all mean? I set myself the task of drawing out ten concerns and ten principles on which we might build early childhood teacher education in the future. Underpinning all these concerns and principles, however, is the heart of the teacher—the person who is the teacher. It is the person who is the teacher who will ensure that the concerns do not become problems. It is the person who is the teacher who will ensure that teaching and learning is wholehearted and grounded on principles.

> 'it is the person who is the teacher who will ensure that teaching and learning is wholehearted and grounded on principles'

Earlier in this Working Forum Roger McClay (2008) encouraged us to cherish children—he said *we need to care for tenderly, to nurture, to value, to hold* [our children] *dear.* Lilian Katz (2008) suggested that *it is a good idea to cultivate our own intellects and nourish the life of the mind.* The advice of both Roger and Lilian is wise and pertinent for our times.

May I also suggest, though, that to nourish and cherish children we must first nourish and cherish ourselves as people as well as teachers. Nourish not only your mind and your feelings towards children, but also the whole person that you are—the thinking, feeling, believing, spiritual person who is the teacher. Then, as student teachers, teachers and teacher educators, we can draw from the fullness of our inner well to serve others.

> 'nourish not only your mind and your feelings towards children, but also the whole person that you are—the thinking, feeling, believing, spiritual person who is the teacher'

References

Amrein-Beardsley, A. (2008). Methodological concerns about the Education Value-Added Assessment System. *Educational Researcher, 37*(2), 65-75.

Cochran-Smith, M. (1995). Color blindness and basket-making are not the answers: Confronting the dilemmas of race, culture, and language diversity in teacher education. *American Educational Research Journal, 32*(2), 493-522.

Cutler, H. C. (1998). *The art of happiness: A handbook for living.* Sydney: Hodder Australia.

Farber, B. A. (1991). *Crisis in education: Stress and burnout in the American teacher.* San Francisco: Jossey Bass.

Foucault, M. (1989). The masked philosopher. (J. Johnson, Trans.). In M. Foucault, *Foucault live interviews 1966-84* (pp. 193-202). New York: Semiotect(e).

Friedman, I. A., & Farber, B. A. (1992). Professional self-concept as a predictor of teacher burn-out. *Journal of Educational Research, 86*(1), 28-35.

Gibbons, A. (2008, May). *The limits of biculturalism: Ka Hikitea and early childhood teacher education in Aotearoa.* Paper presented at the World Forum on Early Care and Education: Working Forum for Teacher Educators, Auckland, New Zealand.

Gibbs, C. J. (2006). *To be a teacher: Journeys towards authenticity.* Auckland, New Zealand: Pearson Education.

Gibbs, C. J. (2009, book manuscript in preparation). *A heart to teach: Moments of abundant teacher presence.*

Guskey, T. R. (1988). Teacher efficacy, self-concept, and attitudes toward the implementation of instructional innovation. *Teaching and Teacher Education, 4*(1), 63-70.

Katz, L. (2008, May). *Challenges in the education of teachers of young children.* Paper presented at the World Forum on Early Care and Education: Working Forum for Teacher Educators, Auckland, New Zealand.

Kristnamurti, J. (1953). *Education and the significance of life.* Ojai, CA: Kristnamurti Foundation of America.

Lawson, M. (1972). *Summerhill: For and against. Assessments of A. S. Neill.* Sydney: Angus and Robertson.

Lerner, M. (n.d.). Retrieved from http://www.reachandteach.com/content/article.php?story=20040812190148765

Locke, E. A., Zubritzky, E., Cousins, E., & Bobko, P. (1984). Effect of previously assigned goals on self-set goals and performance. *Journal of Applied Psychology, 69,* 694-699.

McClay, R. (2008, May). *Cherishing children.* Paper presented at the World Forum on Early Care and Education: Working Forum for Teacher Educators, Auckland, New Zealand.

Ministry of Education (2008). *Ka hikitea—Managing success: The Māori education strategy 2008-2012.* Wellington, New Zealand: Learning Media.

Olson, L. (2004a). 'Value added' models gain in popularity. *Education Week.* Retrieved from http://www.edweek.org/ew/articles/2004/11/17/12value.h24.html

Olson, L. (2004b). NCLB law bestows bounty on test industry. *Education Week.* Retrieved from http://www.edweek.org/ew/articles/2004/12/01/14tests.h24.html

Palmer, P. J. (1993). *To know as we are known: Education as a spiritual journey.* New York: Harper Collins.

Palmer, P. J. (1998). *The courage to teach: Exploring the inner landscapes of a teacher's life.* San Francisco: Jossey-Bass.

Rinpoche, D. P. (1999). Buddhist education: The path of knowledge and wisdom. In S. Glazer (Ed.), *The heart of learning: Spirituality in education* (pp. 51-60). New York: Penguin Putman Inc.

Royal, Te Akukaramū Charles. (2003). The natural world and natural resources: Māori value systems and perspectives. *In Te Akukaramū Charles Royal (Ed.), The woven universe: Selected writings of Rev. Māori Marsden* (pp. 2453). Ōtaki, New Zealand: Estate of Rev. Māori Marsden.

Sanders, W. L., & Horn, S. (1994). The Tennessee Value-Added Assessment System (TVAAS) database: Mixed-model methodology in educational assessment. *Journal of Personnel Evaluation in Education, 8*(3), 299-311.

Sanders, W. L., Saxton, A., Schneider, J., Dearden, B., Wright, S. P., & Horn, S. (2002). *Effects of building change on indicators of student achievement growth: Tennessee Value-Added Assessment System*. Knoxville: University of Tennessee Value-Added Assessment System Research Center.

Smylie, M. A. (1988). The enhancement function of staff development: Organizational and psychological antecedents to individual teacher change. *American Educational Research Journal, 25*(1), 1-30.

Snook, I. (2007). *Learning styles and other modern educational myths*. Paper presented at the Philosophy of Education Society of Australasia Conference, http://www.pesa.org.au/html/documents/2007-papers/Snook,%20I.pdf

Stein, M. K., & Wang, M. C. (1988). Teacher development and school improvement: The process of teacher change. *Teaching and Teacher Education, 4*(1), 171-187.

Wong, L. (2008, May). *Adult learning principles and ethical issues in early childhood teacher education*. Paper presented at the World Forum on Early Care and Education: Working Forum for Teacher Educators, Auckland, New Zealand.

Working Forum for Early Childhood Teacher Educators, 2008: Participants

Pepe Alefaio, New Zealand
Lorrey Arial, Canada
Karyn Aspden, New Zealand
Lindy Austin, New Zealand
Barbara Backshall, New Zealand
Janine Barndon, Australia
Lynn Marie Brennan, Canada
Elsbeth Brown, United States
Margerette Cantwell, New Zealand
Cynthia Carter, Canada
Hui Meng Chen, Singapore
Kathryn S. Clark, United States
Heather Conroy, Singapore
Sharon Cooke, New Zealand
Kirsty Cuthers, New Zealand
Rose Davies, Jamaica
Sean Dolan, New Zealand
Chip Donohue, United States
Barbara Duffy, Canada
Karin DuPlessis, New Zealand
Mary Earick, United States
Julianne Exton, New Zealand
Victoria Farguhar-Ayson, New Zealand
Loryn Feeney, Australia
Iwonna Florczyk, Canada
Kazimierz Florczyk, Canada
Rhonda Forrest, Australia
Lyn Forster, New Zealand
Selena Fox, New Zealand
Rebecca Freier, Australia
Jane Ciumwari Gatumu, Kenya
Andrew Gibbons, New Zealand
Colin Gibbs, New Zealand
Joy Gibson, Australia
Helga Glover-Plant, New Zealand
Julie Godwin, Australia
Emma Gordon, New Zealand
Judy Goth-Owens, United States
Jill Hadley, Australia
Ellen Hall, United States
Catherine Hamill, Australia
Louise Hard, Australia
Richard Heraud, SOMEWHERE
Rita Huang, New Zealand
Lorrie Huggins, Canada
Mary Hynes-Berry, United States
Rebeca Itzkowich, United States
Lilian Katz, United States

Ra Keelan, New Zealand
Natasha Kibble, New Zealand
Sabina Klepp, Australia
Kylie Lamont, New Zealand
Ann Le Marseny, SOMEWHERE
Melanie Lewandowski, New Zealand
Rachel Lincoln, New Zealand
Ros Littledyke, Australia
Raena Lopas, New Zealand
Katrina Ludeman, New Zealand
Alison Lutton, United States
Nanisi Mabbs, New Zealand
Ishbel Macconnachie, Australia
Christine Mayfield, Australia
Fiona McAlevey, New Zealand
Roger McClay, New Zealand
Cheryl McConnell, New Zealand
Jenny McDonald, New Zealand
Bambi McLean, Australia
Karen Miller, New Zealand
Chris Naughton, New Zealand
Bonnie Neugebauer, United States
Roger Neugebauer, United States
Ann Noland, United States
Glennie Oborn, New Zealand
Latika Oud, New Zealand
Lorelie Paraiso, New Zealand
Cheryl Payne, Australia
Saras Pillay, New Zealand
Swati Popat, India
Gillian Postlewaight, New Zealand
Cynthia Prince, New Zealand
Karen Prince, New Zealand
Lucy Quek, Singapore
Leigh Reddish, New Zealand
Sharon Reddy, New Zealand
Bessie Rios, Philippines
Carole Roberts, New Zealand
Katherine Rugg, New Zealand
Angela Russell, China
Debbie Ryder, New Zealand
Roseanne Saluni, New Zealand
Carla Scalia, Australia
Larry Schweinhart, United States
Monika Iyana Sitepu, Indonesia
Wyverne Smith, Australia
Reeta Sonawat, India
Debbie Speed, Australia

Liliana Sulikowska, Canada
Agnieszka Sulikowska, Canada
Rachel Talapati, New Zealand
Relinde Tap, New Zealand
Ann Terry, New Zealand
Marek Tesar, New Zealand
Lavinia Tiko, Fiji
Leanne Tong, New Zealand
Rachel Tong, New Zealand
Julie Treweek, New Zealand
Trish Tucker, New Zealand
Geeta Velu, Singapore
Andy Walker, New Zealand
Amanda Wallace, Australia
Kathy Ward-Cameron, United States
Barbara Watson, New Zealand
Kathryn White, New Zealand
Julie Whittaker, New Zealand
Janet Whitten, Australia
Chantal Williams, Australia
Lily Wong, Singapore
Donna Wrack, New Zealand
Sonja Zoellner, New Zealand

Author index

Subject Index